A Practical
Guide to Ethics

A Practical
Guide to Ethics

*Living and Leading
with Integrity*

Rita C. Manning
SAN JOSÉ STATE UNIVERSITY

Scott R. Stroud
UNIVERSITY OF TEXAS, AUSTIN

Westview Press
A Member of the Perseus Books Group

Published by Westview Press,
A Member of the Perseus Books Group

Find us on the World Wide Web at www.westviewpress.com.

Westview Press books are available at special discounts for bulk purchases in the United States by corporations, institutions, and other organizations. For more information, please contact the Special Markets Department at the Perseus Books Group, 2300 Chestnut Street, Suite 200, Philadelphia, PA 19103, or call (800) 255-1514, or e-mail special.markets@perseusbooks.com.

Designed by Brent Wilcox
Text set in 11 point Adobe Caslon

Library of Congress Cataloging-in-Publication Data
Manning, Rita C.
   A practical approach to ethics : living and leading with integrity /
Rita C. Manning and Scott R. Stroud.
      p.   cm.
   Includes bibliographical references and index.
   ISBN-13: 978-0-8133-4382-2
   ISBN-10: 0-8133-4382-8
   1. Ethics—Textbooks.   I. Stroud, Scott R.   II. Title.
   BJ1012.M353 2008
   170—dc22
                                                          2007033383

10 9 8 7 6 5 4 3 2 1

Short Contents

Contents

Preface

It is not hard to find textbooks today that discuss ethics in a contemporary context; texts that attempt to give readers the practical knowledge to think and act with integrity, however, are rare. That is the admittedly difficult mission of this present work.

We believe that ethics is more than an abstract body of theories, principles, and ideas. Instead, it is a way of thinking through problematic situations and determining the best way to act. This is why we have connected ethics with two other key, but often overlooked, concepts—*living* and *integrity*. Ethics is a lived endeavor that encompasses most of our interactions with others. How should we treat others? What should we do in a situation where we observe someone doing something wrong? Ought we do anything special at all? These are important questions, and they are questions that will substantially affect the direction, tone, and worth of the lives we lead. Thus, ethics demands that we pay attention to what we are actually *doing*, or, in other words, the sort of lives we are living.

Integrity is a difficult word to define, and perhaps even more difficult to instantiate in our lives. We will discuss classical and contemporary issues in ethics with the ultimate goal of relating them back to the ways one can live one's life with integrity—by displaying imagination in ethical decision making, courage in following through on moral commitments, and openness in communicating these commitments to others. This is a rough picture of that illusive goal of integrity. Notice how integrity goes beyond issues of merely knowing what is ethical or unethical; it ventures into the realm of activity and character. Although the text you now hold cannot change you overnight into a person with complete integrity, it can guide you in reflecting on your actions and your character so that you can begin to live a life more in line with principles of integrity.

Besides focusing on integrity, we recognize the need to frame ethics in a lived, social setting. Such interactive situations as those one faces at work or in the family often involve what we call *leadership*—the ethical process of making decisions concerning action and value that involves courage and imagination and that often has major effects on the lives of others. A person who leads with integrity thoughtfully makes decisions and carries them out with vigor. Leadership that lacks integrity also lacks three other things: clear and informative communication about decisions, clear and logical decision procedures, and values that are reflectively known and held. A major part of this book's mission is to offer some examples of what ethical leadership with integrity looks like, and how everyone can start practicing such a lifestyle.

How do we go about helping individuals to lead a life of integrity? Knowledge is a key part of this equation, so we begin with a discussion of moral reasoning and various ways to do it well. We do not shun theory, but instead look at the great ethical theories as guides or perspectives from which one can learn ways of making ethical decisions. Particular ethical perspectives can illuminate particular moral situations and ethical behavior. Our standpoint is simple—no single moral theory captures the entire complexity of ethical life, as each highlights a certain way of analyzing key terms, such as "good" or "bad," "ethical" or "unethical," as well as the objects of the analysis itself (humans, some humans, all creatures, ecosystems, and so on).

We lead the reader through the important ethical theories of Aristotle, Immanuel Kant, Jeremy Bentham, and John Stuart Mill, as well as more contemporary approaches to moral rights and theories of justice. One must also recognize that ethics extends beyond the borders of nations and dominant traditions, so we include extended discussions of ethical theories from other cultures and from traditions within the West that have often been overlooked. Readers will see images of life with integrity through the worldviews of Hinduism, Confucianism, and Islamic thought as well as through the perspectives of feminism and an ethics of care. Even though these are "theoretical" discussions of ethical theory, the reader is still encouraged to relate these theories to their lives—if the ethical theory seems to make no difference in describing the experiences they've been through, or in which they may be in the future, the theory doesn't seem that vital! We believe that each of these theories and the concepts they involve are relevant and provide important ways of analyzing our ethical experience, and that all give some notion of what it is like to be an ethical person who leads with integrity in moral situations. To this end, the text includes many discussion questions aimed at relating the theories and concepts described to the reader's life and experience.

The unique emphasis of this book on the practice of living with integrity continues with our attention to an often overlooked part of ethics—communication. There are very few ethical situations and decisions that do not involve communication with others, either about a decision made or about why one's values are preferable or justified. Additionally, communication is much more than mere talk: it is an integral part of the composite practice of living with integrity. The ethical person is one who can not only reason about ethical matters, but also communicate these ideas effectively and ethically. Part of this process is respecting your ideas and message enough to put them into a form that is persuasive and engaging to your audience; another part is respecting the audience that you are addressing. This is an ethical decision—you can see your audience as equals, or you can see them as mere objects to be manipulated. The amount of effort and forethought you put into the construction and delivery of your message reflects what you think of your audience, their abilities, and their value. We include discussion of effective and ethical communication in formal and informal settings, thereby enabling readers to lead with excellence in the various situations life is sure to throw at them. The variety of discussion questions and activities we provide are designed to help readers internalize what it means to communicate with integrity.

We conclude the book with a trio of issues that are vitally important today. These include issues involving the workplace, issues involving family and friends, and issues pertaining to the global community. As always, we strive to connect discussions of ethical theory to the actual, lived practice of integrity in these settings. Readers will have to confront tough issues about how individuals are treated in the workplace and in the family unit. Most of these issues are complex insofar as they lack one obvious solution; decision making and thinking are called for in the individual who wishes to lead with integrity. Today's readers will face issues that go beyond these localities, however, and we end with an exploration of the difficult issues surrounding *global citizenship*—the engaged and reflective living of one's life in situations that have global effects. Issues such as immigration, pollution, war, and terrorism are explored as test cases for the student's moral reasoning skills. Leaders of tomorrow will need to be able to think through these issues, come to various decisions, and communicate about these issues with others, and we hope that our mix of ethical theory and practical engagement will stand as a decent way to prepare individuals for such tasks. Attaining the ability to lead with integrity is a lofty goal, but we have tried to emphasize that *we all can be leaders insofar as we interact and affect others and insofar as we have the chance to live a life with integrity or without it.* This text is our attempt to point readers toward a path of continual development.

Like ethics itself, the task of writing an ethics textbook is not a solitary endeavor. Many individuals have been vital in producing the present book. Rita Manning would like to thank Scott Stroud for his insight and breadth; her students over the years, who were the inspiration for the book; and early readers of the manuscript as it was in progress. Scott Stroud would like to thank Rita Manning for being a great teacher and colleague as well as an inspirational coauthor. He would also like to thank Sandra and Herman Stroud for their continuing care and encouragement, as well as his wife, Natalie (Talia) Stroud, for her tireless belief in him and his academic pursuits.

CHAPTER 1

Introduction

In our many discussions of ethics, both in the classroom and in other settings, we hear the same question: How can I do what I think is right even when I am pressured or tempted to do otherwise, and when doing the wrong thing is even rewarded and the right thing penalized? In this book we are not going to tell you exactly what to do in difficult situations, because the answers are not always that simple or clear-cut. Living with integrity takes some thought: It means living with compassion, courage, and conviction, a conviction based on careful reflection about your own values, informed and respectful exchanges with others, and careful research into the situation you are facing. But we will offer practical guidance to help you identify your current values, show you how to subject these values to rigorous assessment to make sure they are the values you want to endorse, and discuss many of the key issues that can help you to determine how to live your life with integrity and inspire others to do the same.

In this chapter we outline three important ideas: living, leadership, and integrity. We then look at some common causes and cures for doing the wrong thing. In Chapter 2, we'll look at basic principles for reasoning and communicating about values. In Chapters 3 and 4, we'll introduce strategies for deciding what is right and wrong and for justifying your decisions. In Chapter 5, we'll extend this to a global setting, and in Chapter 6, we will look at what it means for a society to be just. Chapter 7 offers practical guidance for taking your newfound insights into effective communication with others. In Chapters 8, 9, and 10, we look at three areas of life where ethics is of paramount importance and where temptation, confusion, and indecision often reign: the spheres of work, family and friends, and the global community.

Living

People sometimes talk about living a full human life. You might think that everyone knows what this is, but if there is one thing we've learned by studying philosophy, it is that nothing is as obvious as it seems. Our philosophy here, as elsewhere in this book, is to guide you toward answering this hard question for yourself.

We might start by looking at each part of the phrase. What does it mean to be alive? Well, it is the opposite of being dead, but if you look at biomedical ethics you'll see that there is a lot of controversy about what it means to be dead. This controversy is reflected in different cultural practices around death. In much of the world, you're not considered dead until your heart stops and your body becomes cold. In places where organ-transplant technology has taken hold, you're considered dead when your brain stops working, even if processes are still going on at the cellular level. Unless you are faced with the medical question of death, though, we might rely on a fairly commonsense idea of life—it involves growth, maintenance of essential processes, and sometimes reproduction.

When we add the notion of humanness, we add another level of complexity. But it's not enough to talk about human biology. It's no accident that in the English language, we often refer to people we consider evil in terms that deny their humanity; we call them "monsters" and "animals." It appears then that the very idea of humanness involves a moral component. This becomes especially clear when we talk about a full human life. The idea of a full human life seems to include other things that humans can do and desire: friendship, a basic level of material comfort, intelligence, and appreciation of beauty. But whatever else it means, living a full human life involves consciously living a morally sensitive life.

Leadership

In an influential book about leadership, James Kouzes and Barry Posner described five essential features of good leaders: They model the way, inspire a shared vision, challenge the process, enable others to act, and encourage the heart.[1] As we thought about this model of leadership, we realized that integrity is the foundation of each of these features. When you live with integrity, you carefully consider how to do the right thing and you try to live up to your ideals. Whether you have a formal position of leadership or not, when you live with integrity you set an example for others to follow. Your courage and conviction as you do this will be a source of inspiration to those around you. When you are living with integrity, you will often find yourself out of step with the people who are doing what is easy or comfortable. This is one of the characteristics of good leadership—doing what you think is right, even when this means leading and not following the crowd.

When we hear about things like the Enron scandal, we often find ourselves at a loss. How did this happen? What can we do to prevent things like this from happening in the future? We often look to people in positions of leadership—CEOs, boards of directors, outside auditors—to prevent things like this from happening, but in this case these people were themselves implicated in the scandal. If there is a hero in the Enron affair, it is Sherron Watkins, Enron's vice president for corporate development, who was far enough down in the organizational hierarchy that she couldn't share her concerns with CEO Ken Lay directly; she had to write him a letter. Her letter and her phone calls to Arthur Anderson, Enron's auditors, provided a glimpse into the accounting practices that in 2001 led to the biggest bankruptcy in US history. But her letter tells us something else as well; it tells us what a person of courage and integrity can do, even when he or she is not seen as a leader.

This provides an important lesson for all of us. People sometimes like to think that bad things happen because some people are just evil. We have a more complex view of evil. We think that it happens when institutional arrangements make it possible for some morally challenged people to give in to their temptations—and when the rest of us look the other way. In the Enron case there were institutional arrangements that made it possible for the questionable accounting to occur—the lack of real autonomy for its auditors and lax oversight, for example. But the Enron scandal wouldn't have happened if good people had not been looking the other way. This is the core of leadership: standing up for what you believe is right. You needn't be a CEO to exercise this kind of leadership. We can all be leaders in this respect. It's up to you to decide whether you want to take responsibility or look the other way.

Integrity

Many people worry about a crisis of leadership in our country. Too many people are only interested in themselves, lack personal ethics, or are afraid to stand up for what they believe in. Often these same people are highly skilled and technologically sophisticated, but still there is something missing. In this chapter we will begin to sketch this missing feature—integrity—and throughout the book we will consider integrity in more detail, in the process taking a journey through more than 2,000 years of human thought and experience to shed light on the subject of how we can live a life of integrity as individuals and in groups in the twenty-first century.

The picture of integrity that emerges will be complex, but it is possible to provide a snapshot of integrity at the outset. People with integrity understand and can communicate their own values, but they also are able to understand and communicate with people who have different values. They are imaginative and they are good at thinking about both the long- and short-term consequences of different strategies. They respect the people they interact with—family, friends, colleagues, employees, peers, customers, and fellow citizens—and are able to build successful relationships with all these groups. This does not mean that they always agree with everyone, but when they disagree they are able to do so without losing their cool or treating people with contempt. They also care about the people they interact with. They are brave, honest, humble, and fair. They understand the role of ethics in their personal, civic, and working lives. Finally, they have a robust sense of justice and work to create more just institutions.

Integrity and Personal Growth

At this point, you may be tempted to say, "Well, I sure would like to have a boss with integrity, but why should I have integrity?" This is a question that humans have been asking for thousands of years, and philosophers have offered a number of answers. Plato discussed this question in his dialogue *The Republic*. Suppose, he said, you had a ring that could make you invisible. What would you do with it? Some of the people in the dialogue said they would use it to make themselves rich or to have things they couldn't otherwise get. Socrates, who was Plato's teacher and the main character in the dialogue, said that the wise person would act with integrity regardless of whether he was visible or not. So for Socrates, integrity is a part of wisdom. In everyday terms, we might say that as you become wiser, you just begin to see why it makes sense to do the right thing. Aristotle had a slightly different view. He thought that having integrity is just part of living a full, complete, and happy life. Take a moment to do a thought experiment to see if he is right.

> ▶ **Exercise 1.1**
>
> Suppose you die tomorrow. On your deathbed, will you look back on your life and say you'd had a good life? Will you have any regrets? What will they be? Suppose you could watch your own funeral? What do you suppose people would be saying about you? What would you want them to say?

Integrity and Effective Organizations

Whenever we ask people to describe the worst job they've ever had, they almost always describe working in a dysfunctional organization where employees are not treated decently and there is no sense of solidarity or trust. Integrity alone will not make organizations effective, but without integrity, no organization can be effective. Organizations that lack integrity can never develop the kind of teamwork and commitment it takes to serve customers and clients or to meet organizational goals. Thousands of years of human history illustrate that shared moral understandings provide the glue that holds groups together and the grease that makes it possible for people to interact with a minimum of friction.

Most people do not need to be convinced that integrity is a valuable thing for both individuals and organizations. The more difficult task is trying to decide exactly what is involved in having integrity. The most difficult and long-term task is actually developing integrity in individuals and organizations.

Integrity and Justice

Persons with integrity understand that one cannot do the right thing in a vacuum. Just institutions, whether social, political, or financial, are the underpinnings of personal integrity. Persons with integrity also care about their neighbors, their nation, and the world, and they manifest this caring in conscious political activity. Although for the bulk of this book we will be concerned with developing one's own character and conscience, we will also look at the larger social forces that either support or undercut this task. Before we look at the larger social forces, let's take a moment to reflect on some of the causes of personal misconduct, some of the ways in which our individual integrity can be challenged.

Why Is It So Hard to Do the Right Thing?

Philosophers have been asking this question for a very long time. From Plato and Aristotle through Immanuel Kant, David Hume, Jean Paul Sartre, and others, and in numerous systems of thought around the world, it is a question that has inspired different sorts of answers. Philosophers have broadly addressed two types of misconduct in these discussions: personal misconduct and group misconduct.

Personal Misconduct

The standard case of wrongdoing is when one person does something that harms another person. This is personal misconduct. But it is possible for wrongdoing to be done by a group of people. Many people have tried to explain group misconduct by finding individuals within groups who did something wrong, but this is problematic for two reasons. First, group dynamics make a big difference in how individuals behave, so it is important to look at how misconduct occurs in a group setting. Second, sometimes the misconduct cannot be laid at the feet of any particular individuals because it involves group culture or practice. For these reasons, we will be looking at personal misconduct and group misconduct separately.

Causes of Personal Misconduct. Plato thought that people did the wrong thing only out of ignorance. This view was shared by Kant, a very influential eighteenth-century German philosopher. Buddhists offer a similar answer, though their idea of what we have to know to do the right thing is more complex than Plato's and Kant's views. Aristotle also had a more complex view. He thought that misconduct was either a product of ignorance, weak will, or malice. Ignorance can take two forms: We can be ignorant about what is right or wrong, or we can be ignorant about whether a particular thing is in the category we identify as right or wrong. For example, someone may tell a lie because he or she does not understand that lying is wrong. This is an example of ignorance of the first kind. But one may also tell a "lie" by just "bending the truth a little," perhaps to avoid hurting someone else's feelings. In this case, the person who lied may not think it was wrong to tell the lie; after all, hurt feelings were avoided. This might be considered an example of ignorance of the second kind.

The discussions in this text should help you to dispel ignorance of both kinds. Malice is a different thing altogether. A person of malice does the wrong thing simply because he or she wants to do wrong. This individual realizes that what he or she is doing is wrong and wants to do it anyway, perhaps *because* it is wrong. This is true evil, and luckily it is not very common.

This leaves Aristotle's third category: weakness of will. A person with a weak will wants to do the right thing, but he or she has desires that conflict with doing it. The desire to gain something for ourselves, the desire for approval, and the fear of disapproval or punishment all may conflict with the desire to do the right thing. Often we rationalize our behavior in these cases: "Everyone else is doing it." "I'm not powerful enough to really make a difference." "I'm a nice person so this can't really be that bad." "Being a good friend means looking the other way." A more damaging kind of rationalizing is denial. We deny that we are doing anything wrong. We blame our victims. We say that the world just isn't fair. We say that it's not our fault, point out that there are people who are much worse than we are, claim that we are only doing what we are told, or blame our parents, our therapists, our spouses, or our children. Jean Paul Sartre, a famous French philosopher who was one of the founders of Existentialism, described this kind of person as lacking authenticity. In both kinds of rationalizing, we are trying to deny our moral responsibility. We feel the need to rationalize because we are uncomfortable with our actions.

A final cause of personal wrongdoing is a failure of empathy. Eighteenth-century British philosophers like David Hume, Francis Hutcheson, Lord Shaftesbury, and Adam Smith thought morality was primarily a function of having the right kind of sentiments.[2] Many philosophers have described care as the central sentiment. We'll discuss this view in some detail in Chapter 4. Moral psychologists like Martin Hoffman have seen empathy as the appropriate moral sentiment.[3] Ordinarily empathy is a very powerful motive to help others. Hoffman claimed that it is part of our evolutionary heritage and is present even in newborns. In the normal course of moral development, one becomes more able to figure out how others are feeling and to respond appropriately.

But empathy does not always prevail, and it can sometimes even let us down. Hoffman described how we can blame the victim to reduce our desire to help; we can sometimes become so overwhelmed that we begin to be much more attentive to relieving our own distress than we are to relieving the distress of others. Empathy can also be a cause of wrongdoing. Hoffman described what he called familiarity and "here and now" bias. It is natural to feel more empathy for those we are close to or those with whom we identify, but it can sometimes cause us to neglect our other duties. Michael Slote, another contemporary philosopher, has argued that the morally best person balances sentiments in favor of helping those near and dear with some concern for self as well as humanitarian concern for all.[4]

Cures for Personal Misconduct. Humans are creatures of habit, and our actions today influence the person we will become tomorrow. If we wallow in ignorance, we will become less and less sensitive to the moral dimension of life. If we rationalize our behavior, we will find it easier to give in to our desires, harder to maintain our sense of what is right, and harder to do what is right. If we think of ourselves as members of a special privileged group, we will find it easier and easier to dismiss the needs and perspectives of people who are not like us. Life is a journey. You have to decide what road to take—the road to virtue and integrity, or the road to selfishness and irresponsibility.

If you're still reading, we're assuming you are interested in the road to integrity. How can you guard against misconduct? First, banish ignorance. Pay attention to the moral dimension of life. Come to understand what you think is right and wrong and why you think this. Be open to different perspectives while maintaining your commitment to living a good life. See how principles apply in practice. Second, work on your weakness of will. Fear is a powerful barrier to doing what you think is right. We think of ourselves as little fish swimming out there in the shark tank. But the world is not an aquarium, and you are not just a little fish. You're a growing fish swimming in the open ocean, and your actions will reconfigure your world. Ask yourself what kind of a world you want to swim in and make it so. Cultivate a sense of pride in doing what you think is right. The more you cultivate integrity, the easier it will become.

Be aware of all the excuses we use for not doing the right thing: "Everyone else is doing it." "I'm not powerful enough to really make a difference." "I'm a nice person so this can't really be that bad." "Being a good friend means looking the other way." "I'm not doing anything wrong." "He had it coming." "The world just isn't fair." "It's not our fault." "There are people who are much worse than I am." "I am only doing what I was told." Look yourself in the mirror every morning and try to be honest. Take responsibility for your behavior. Ask yourself what you would do if this were the last day of your life. Finally, cultivate your ability to empathize with others. Educate yourself about what is going on in your family, among your friends, in your community, your workplace, your society, and the world. Be sensitive to the concerns of those near and dear to you, but not at the cost of being indifferent to everyone else.

▶ Exercise 1.2

Think back to a situation where you were very tempted to do the wrong thing. Why were you tempted? If you resisted, what factors helped you to resist? If you gave in, what factors influenced your decision? Suppose you were faced with the same decision today. What kinds of things would you tell yourself to keep from doing the wrong thing?

Group Misconduct

We do not exist as isolated individuals. We live and work and play in social groups, and our actions, both right and wrong, are done in a social context. For this reason, we need to look at group misconduct. We believe that collective misconduct, whether it occurs in corporations, in nonprofits, or in political organizations, has multiple causes, and in this section we will look at some of those causes. Since a person of integrity is not content to place blame but is committed to working toward solutions, we will also look at a number of possible cures.

Causes of Group Misconduct.   Group misconduct can occur in many different scenarios and can involve different types of personalities and different group dynamics. Some causes are as follows:

A Few Bad Apples. Some have argued that the system is basically fine and that a few bad apples have spoiled the environment for the rest of us. Though some people are comfortable explaining misconduct in terms of a few evil individuals, we do not believe that this view is supported by the evidence. We are not denying that there are evil people. Hitler is an example that is widely cited. But luckily people like Hitler are rare.

The Banality of Evil. Though we do not dispute the claim that there are, and have been throughout history, people of great evil, we think that far more evil is done by basically decent people going along and looking the other way. How often have you heard people say: "Everyone else is doing it." "I'm only one person. I can't make a difference." "I try not to involve myself." "I can't afford to complain. I need this job." "They probably know better than I do." "This is what it takes to get ahead." "Morality is not part of my job description." "If I don't do it, someone else will." "As long as my accountant (lawyer, boss) thinks it's legal, it must be okay." "I was only doing what I was told." The justifications go on and on. But every justification ends up serving the same purpose: enabling and allowing immoral behavior to continue.

Primary Focus on Insiders. This cause is particularly relevant to the case of for-profit corporations but can affect many types of organizations. It occurs when the members of an organization focus on their primary mission and their own membership and forget that their actions affect many others outside this circle. Some have even argued that for-profit corporations have no obligations but simply exist as profit-making machines. This is a view with serious implications, given the power that multinational corporations wield in today's world, so we will return to this view when we talk about whether "business ethics" is an oxymoron.

Primary Focus on the Short Term. Another part of the story is the emphasis on short-term gain, often to the detriment of long-term gain. Many things look reasonable when we consider only the consequences in the short term. That ice-cream sundae looks great until we think about the extra weight and effect on our health. Falling into bed without flossing your teeth looks reasonable when you're really tired, but it's knowing that flossing is required to keep your mouth in good repair for the long haul that makes you put in the effort to floss. Organizations can suffer from the same shortsightedness. For-profit corporations have another reason for the emphasis on the short term. The wave of corporate takeovers created a reasonable focus on stock prices—undervalued stock made companies ripe for takeover. While there are good consequences for many takeovers—for example, constraints may be put on incompetent management—this emphasis on the short term can be a cause of unethical practices.

Failure of Leadership. Sometimes we think of leadership in terms of position and power. But having a position of power and responsibility does not automatically make someone a leader. Regardless of power or position, we are all leaders when we are willing to stand up and be counted. Cynthia Cooper, an auditor, changed the entire course of WorldCom and corporate oversight in the United States in 2002 when she went against the express wishes of her bosses and detected the largest accounting fraud in US history. Scott Sullivan, WorldCom's former chief financial officer and Cooper's boss, failed at leadership when he ignored his responsibility to WorldCom's stakeholders in favor of lining his own pockets. Sullivan's inaction fueled Cooper's search for WorldCom's financial misdeeds. Cooper inspired her small team of Gene Morse and Glyn Smith to a heroic and frightening effort that ultimately brought the massive fraud to light.

Dilution of Personal Responsibility in Groups. Many people have pointed out that personal responsibility can often be lost in groups. Consider how often you've passed someone who is pulled over on the side of the road with car trouble. It is easy to rationalize your failure to help by telling yourself someone else will stop. Corporations add another layer of complication to the story of diluted personal responsibility in group settings because corporations are set up to assign legal responsibility to the corporation itself instead of to its members. There are other complex organizations in which the individual members are often not sure of their impact or power to effect change. In this kind of culture, "someone else will do it" is a common refrain.

People often worry about rocking the boat and endangering their careers and even their jobs. They tell themselves that they couldn't really make a difference anyway. But they are wrong. Coleen Rowley was an FBI employee two and a half years from retirement and her family's sole breadwinner. She wasn't in a position of great authority; she was a mid-level lawyer in a midwestern field office. Nevertheless, her revelations to then–FBI Director Robert Mueller as well as to the Senate Intelligence Committee about failures to investigate terrorism were the spark that ignited a serious look into the internal workings of the FBI in the aftermath of the 9/11 attacks.

Organizational Process and Structure. The *Challenger* space shuttle disaster exemplifies a number of ways that things can go tragically wrong. One of the problems was the way the launch process was structured. Engineers did not have the final say over whether the *Challenger* would launch, even though they were in the best position to assess the safety of the launch during various windows of opportunity. In addition, they did not have a formal process by which they could raise their concerns about safety to someone who would both understand the engineering issues and make a final decision. Although there were other kinds of wrongdoing in this case, it shows that it is actually possible for something bad to happen even in the absence of deliberate individual wrongdoing. If we couple a badly organized process with human wrongdoing, we have the possibility of serious catastrophes. How common are these system failures? According to two prominent risk analyzers, these failures account for the vast majority of preventable errors.[5]

Organizational Culture. Organizations have cultures—values and ways of doing things—that can either support or undermine integrity. Some organizations encourage a "cowboy mentality" where doing the right thing takes a back seat to personal aggrandizement. Some organizations stress secrecy and put the health of the organization above its stakeholders. Some organizations are punitive and disrespectful of the rank and file, who feel powerless and resentful. All of these cultures are ripe for misconduct.

Lack of Oversight. For many people, the accounting scandals of the past decade are evidence that lax oversight is the oxygen that allows the match of greed to ignite an inferno. There is a great debate about regulation and oversight. Some have argued that a free and open market will constrain companies from fraud, bad products and bad service, and inefficiency because customers will shift to the ethical, productive, and innovative companies. But even if this were so, it's not clear that it would solve our problems, because we don't really have completely free or open markets. Second, even if markets could work to root out problems, many people would suffer in the meantime. For this reason, many people are convinced that we need some regulations to constrain corporate misconduct and oversight bodies to see that the regulations are followed.

Misalignment of Incentives. Sometimes organizations are trying to create ways to encourage their members to do the right thing, but their strategies misfire. Stock options are a great example here. A stock option gives one the ability to buy company stock at a fixed price. Say you join the Northwest Widget Company, whose stock is trading at $1 a share. As part of your compensation package, you get 1,000 options to buy Northwest stock at that price. If Northwest's stock goes up, to $2 a share, you can exercise your option and buy 1,000 shares at $1. You can turn around and sell them for $2,000, realizing a $1,000 profit.

The initial idea behind stock options was to get managers to share the interests of shareholders. Both groups would then want the company to do well so that the stock would do well. Unfortunately, the example of Enron and others showed that often stock options don't work very well; sometimes, instead of aligning the interests of management and shareholders, they provide a way for unethical management to pursue self-interest. When managers own a large number of stock options, they have a reason to increase the stock price. This can be done by increasing the real value of the company, but it can also be done by manipulating the financial reports of a company, as happened in the case of Enron.

Corrupt Political Environment. Organizations exist in a larger political context. If this larger context either supports corruption or simply looks the other way, then the organizations that exist within it are liable to become corrupt. We will return to this topic in Chapter 6.

Influences of Globalization. Suppose we succeeded in reining in corporate misconduct in the United States. Suppose all corporations operating on our shores were models of financial propriety and shareholder responsibility, responsive to customers, fair to the workers, and responsible stewards of the environment. Would we be able to rest on our laurels? Obviously not, because we live and work in a global environment. Globalization raises a myriad of questions about corporate responsibility. Should an ethical company in one country avoid dealing with unethical firms elsewhere, for example? And how can this be accomplished when companies find themselves in a complex web of international business relationships?

In addition, although the returns on corporate responsibility are clear and convincing, they often accrue to parties outside the companies themselves. Being socially responsible is often costly to companies. For example, air pollution is a cost to everyone who breathes, whereas clean air is a clear benefit. Socially responsible companies that use processes involving air pollutants will want to make investments in clean technology to keep the air clean, but this technology is not free. The companies that do not shoulder the additional cost can sell their products at a lower price, thus crowding out the cleaner products. This is what happens when one country or group of countries sets a standard for corporate conduct while other countries or regions set the bar at a lower level.

Cures for Group Misconduct. The cures for group misconduct will be at least as varied as the causes, depending on the situation, the personalities, and even the theory of justice and the legal system involved. Some examples of the cures are as follows.

A Renewed Emphasis on Integrity (Isolating the Bad Apples). There are bad apples, people whose greed and self-importance make them insensitive to the demands of morality. Though it's often difficult to see the harm in the case of white-collar crime, the cost is enormous. In the WorldCom case, over $3 billion disappeared, and that money belonged to someone: to the employees, customers, vendors, and shareholders.

In our opinion, part of the cure for these bad apples is punishment inflicted promptly and fairly. But in the United States, the more common legal response to corporate misconduct is either administrative or civil sanctions. Many have argued that prison would be both more effective and fairer. White-collar crime is more costly than street crime, but someone who commits a street crime is treated much more harshly by the criminal justice system. This is both unfair and inefficient. In addition to the stick approach, we also need the carrot: that is, we need to make it easier for people to do the right thing. One way we can help people to stand up and resist corporate misconduct is by protecting whistle-blowers.

People who remain in blissful ignorance or who simply go along with the unethical decisions of others are both more common than those who make those decisions and, because they are more common, more of a problem. Punishing bad apples promptly and fairly will go a long way toward strengthening the backbones of the apathetic and the blissfully ignorant. The rest of the work must be done by social pressure and individual conscience.

Leadership with Integrity and Personal Responsibility. If weak or misguided leadership causes or allows misconduct, leadership based on integrity, communication, and personal responsibility is the cure. One way we can encourage more personal responsibility and leadership is by building it into our organizations—and that means we need whistle-blower protection as well as evaluations that focus on personal integrity and responsibility, not just the bottom line.

Systems Organized for Integrity: Moral Risk Management. To counter faulty processes and badly designed systems that cause avoidable errors, we must design and test systems with the express goal of avoiding harm. Since it is impossible to design perfect systems or processes for moral risk management, we need to make sure the system includes reporting procedures to empower users and designers to report problems.

Ethical Cultures. Ethical organizations reward integrity and discourage wrongdoing. They have an explicit set of values, and these values permeate the organization. The tone is set at the top, and the members of the organization incorporate these values in their day-to-day activities. They understand their responsibilities to their stakeholders and develop practices that are attentive to these responsibilities. The members feel trusted and valued, and they bring a sense of commitment to their activities on behalf of the organization.

Meaningful Oversight. Regulation and oversight are part of the recipe for minimizing organizational misconduct, but we must be careful to balance efficiency and fairness with the desire to prevent wrongdoing. Many of us have had the misfortune of being blamed for the wrongdoing of others. Being constantly treated as a possible criminal is demoralizing, and ultimately, treating people as if they were under suspicion undermines the very trust and commitment that are needed in an organization to help people to do the right thing. Arriving at the right balance is something that people must work very hard to achieve, and it is a task that is never finished.

Realignment of Incentives. There are many ways to provide incentives for doing the right thing and disincentives for doing the wrong thing. The first thing to do is to have such incentives and disincentives in place. For example, let's return to our example of stock options. Here we see a range of possible solutions. The two goals of reform are (1) aligning the interests of stockholders and managers, and (2) minimizing the role of stock options as a temptation for misconduct.

One might give options only when a company outperforms its competitors, thus reducing the payoff for managers who merely ride an industry wave to success. We could require that stock options be held for a longer period of time, thus minimizing the push toward short-term over long-term gain. We could put limits on the amount of compensation given in stock options. We could abolish stock options altogether. Expensing stock options is a related strategy whose principle aim would be to give shareholders a clearer picture of the corporation's finances. Because stockholders would be able to see the real cost of the options, it might also have the effect of limiting the number of options that are issued.

Responsible Political Environment: The Just Society. Since organizations operate within a larger economic, social, and political context, we can't expect organizations to be morally responsible unless we create and sustain a just society—that is, just social institutions. Since the question of what counts as a just institution is such a big one, we will devote all of Chapter 6 to it.

Integrity in Globalization. If the primary problem of globalization is that we do not have a level playing field for scrupulous and unscrupulous organizations, then the ultimate solution is to have international agreements to ensure that organizations do not benefit from corporate misconduct. These agreements, obviously, would have to be suitably enforced, and obviously this is not something that can happen overnight, but it is certainly something to strive for. We will return to this issue in Chapter 10.

▶ Exercise 1.3

In 1970, a donor gave the Franciscan Friars of California a copper mine. For over thirty years, the Franciscans got a small income from the mine, but it wasn't until 2003 that they became aware of the amount of pollution that had been generated by the mine. Because they were committed to the value of kinship to the land, they wanted to clean it up. Because they also have a vow of poverty, they lacked the funds to carry out the cleanup, and the value of the land fell far short of the $2.2 million needed for the project. The Friars could have abandoned the polluting mine, as the owners of more than 100,000 other mines in the West had done, but instead they decided to make a commitment to putting things right. By 2007, through the efforts of many donors as well as through government assistance, the land was almost completely restored.[6]

Answer the following questions about this case. What possible explanations can you think of for why more than 100,000 mines had been abandoned without cleanup? What features of this case explain why this mine was cleaned up? What solutions would you suggest to make sure all abandoned mines would be cleaned up?

Is "Business Ethics" an Oxymoron?   Before we end this discussion of group misconduct, we would like to anticipate an objection. Many people have argued that certain kinds of organizations fall outside the scope of morality. Business is a common example. Many people argue that business has no responsibility to do the right thing, or even that business is fundamentally at odds with morality. Robert Solomon, a professor of business and philosophy, wrote an entire book on this subject, supplying a very cogent account of the importance of integrity to leadership and business success.[7] We agree with Solomon that "business ethics" is not an oxymoron, but before we offer our thoughts, we want to look at why someone might make this claim.

There are two prominent arguments for the claim that business cannot be held morally accountable. The first rests on the assumption that the environment of business is so cutthroat that the rules of morality simply do not apply. Doing business is like being on a deserted island without enough food and water to survive. In this kind of environment, people have a primary obligation of self-defense that trumps their obligations to others.

To counter this argument, we would respond that it's not at all clear that even on the deserted island we would have no obligations to others. Indeed, it was in thinking about issues like this one that important political philosophers like Thomas Hobbes and Jean-Jacques Rousseau developed their social contract theories. They argued that when people realize that they cannot survive by themselves because nature and human action have become a danger to all, they commit themselves to civil society. In *The Leviathan,* Hobbes described the alternative as a state of nature, a "war of all against all," where "life is nasty, poor, brutish and short."[8] In civil society, everyone makes a commitment to be subject to the rule of law because it is only through cooperation that they can improve their odds of survival. One could argue that the business environment is similar. If business were completely unregulated, and if doing business were a requirement for survival, and if there were not enough customers and resources to go around, then it would be prudent for business to commit to a system of morality that would provide a level playing field for all. The bottom line is that even if we grant that the business environment is cutthroat, this is not a reason to abandon morality. Indeed, it is a reason to adopt it and to advocate for a system where all the players are committed to a playing field that is made fair for all.

The second kind of argument is that business does have a social responsibility, but it consists solely in maximizing shareholder return. Maximizing shareholder return requires that employees focus solely on creating maximum profit. Milton Friedman defended this argument in a famous essay, "The Social Responsibility of Business Is to Increase Its Profits."[9]

There are a number of problems with this argument, and we will look at three of them here. First, it assumes that all employees stand in an agency relationship with shareholders and that this agency relationship trumps all other moral considerations. In a typical agency relationship, one party acts as an agent for another. If I hire an attorney to represent me in a commercial venture, the attorney is acting as my agent. In this capacity, the attorney is to represent my wishes rather than his or her own. But agency does not eliminate moral obligations. If I want my attorney to violate legal ethics, for example, my attorney is within his or her rights to refuse. Even if we assume that my agent has obligations solely to represent my interests, I am still a member of the moral community, so I have obligations. Responsible agency would require that my agent represent my moral obligations along with my other interests. The bottom line here is that agency relationships do not cause morality to disappear.

The second major problem with this argument is that it assumes that employees have an obligation to maximize shareholder return because the shareholders are the owners of the company. But the owners are not the only people who are affected by the actions of business. Consider a simple example. If I set fire to my barn on a hot and windy day, I am endangering all my neighbors. The danger to them gives them legitimate grounds to protest my action. This example suggests that owners are not the only people who have a right to control over their property. Anyone who is importantly affected by my actions also has a legitimate right to limit my actions. Thus, even if employees do have obligations to shareholders, they have other obligations as well. This fundamental insight is the basis of stakeholder theory, which is now the predominant view about the social responsibility of business.

The third problem with Friedman's view is that even if we agree that the responsibility of business is to maximize profit, focusing solely on the bottom line is paradoxically not the best way to maximize profit. If we look at successful organizations, we see people focused on the central mission of the organization. Apple, for example, is successful because it has continued to focus on it core mission: creating high-level design and functionality in technology products. Profit is certainly a necessary condition of success; without a constant reliable return, companies cannot continue to exist. But this is not the same as saying that companies exist solely to make a profit. The internal structure of successful organizations reflects this reality: Someone counts the money while others focus their primary attention on creating goods and services.

At this point, we think we've shown that morality and business are not incompatible. Now we turn to our positive argument: that morality is actually the cornerstone of a successful business environment. Recall Hobbes's argument that the only prudent course for people living in a state of nature is to come together to form a civil society in which individual actions are limited in support of greater freedom and security for all. These limits can be legal and moral. We can make a similar argument about business. A totally unregulated environment is a danger to all, and the most prudent course of action is to limit the freedom of each enterprise in support of greater freedom and security for all.

There are two other arguments we offer in support of our view that ethics is not only compatible with business, but a necessary condition for success. The first is that public relations are an increasingly important factor in the success of organizations, and a reputation for integrity is crucial to a positive public perception. The second is that the success of any organization depends on the ethical behavior of its members. If a company encourages its employees to shortchange customers, why should they expect these same employees to be fair in their dealings with their employer?

Conclusion

In this chapter, we've described what it means to live and lead with integrity.

We've also looked at some of the common explanations for misconduct, both personal and organizational, as well as suggestions for cures. In the next chapter, we'll begin to describe the kind of thinking you'll need to do to figure out what you believe is right and wrong.

▶ Study Questions for Chapter One

1. What are the basic characteristics of people with integrity?
2. What is the relation between integrity and personal growth?
3. What is the relation between integrity and effective organizations?
4. What is the relation between integrity and justice?
5. What are the basic causes of personal misconduct?

6. What are the basic cures for personal misconduct?

7. What are the basic causes of group misconduct?

8. What are the basic cures for group misconduct?

NOTES

1. James M. Kouzes and Barry Z. Posner, *The Leadership Challenge* (Hoboken, N.J.: Jossey-Bass, 2003).

2. See Rachel Cohon, *Hume: Moral and Political Philosophy* (Aldershot, UK: Ashgate, 2001); Francis Hutcheson, *Illustrations on the Moral Sense* (Cambridge: Belknap Press of Harvard University Press, 1971); Adam Smith, *The Theory of Moral Sentiments* (Oxford: Oxford University Press, 1976; Lord Shaftesbury, *Characteristics of Men, Manners, Opinions, Times* (Boston: Adamant Media, 2005).

3. Martin Hoffman, *Empathy and Moral Development* (Cambridge: Cambridge University Press, 2000).

4. Michael Slote, *Morals from Motives* (Oxford: Oxford University Press, 2003).

5. See Neil Johnston, James Reason, and Rob B. Lee, *Beyond Aviation Human Factors: Safety in High Technology Systems,* edited by Daniel E. Maurino (Aldershot, UK: Avebury Aviation, 1995); James Reason, *Human Error* (Cambridge: Cambridge University Press, 1990); James Reason, *Managing the Risks of Organizational Accidents* (Aldershot, UK: Ashgate, 1998).

6. These details are from *Wall Street Journal,* April 20, 2007.

7. Robert Solomon, *A Better Way to Think about Business: How Personal Integrity Leads to Business Success* (Oxford: Oxford University Press, 2003).

8. Thomas Hobbes, *The Leviathan* (originally published 1651).

9. Milton Friedman, *New York Times Magazine,* 1970, reprinted in *An Economist's Protest: Columns in Political Economy* (Glen Ridge, N.J.: Thomas Horton, 1972).

CHAPTER 2

Reasoning and Communicating about Values

There are effective moral reasoning styles, and there are not-so-effective moral reasoning styles. Let's clear the brush a bit by looking first at the common ways in which moral reasoning can be defective. We begin this chapter with two exercises. The first exercise is meant for you to do by yourself, and the second is intended for a group of about five.

Exercise 2.1

Think of a communication about moral values that you found ineffective. What was it about the communication that bothered you? (If you cannot think of an example from your own life, you might try to recall one from TV, literature, politics, etc.)

Exercise 2.2

In your group, share the answers that each person came up with for Exercise 2.1. List the examples along with the reasons they were thought to be ineffective.

A great deal can be learned from doing exercises like these. Be open to the possibility that your example may be quite different from the ones offered by the others in your group. Despite the differences, we predict that many, if not most, of the lists will include some of the following reasons for ineffectiveness: arbitrariness, relying on gut feeling, being overly emotional, being partisan, and appealing to moral authorities.

Mistakes in Moral Reasoning

When coauthor of this book Rita Manning was a little girl, it drove her crazy when she was not given a reason for something. "Because I said so" was for her the most irritating sentence in the English language. Now that she has children of her own, she understands how irritating it can be to have to provide reasons for everything, so she's forgiven her parents for saying this so much. But there are situations in which we still hear these words, and they still have the power to irritate. When we are communicating about values, it is upsetting to say or hear that something is right because someone else says so.

When someone says that something must be right or wrong simply because it *is* right or wrong ("Because I said so . . . "), that is arbitrariness. For example, consider the following argument about stealing. In this case, one employee of a shop (Toby) has stolen merchandise, and the other employee (Joan) thinks the theft is wrong.

JOAN: I cannot believe that you would do something as wrong as stealing merchandise.

TOBY: Why is it wrong to take the merchandise? There are things here that we will end up giving to charity because we will never be able to sell it.

JOAN: Yes, but it's wrong to do it because it is stealing!

In other words, Joan is saying that this instance of stealing is wrong simply because stealing is wrong. Now Joan deprived herself of a good argument and irritated Toby because she just couldn't think of a good reason why stealing is wrong, when there are really lots of good reasons. The moral of the story is that if you are tempted to be arbitrary and say that something is wrong because it just is, give it some more thought. See if you can find a reason for your strong sense that it really is wrong.

A close cousin to being arbitrary is relying on gut feeling. Let's add to the dialogue above:

TOBY: I don't see what the problem is.
JOAN: I just know it's wrong to steal. I can't believe you don't have the same feeling about it.

We can see where this argument is headed. Pretty soon they will be insulting each other and Joan will have lost the opportunity to see if Toby is an employee who could be salvaged. Indeed, it is possible that Toby really did think the merchandise was on its way to charity and was taking it directly to Toys for Tots himself. Joan will never know if she relies on her gut feeling to explain her point of view.

One day when Rita Manning was at the gym, a talk show that relied on heated reactions to hot topics came on TV. She found that she could hardly be in the same room when people on TV were screaming at each other about an incident where values were in conflict. It came as no surprise when the screaming degenerated into fisticuffs. Now some people enjoy such conflict, even in their own interactions. If you are one of these people, you will not be too upset when people get overly emotional when discussing values. But lots of people don't enjoy such interactions and, perhaps more importantly, emotional slugfests seldom result in any meaningful resolution. They more often result in hurt feelings and ruptures in relationships. Some people go so far as to avoid ever discussing values for fear that the discussion will turn emotional. There are good reasons for avoiding lots of value issues, but people often need to discuss issues with important value dimensions. If we try to ignore the value dimension, we risk undermining the trust and consistency we need in effective interpersonal relationships and/or we are left feeling like we are selling our souls.

Sadly, too many of us have worked in organizations where "friends-of-Bob" seem to get all the benefits. This can happen in moral reasoning as well. The partisan person always tries to benefit the same group of friends or sycophants, not because they have a particular need, but simply because they are friends. There are times when we owe something special to our friends, but the partisan person seldom seems to think in any other way.

Finally, appealing to a moral authority means doing something just because someone whom you regard as your moral authority tells you to do it. When we are small children, we look to our parents and teachers as our moral guides. As we get older, most of us begin to think for ourselves. It is always a good idea to go to people you trust for moral advice, but seeking advice is not the same thing as doing what you are told. We weigh advice and decide whether or not to take it. The person who appeals to a moral authority is stuck in childhood patterns. In addition, because we don't all have the same moral heroes, not everyone will be impressed by what our particular moral authority had to say.

Some other problematic forms of moral reasoning are described below.

Self-Interest

All of us are strongly motivated to pursue our own self-interest. This is not a bad thing. In fact, it is probably one of the impulses that has helped humans to survive and thrive for thousands of years. Sometimes, though, we allow our concern for self-interest to cloud our views about what is right. We have all been in situations where everyone was so busy protecting self-interest that nothing could get done. When someone invokes self-interest at the same time that you are trying to invoke moral values, there are two things you can do. First, you can try to get the person to recognize that he or she is appealing to self-interest and that this is a situation that calls for a broader perspective. Second, you can defend your view by pointing out that it is really more in tune with his or her long-term good.

Some philosophers and popular thinkers have suggested that the best moral strategy would be for everyone to do what is in his or her own self-interest. This view is often called Moral Egoism. It is different from other appeals to self-interest. You can make an appeal to self-interest without thinking that it is a moral appeal. Moral Egoists argue that there is really no difference between appealing to morality and appealing to self-interest—

one should appeal to self-interest and self-interest only when taking the moral point of view.

There are several problems with this view. First, if everyone followed it, we would live in a much more combative world. Second, if this view were correct, then there would be no difference between altruism and self-interest. On this view, altruists are just being generous because it is in their self-interest. This does not jibe with most of our intuitions. Most of us think that there is a difference between people who never seem to think about others and people who are tuned in to the needs of others.

The Moral Egoism debate is an important one in philosophy, and it is still going on. If you find it interesting, we encourage you to pursue it, but we think that it is problematic enough that we will not be referring to it further as a way of making moral decisions.

Morality and Religion

Some people think that morality depends on religion. What might they mean by this? One possibility is that they think that only religion can motivate people to do the right thing. The problem with this view is that we all know people with no real religious convictions who are basically good people nonetheless. In addition, we need only look at history, or today's newspaper, to see many examples of how religion has been used to motivate people to do terrible things. Still, religion can be a powerful motivator to do good, and when moral philosophers say that morality does not depend on religion they are not denying this or putting down religion. They just think that the relation between morality and religion is a bit more complex.

When people say that morality does depend on religion, they are saying that religion is the only way we can justify any moral perspective. These people think that if God (or some other higher power) did not exist, we could just say "Anything goes." This view was refuted in a dialogue written by Plato over 2,000 years ago. In his dialogue, *The Euthyphro,* he depicted Socrates questioning someone about what it is to be pious. "Piety" in this dialogue is an ancient Greek notion, but we can get close to the meaning by substituting "right" for "pious." One of the answers he considers is that something is right because the gods think it is right.

Socrates had a fairly complex response to this definition, but we can summarize and update it in the following way. There was a character named "Q" on the series *Star Trek: The Next Generation* who appeared to have many of the qualities that Christians associate with God. He seemed to know everything, he had the power to do anything, and he was immortal. He was missing one crucial thing: He was not all good. The crew of the *Enterprise* (and later the *Voyager*) did not think of him as a God precisely because he was not good. What this suggests is that goodness is part of our view about God.

Now, in Plato's time, the Greek gods could be as petulant and arrogant as Q, and they often were in conflict with each other (just as Q was sometimes in conflict with the rest of his "continuum" on the show). How could piety be based on the gods if the gods themselves did not always agree? In Plato's dialogue, it is posited that something is then right if it is something that all the gods agree is right. This notion allows us to make a leap: We can use the same reasoning for a single god as for the Greek pantheon because now we are talking about those things which all the gods agree is right (what all the gods agree is right would be like what one god says is right). But then, using reasoning similar to Socrates' reasoning in the dialogue, we might go on to say the following: Perhaps it is not that God's thinking something good makes it good, but rather that we only consider a powerful person a god when s/he already approves of things we think are good. To put it another way, something is not good merely because God thinks it is. We honor God because, among other things, s/he thinks the right things are good.

Again, we could spend a lot of time playing with this idea, and philosophers, who are people who really love ideas, have done that. But even if you don't agree with Socrates, there is a serious practical problem in appealing to religion as the source of morality: People with different religions will not be able to share moral reasons.

Cultural Relativism

Cultural Relativism (also called Ethical Relativism) is the view that you morally ought to do whatever your society thinks is right. This view is often heard expressed in terms of one's traditions ("This is the way we do it in my tradition") or family ("My family would be upset if I didn't go along with them"). Cultural Relativism says that what is right and wrong is relative to society. What is right in one society might be wrong in another one.

Cultural Relativism needs to be distinguished from two other defensible views. The first is that we ought to be tolerant and respectful about cultural difference. The second is that we ought to be respectful of our own traditions. Cultural Relativism is a much different view than merely advocating tolerance. Remember that Cultural Relativism says that you should always do what your society thinks is right. Tolerance would only be a virtue if it were a virtue in your society. If you came from a society that thinks tolerance is wrong, then you would be obligated to be intolerant if you were a Cultural Relativist. Cultural Relativism is also a much stronger view than the view that you ought to respect your own traditions. You can respect your own traditions even while you do not think it is right to follow them all the time. Cultural Relativism says that you should follow your traditions no matter what. It also says that if you think your traditions are wrong sometimes, it is you and not your traditions that are wrong.

You can be a relativist of another sort even if you reject Cultural Relativism. For example, many philosophers are Meta-Ethical Relativists. This means that they think that there is no ultimate way to show that one moral perspective is superior to another. As you will see when you look at some of the moral perspectives still to come, you can also be a relativist in a less radical sense. You might think that what is right and wrong depends in part on the circumstances. You can believe this even if you believe that there are moral rules that apply in all times and places. For example, suppose Joe tells Manuel that he thinks his new car is "totally you." Suppose that Manuel interprets this as a compliment even while Joe was thinking that it was just like Manuel to display his vanity with a flashy car. Did Joe do something wrong? People can disagree about this even if they agree that it is always wrong to deliberately mislead others. They may disagree about whether Joe intended to mislead Manuel. Perhaps Joe was just trying to avoid hurting Manuel's feelings.

Though these two kinds of relativism are reasonable, Cultural Relativism is much less so. It requires that morality is just a matter of where and when we live, and it requires that we always obey our society even when we feel our society is wrong. In fact, if Cultural Relativism were true, we would be forced to condemn many of our moral heroes. People like Martin Luther King Jr. and Mahatma Gandhi stood up to their societies. A Cultural Relativist would say that their resistance was wrong, but most of us think that they were not only morally right but courageous for standing up against injustice.

Good Moral Reasoning

It's obviously not enough to know what not to do, so now we will suggest what you should do when you reason morally. Later, we will look at specific ways of making moral decisions (these will be called "moral perspectives"). After we look at all of them, you will be on your way to a clear understanding of what your moral values are and why you hold them. Once you've completed this step, you will have some fairly specific decision procedures to follow. For now, our suggestions will be fairly general and will apply to any moral perspective.

First, try to give yourself some calm time to think things through. It is hard to do any clear thinking when we are feeling emotional. This doesn't mean that we should leave emotion out altogether. Our emotions are an important resource when we make moral decisions and carry them out. We do want to avoid being overly influenced by emotion, though.

Second, try to make your decision on the facts. All of us have a built-in desire to see things in a certain way. Some of us are Pollyannas—we see good outcomes everywhere. For others, the glass is always half empty. To reach a decision you can live with, you must avoid both extremes. Seek out information during this stage, and don't be afraid to seek advice.

When you have come to a tentative decision, make sure that you can clearly articulate what it is and that you can defend it to others. It is not enough to say, "I think we should do it this way because I have a gut feeling that this is the way to go." Instead, investigate your gut. Why is it telling you this? Is it simply indigestion? If it is a good intuition, there are reasons for it. Try to figure out what they are.

▶ Hints for Developing Good Moral Reasoning

Always give yourself time to reason calmly. When a moral issue arises that you are not prepared to discuss, try to table the discussion until everyone has had a chance to think about the issue a bit. Do not simply shelve it forever!

Take time to write out your reasoning. Make sure you take all the relevant facts into account. Look for reasons that can support your view. When looking for reasons, try to do some reflective moral reasoning: Look for reasons that both support your view and are cast in terms of the values and reasoning of the other people involved.

▶ Hints for Avoiding Mistakes in Moral Reasoning

Review the hints for developing good moral reasoning.

Ask yourself what outcome would be in your best interest. Once you have some idea about this, you will be able to assess how much this is influencing your decision.

Don't be afraid to seek advice from your spiritual advisers and elders in your community, but make sure that any decision is really your own.

Once you've decided what is the best thing to do, use whatever it takes to motivate yourself to follow through.

Prepare yourself to justify your decision to people who are not members of your community or religion.

Communicating about Values

You now have some idea about how to reason effectively about moral issues. Now it's important to see what your own values are. In the next chapter, we'll help you to reflect on these values and see whether you want to recommit yourself to them or restructure them in some way. Our goal in this section is to help you communicate respectfully and effectively with others on the volatile issue of values.

Understanding Your Own Values

Before you can successfully communicate about values, you first have to understand your own. There are lots of things that we all care about: our families, for example. Some of the things we care about are abstract; for example, we may value beauty or strength or courage. Some of the abstract things we care about are moral values. Morality has come to have a limited meaning in our public discussions recently, and lots of people think it refers just to matters of family or of sex. But moral values include much more than values about sex and family. A *moral situation* can be defined as any situation that has a real potential for harming things that are important to us. The clearest moral situations are those that involve harm to a person, although for many people they would include harm to communities, animals, the natural environment, works of art, important artifacts such as historic buildings, and other types of property. Part of your task is to see what you think is included in the realm of morality.

It is important to see what our own moral values are, and the best way to think about this is to consider a situation that we could clearly describe as a moral situation and then see why we understood the situation this way. But understanding your own moral values requires more than coming to see what you care about. You also need to see what your moral reasoning is—what strategies you use in coming to a decision about what to do in a moral situation. To help you do this, the following activity is provided. First, by yourself, answer the question in Exercise 2.3. Then, for Exercise 2.4, discuss your answers in groups of about five. Have each person tell his or her story and explain his or her moral reasoning. Next, take a few minutes for everyone to think about all the different strategies group members used. How would you describe each person's strategy? Finally, review the sorts of answers you came up with as a group.

It is important to answer the questions in Exercise 2.3 by yourself first, and then, in Exercise 2.4, to take the time to think about the moral reasoning of the others alone before discussing them. If you don't, an interesting group dynamic emerges. The first person to describe someone else's moral reasoning will likely set a pattern for everyone else's descriptions. This happens because, though we may be very clear about what is important to us morally, we often are not clear about our own moral reasoning. We are not at all clear about what other possible strategies could be used because we seldom discuss these types of issues outside of a philosophy course. Expect a bit of uncertainty about this, but as you gain more practice in moral reasoning, your confidence will grow, though moral decisions will always be a challenge.

▶ **Exercise 2.3**

Describe a moral situation that you had difficulty resolving. How did you decide what to do? If someone asked you to defend your decision, what would you say?

▶ **Exercise 2.4**

Discuss your examples in a group. Think about how you would describe the moral reasoning used by other members of your group. Then discuss your answers.

Understanding the Values of Others

By now, you have some idea about what your values are and how to describe your moral reasoning. You also have had some practice defending your moral decisions. You have also noticed that other people have different values and different styles of moral reasoning. It is important to understand these different styles, because communicating about values requires understanding all the different views expressed. When we understand our own values and moral reasoning and a good cross-section of other values and moral reasoning styles, we are prepared to have a calm discussion with some hope of resolution when values enter into the discussion. Now some people would probably rather have a heated style of interaction when values are involved, but though this may be entertaining, it is unlikely that a resolution acceptable to all will emerge, and it is almost certain that relationships will not be enhanced.

Discussing Values with Others

Because discussing values can be such a difficult thing to do, many times we simply avoid doing it. But avoiding these discussions in itself can be a questionable moral choice. Consider this hypothetical situation. Van is a respiratory therapist who is working in the Intensive Care Unit of a hospital. One of her patients, Fred, is dying of bone cancer and is in great pain. He develops pneumonia, and the primary physician advises the family to allow Fred to be intubated and connected to a ventilator that will do all his breathing for him. Van privately thinks that it would do the patient little good and that intubation will be uncomfortable for him, but she decides not to try to discuss this with the physician because she and the physician may have very different values. The patient is mechanically ventilated for three weeks and dies in great pain. Did Van do the right thing in not talking to the doctor?

Now that you've had a chance to think about your own values and the values of others, it is time to think about questions like this. Some people think that we should never try to discuss values. This is why some advocate never talking about politics or religion. It certainly makes sense to keep some things to yourself, but core values are often involved in the decisions we need to make with others. We think, and we hope you agree, for example, that Van should have communicated her concerns. Granted, the politics of medicine make it somewhat difficult for a respiratory tech to challenge a doctor, but Van could have done this diplomatically. She might have been surprised at the outcome.

Coauthor Rita Manning has a friend who is a chaplain at a hospital, and she gets called in for all code blues. She says that doctors are often relieved when she tells them, "Doctor, I think you've done enough." The doctors agree with many of her values, but in a crisis, they are often relying on years of training, in which they have learned the important general rule that says "do whatever you can," rather than reflecting on their values. It often helps to have someone remind them of their values. Perhaps Van would have had a similar experience. Even if the doctor disagreed, it would be good practice for her to question him. If she keeps silent, she is training herself to ignore her own values, and this can have long-lasting, grave consequences.

Here are some useful steps to take in communicating about values. You first need to be clear about your own values and have some idea of the range of values others might hold. The next thing you need to do is gather the appropriate information. You first have to see what interests and values are at stake. Van, for example, needs information about her patient, his prognosis, his current condition, his family's condition, and their values. But in some cases, we have the time and the resources to gather comprehensive information, whereas in other cases we simply cannot gather every bit of relevant information. We need to balance several factors: how much information we need to make a minimally informed decision, how much time we have to decide, and what other pressing concerns we have to address. As Fred's respiratory therapist, Van probably already has a lot of the information she needs, but her time may be limited, as she has other patients who require her services. If she feels she needs more information, she needs to simply do her best with the time she has available.

The next thing she must do is sort through these details and see which are concerned with values. In the case of Van's patient, we have the important values of life, of avoiding suffering, and of maintaining good relationships. There are three sorts of relationships that are important. One is Van's relationship to the doctor and the other members of the health-care team. She must resolve this case without sacrificing her ability to be an effective member of the team. If she doesn't do this, she will be unable to take adequate care of her future patients. The second important set of relationships is that of the family members. The families of patients are going through a great deal of stress and providing much of the comfort and care that the patient requires. The final, and some would argue most important, relationship is between the health-care practitioner and the patient.

The next thing to do is to listen to what all the interested parties have to say. In health-care settings, anyone can ask for a family meeting, which is a fairly formal way to come to a decision. Even if Van cannot get everyone together in a family meeting, she can listen to each of them separately. Good listening is a real skill, and it is especially important in communicating about values. Good listening requires hearing what is said, as well as what is implied, and reading body language. When we communicate about values, we need to be listening carefully to hear what interests and values are expressed, what others see as the morally relevant facts, and what styles of moral reasoning are being used. This requires sophisticated listening skills because people are often not very good at expressing values, especially in a time of great stress.

When discussing values it is important to avoid jumping to conclusions. We often think we know what a speaker is trying to say, so we stop actively listening to their arguments and claims; of course, what we miss when we think we "know it all" is often something that is important to the other person's perspective. This is a bad habit. A conscientious listener should really *listen* to everything the other person has to say, without jumping to conclusions, thinking about counterarguments, and so on.

Good listening also includes time for reflection. When we stop to reflect on what is being said, we not only give others encouragement to say what is on their mind, we give ourselves and others time to think about what is being said. Some TV talk shows provide examples day after day of what happens when we don't do this. Everyone is talking at the same time, and pretty soon everyone is shouting. Some of this reflection can be done as a group, in a brainstorming format. First, we need to reflect on our options. What possible actions can we take? Second, we need to consider the moral pros and cons of each option. As we do this, we recognize that we won't all agree. Here we must each state our own moral commitments and hear the moral commitments of others.

The final stage is to let each person (or spokesperson for a group) say what he or she believes would be the best course of action and why. During this phase, common ground will often emerge, and this should be encouraged.

One of the real obstacles to effective communication about anything, and particularly about values, is that not everyone is willing to abide by ground rules for effective communication. That is why it is often helpful to have a specific forum or policies about such. We can look to health care for some good examples. Hospitals often have organized ethics boards with specific procedures to ensure good communication, and family meetings are widely used. The quality of these boards and meetings differs widely, but the fact that they exist at all is a step in the right direction.

▶ **Hints for Becoming More Effective at Communicating about Values**

Keep a journal in which you record the situations when you find yourself thinking about moral values. List the moral values you find yourself attracted to. Then see if you can describe your moral reasoning.

Practice reflective moral listening about values. When you are discussing a situation that involves moral values, see if you can tell what values are being expressed by others. Test your understanding of their values by asking a question of the form: "You value _____ and that is why you think we/you should do _____."

Practice reflective moral dialogue by first coming to an understanding of your values and reasoning and the values and reasoning of others. Try to form your responses in terms of the moral values and reasoning you hear expressed by others.

Conclusion

In this chapter, we have discussed both good and bad forms of moral reasoning. The forms to be avoided include appealing solely to self-interest, relying on religion as the only justification for morality, and following the dictates of one's culture without reflection. Good moral reasoning first assumes that one must *have* reasons for one's moral decisions; relying on gut intuition is not a reliable guide, nor is it a foundation for discussing issues with those who disagree. Next, it is important to think through difficult issues in a calm frame of mind, with a good understanding of the facts involved. In the next few chapters, we will give you concrete guidance about the kinds of considerations that will help you to become reflective moral decision-makers.

▶ Study Questions for Chapter Two

1. List five key mistakes in moral reasoning.
2. Why is self-interest a problematic moral decision-making strategy?
3. Why might someone object to religion as a moral decision-making strategy?
4. What is Cultural Relativism? Why might someone call it a problematic moral decision-making strategy?
5. What are the three features of good moral reasoning?
6. Describe some effective strategies for communicating about values.

CHAPTER 3

Moral Perspectives I

Consequences, Respect, Character

We have seen some of the ways that moral reasoning can fail and some of the ways that moral communication can be ineffective. Now we will focus on different moral strategies that are effective both for thinking about your own ethical concerns and for living and leading effectively and with integrity. We begin with our description of the characteristics that people with integrity share. In the next two chapters we will show what is involved in each of these characteristics and provide guidance about how to develop and implement them in yourself.

Characteristics of People with Integrity

Awareness
- of one's own values
- of the values of others

Ability to communicate
- one's own values
- using common values

Ability to assess short- and long-term consequences
Respect for others
Care for others and an ability to foster relationships

Virtues, e.g.:
- Courage
- Honesty
- Humility

Fairness
Understanding of Professional Ethics

It should come as no surprise that this work will draw heavily on philosophy to explain all these characteristics. After all, philosophers have been thinking about basic questions of integrity for over 2,000 years. We have already talked about how to develop awareness of one's own values and the values of others, as well as how to communicate about values. Now we turn to the next characteristic: the ability to assess short- and long-term consequences. The idea that assessing consequences plays a key role in making moral decisions is the foundation of a moral theory that philosophers call Consequentialism. The most famous version of Consequentialism is Utilitarianism. In the next section we will discuss Utilitarianism in some detail.

Utilitarianism: Assessing Short- and Long-Term Consequences

We often make decisions by assessing the short- and long-term consequences of various options, but we do this fairly unsystematically. We all know how to brainstorm and how to gather information, and we all have some decision strategies based on these two competencies. There is even a special branch of philosophy and social science called decision theory. We think individuals can benefit greatly by making their decision making more systematic, especially when setting a standard for others to follow. Utilitarianism is the philosophy that is based on a common argument form—one involving consequences. Here is a typical format for such an argument:

1. We have a serious problem.
2. There are these options: A, B, C.

3. The consequences of doing A are bad.
4. The consequences of doing B are bad.
5. The consequences of doing C are good.

Therefore, we should do C.

▶ **Exercise 3.1**

Come up with your own argument based on consequences using the format described above. It might be helpful to write about a fairly simple problem that has only a few well-defined solutions.

Act Utilitarianism

Utilitarianism builds on the simple intuition that doing the right thing involves thinking about all the possible consequences of our actions and picking the alternative that has the most good and the fewest bad consequences. Here is our definition of one simple version of Utilitarianism, Act Utilitarianism: *One ought to do the action that will create more social utility than any alternative possible action.*

There are a number of terms in this definition that need elaboration. Let's start with "social utility." For now, "utility" will just mean good or bad consequences. Later we will be more precise. "Social utility" is the overall balance of negative and positive utility, over the long term, for all concerned. There are three parts of this definition. First, we do not count just the bad consequences or just the good consequences. Our choices are seldom between doing something with only good or bad consequences. Most of our choices involve some pros and some cons. To come up with a measure of social utility, we add up all the good and bad consequences and subtract the bad consequences from the good. What is left is on its way to being social utility.

The second part of the definition of social utility is that it must be measured not just in the short term, but over the long term. It is sometimes difficult to decide how far into the future we should go in determining the likely consequences. If you are trying to decide whether you will help a sick friend or visit your lonely aunt, you needn't imagine how your actions will affect future generations. In this case, you need only figure out how it will affect things over the course of the next few days. If you were deciding whether to vote for a nuclear waste dump in your state, you would need to think about future generations, because the effect on them would be considerable.

The final factor we need to stress is that social utility is the measure of utility for all concerned. This is what distinguishes Utilitarianism from self-interest. When we are making a self-interested decision, we need only consider the consequences to ourselves. When we are measuring social utility, we must consider all the people who would be affected by our different options. Again, we needn't consider every person who is remotely affected, but we should not be too hasty in deciding to limit our investigation into the effects of our various options.

Here's how Act Utilitarianism works. Suppose you have promised your daughter that you will take her to the mall to get a second set of holes pierced in her ears. On the day you are scheduled to go, an old friend calls to say he is unexpectedly in town and would like to see you. Act Utilitarianism says that one should do the act that will create the greatest amount of social utility. It appears that you have three obvious alternatives. You can either meet your friend, take your daughter to the mall, or get your friend to go to the mall with you and your daughter.

You must now consider your options. What you want to know, if you are a conscientious Utilitarian, is what good and bad consequences will follow from each option. If you just take your daughter to the mall, you will miss your friend. This will be bad for you and your friend, but good for you and your daughter. If you just spend the time with your friend, this will be good for you and your friend, but bad for your daughter. If you can get your friend to meet you and your daughter at the mall, you will be happy to see your friend, and your daughter will get to spend time with you and get her ears pierced, which is something that she wants. Act Utilitarianism says that you should count up all the pluses and minuses for all the people concerned and do what will create the best consequences overall, so this looks like the best solution from an Act Utilitarian point of view, even though both your daughter and your friend might prefer to spend time alone with you. In a nutshell then, here is how you decide if you are using Act Utilitarianism.

▶ **Decision Procedure**

1. List all concerned.
2. Consider all alternatives.
3. Calculate the overall utility of each alternative for all concerned.

___

It's now time to go back and clear up some confusion and create some more. The first thing we need to do is discuss the concept of utility. We started out by defining it as good or bad consequences. We now need to get more precise. It turns out that people have very different ideas about what would be a good consequence or a bad consequence. It depends on what they value. "Utility" is a placeholder. You have to decide what to put in its place.

Utility.   Over the years, Utilitarians have offered different definitions of utility. Jeremy Bentham,[1] the first systematic Utilitarian, defined it as pleasure and the absence of pain. John Stuart Mill,[2] another famous Utilitarian, objected to this definition because it counted all kinds of pleasure equally. Suppose, for example, that you had $100 to give away and you wanted to give a prize using Utilitarian considerations. Suppose further that there were just two candidates for the prize. The first said that she would throw a party for her friends and that they would all have a great time. You know her friends, and you believe that she would indeed give pleasure to many. The second says that she would spend it to buy more calligraphy paper so that she could finish a project she is working on. She is pretty low key and says that though her work is very important to her, she doesn't anticipate getting a whole lot of pleasure. Typically, she frets a great deal about her work and often destroys it because it was not up to her standards. If pleasure is the measure of utility, who should get the money? It looks like we throw a party. Bentham might well agree with this decision. After all, he said that a game of darts was just as good as poetry.

Mill would not be satisfied with this response. His solution was to distinguish between what he called higher and lower pleasure. Higher pleasure involves the use of our higher faculties like our intellect and our imagination. Run-of-the-mill partying creates only lower pleasure, but creating a work of art is capable of creating higher pleasure in both the artist and the audience. Mill even goes so far as to say that most humans would choose to be "Socrates dissatisfied" than a "pig satisfied," implying that we would realize the lack of value of sating only lower pleasures.

There is an additional problem with using pleasure as the measure of utility. The original argument for using pleasure as the standard of right and wrong was that all people value pleasure above all else. But this may not be the case. We often sacrifice pleasure in pursuit of other goals. Bentham's response was to distinguish between different characteristics of pleasure—intensity, duration, certainty, fecundity (the ability to generate future pleasure), and purity (not being mixed up with pain). He would say that we rationally forgo present pleasure in the interests of future greater pleasure. But not everyone agrees with Bentham about this. People like Aristotle and J.S. Mill think that humans care (or should care) about more than pleasure. They describe this "something more" as happiness. We now turn to happiness as a measure of utility.

Happiness involves a higher-level mental state than pleasure. It involves feeling pleasure (and pain), but more importantly it involves making judgments about our pleasures in the context of our life plan. Aristotle said that no one could judge whether they were happy until they were on their deathbed. What he meant was that happiness is the recognition that we have achieved our important goals and lived the kind of life we now wished we had lived. If we had to wait till our deathbed, happiness would be a poor choice for a measure of utility, but we can understand happiness as the satisfaction we gain from recognizing that we are achieving our important goals.

It is hard to measure mental states like pleasure and happiness, and for this reason some Utilitarians have argued for more concrete measures of utility. Fans of the original *Star Trek* and the movies it spawned will recall that Spock could use the "Vulcan mind-meld." In this way he could very accurately measure and compare the pleasure and happiness of others.

This is another way in which he was the perfect Utilitarian. Some other measures are well-being, preferences, and a mixed bag of measures. The advantage of well-being is that we can come up with more or less objective standards for well-being. The disadvantage is that people will contest each other's standards. The advantage of using preferences is that we can simply ask what people would prefer. This makes it fairly easy to crunch the numbers when we have a complex decision with many variables and lots of people affected. The disadvantage is that people don't always understand what they want. Even when they do understand what they want, what they want is not always seen by others as conducive to their well-being. Finally, you could measure a mix of things that you think are good.

The bottom line here is that you have to decide what you think is the best measure of utility, and, when you are communicating with others about values, you have to listen carefully to see what others are identifying as the good to be promoted. If you disagree with them about what good is worth promoting, you must be ready to explain why you think your measure of utility is better.

Another related issue is who should be counted. When making our utility calculations, we could count all humans; some humans; humans and animals; humans, animals, and the biosphere; or some other combination. There are good arguments for all these choices, but here again, you do have to choose, and you have to think about why your choice seems like the best one. Notice that this choice is related to the earlier one. If you think pleasure is the utility worth maximizing, then you will need to consider all creatures that can feel pleasure and pain (sentient creatures). If you think happiness is better, you will be hard pressed to include animals with a less complex mental life than humans.

Some Problems for Utilitarians.   We have seen that Utilitarians have different views about what should count as utility and who should be counted. In addition to these differences, there are special problems that Utilitarians have to solve.

The first problem involves measuring utility. How do we measure how our actions will affect persons in the future? This is a problem shared by everyone who has to plan for the future, and there are many ways of doing it. They include looking to the past, looking to similar situations elsewhere, and creating models for predicting outcomes. None of these are perfect, and for those who think that the dictates of morality must always be crystal clear, this counts as an objection to Utilitarianism. Utilitarians would reply, however, that this is not a perfect world, that we are not perfect beings, and that under the circumstances, Utilitarianism is as good as it gets.

There is another problem for Utilitarians. Do we measure the total utility or the average utility? Total utility is the amount of utility we have when we add up the utility of each person. Average utility is the utility we have when we average the amount of utility among persons. This may seem to be just a theoretical problem, but it becomes very real when we look at issues like immigration. Let's take the example of California. Critics of immigration say that when there are more people in the state (regardless of where they are from), everyone suffers from a lower quality of life than was available before the population increased. Defenders of immigration say that there is more utility because more people get to share in the dream.

There are other practical problems for Utilitarians. What do we do when we are in a hurry? How do we teach our children? One solution is to rely on rules of thumb in both of these cases. The rules of thumb come from our past experience in similar situations.

There is one more problem that critics of Utilitarianism have suggested, and that is that Utilitarianism can be unfair. What if the action that maximizes utility results in inequality or unfairness? We've all experienced this kind of unfairness. Teachers punish the whole class because this is the most effective way to control the class. Someone is sent to jail for life for stealing vitamins because "three strikes" laws are thought to decrease the crime rate. Utilitarians have responded in three ways. One is to endorse such inequality if it maximizes utility. The second is to point out that when we calculate utility over the long term, much of the most egregious inequality is indefensible. People just get too angry if they are treated unequally for too long. Finally, some have responded by coming up with a version of Utilitarianism called Rule Utilitarianism.[3] We will turn to this in a moment. First, let's take one last look at the decision procedure for Act Utilitarianism.

▶ **Decision Procedure**

1. Describe morally relevant features of the case.
2. List all options.
3. List all concerned.
4. Calculate utility for each option for all concerned.

▶ **Exercise 3.2**

Describe a moral problem that you have faced. Apply the Act Utilitarian decision procedure. What did this procedure tell you to do? Now, find a partner and use this procedure to defend the action you actually took. In your interaction, keep in mind all the strategies for effective communication about values.

Rule Utilitarianism

According to Rule Utilitarianism, one should *do the action that is in accord with the rule that would, if generally followed, create more social utility than any alternative rule.*

Let's go back and see how this method would work. Consider the trip to the mall with your daughter versus a visit with your friend. Rule Utilitarianism says that we should not make decisions on a case-by-case basis. Instead, we should consider which rules would create the most utility overall. What rules might we appeal to in this case? This is really a difficult question, and it requires that we first say a few things about what a moral rule is. A moral rule is in the form of an imperative, a "should" statement. It is designed to guide us about what to do. In order to provide guidance, a rule must be general enough to provide guidance in similar cases, but specific enough to tell us what to do. In the case described above, we don't want a rule like "Be nice" because it is too general to help us. Neither do we want a rule like "Always consider the needs of your daughter first." This rule would not apply to our sons, our parents, a spouse, and so on. A less specific rule might be "Always consider your family first."

Rule Utilitarianism tells us to consider the utility of alternative rules, so now we must think of alternatives. How about "Do not give your family priority over other persons in making decisions." There are lots of interesting questions that come up as we consider these two alternatives. If we always consider our families first, aren't we in danger of providing for a whim of a family member instead of the pressing need of someone else? Considerations like this suggest ways in which we might amend our rules to make sure they maximize utility. We might end up with a rule something like this: "Always consider the important needs of your family first." Utilitarians defend rules like this by saying that they do maximize utility; when people can depend on their families, everyone is better off overall.

Many people would dispute this, but suppose you agree. If you are a Rule Utilitarian, you would then follow this rule. Even when two people follow the same rule, there is room for disagreement. Some people would think that always giving in to our children's desires is not good for them in the long run. How do we decide? We might just see whether it would create more utility in this case to give in to the daughter. But then, Rule Utilitarianism looks just like Act Utilitarianism, doesn't it? This is a criticism that has been lodged against Rule Utilitarianism, and it's tricky to refute.[4]

In any case, even if you think that Rule Utilitarianism reduces to Act Utilitarianism, there are many cases when we are really looking for a rule. When we are making laws and policies, and when we know our decision will create a precedent, we need to consider the utility of rules. Now there are many moral perspectives to choose from in considering rules, and utility is just one way to think about rules. Later, we'll see other ways to think about rules. In any case, Rule Utilitarianism is in agreement with Act Utilitarianism in saying that we should only consider consequences and measure utility when we make moral decisions, including decisions about what the moral rules should be. Here, then, is the decision procedure for Rule Utilitarianism.

▶ **Decision Procedure**

1. List possible rules.
2. Consider the consequences of adopting each rule.
3. Select the rule with the most utility.
4. Apply the rule.
5. Describe the actions that would conform to the acceptable rule(s).

▶ **Exercise 3.3**

Go back to the situation you described in Exercise 3.2. Now apply Rule Utilitarianism. What is the outcome? Did you have a different outcome when you used Rule Utilitarianism? Now find a small group and defend your action using Rule Utilitarianism. As you do this, keep practicing effective communication about values.

Respect for Others: Kant

Think about someone whom you consider a person of great integrity and an effective leader. Now think about someone who is a bad leader. We would guess that a key characteristic of the effective leader is that s/he treats people with respect. This notion of respect is central to integrity and leadership, and it is also interestingly complex. Just how do we treat people with respect? We can begin to answer this question by looking at two traditions in philosophy: Kantianism and the moral rights tradition.

Immanuel Kant was a late eighteenth-century philosopher who described ethics in terms of two central and related notions: right intentions and respect for persons.[5] To explore the first idea, let's start with an example. Suppose Maria goes out of town and does not leave her sprinkler system on during a long, hot, dry spell. She has four neighbors who all pitch in to water the lawn: Carlotta, Mei, Josh, and Bart. Carlotta, Mei, and Bart assume Maria forgot to set the sprinkler system to automatic. We'll return to Josh. Carlotta decides to water Maria's lawn because she is concerned about how a brown lawn will affect the sale of her nearby house. Mei waters the lawn because she is genuinely fond of Maria. Bart doesn't like Maria but he decides that watering the lawn would be the right thing to do. Josh has some inside information: He overheard Maria talking to a landscaper and knows that she left the lawn unwatered to kill it so that she could put in some new drought-resistant plants. He decides to water the lawn because he thinks it would be fun to undermine her plans and because he knows that he can get away with it by pretending that he did it to be neighborly.

What do we say about these neighbors? First, notice that they all did the same thing—they watered the lawn. I think we would all agree that Josh is simply malicious. Carlotta is merely self-interested; Mei is acting out of affection for Maria; and Bart is watering the lawn because he thinks it is his duty. Kant describes Bart as the only person who deserves moral praise for his action.

The moral of this story is twofold. First, morality is not simply a matter of our actions, regardless of their intentions. In this case, the consequences of watering Maria's lawn were negative, but we don't blame those who had no reason to think that the consequences wouldn't be good. Second, morality seems to be fundamentally concerned with intentions. Kant captures both of these insights in his first formulation of what he calls the Categorical Imperative: "Act only according to that maxim by which you can at the same time will that it would become a universal law."[6]

"Maxim" is a complicated notion, but for our purposes, we can understand a maxim as a moral principle. So we can say that Kant thinks that we should be basing our actions on moral principles, and not solely on the consequences that we think we can produce. Our duty then is to act on the basis of the right intention—the intention to follow the right kind of moral principle. How do we decide what the right kind of principle is? The right kind of maxim is the one that we think all rational persons would accept as universal. Here we can appeal to two ideas—reversibility and universality. Universality means that I recognize moral principles as applying to all human beings. Reversibility means that I accept a principle even as it applies to me.

Let's now return to the lawn example. The basic moral principle here might be "help others." We would probably want to add a qualification such as "as long as doing so does not harm yourself or others unduly." Is this principle universal? That is, does it apply to all persons? It would seem so. Presumably we would want everyone to help others, just as we would want everyone to be helped when they need it. Is it reversible? In other words, would I accept it if it applied to me? Again, it seems to pass the test. I would want to be helped, and thus I should accept the duty to help others.

The question that seems to arise here is: Why should I accept that I have duties to others? Here Kant offers his second version of the Categorical Imperative,[7] which says, "Act so that you treat humanity, whether in your own person or in that of another, always as an end and never as a means only."[8] There are two parts of this imperative. The first is the minimal one—don't use people. The second is a bit more complex—treat persons as ends in themselves. We're going to cash this out in terms of seeing persons as moral equals. We begin with the injunction against using people.

It is pretty easy to understand the idea of using people. Let's look at another example. Jack is notorious for being unable to keep administrative assistants. He is not good about keeping track of their names, but it doesn't really matter because he refers to all of them as "my girl." He is totally indifferent to how many hours they work, or whether their work affects their health or their personal life. We all know people like Jack, who seem to think that the people around them are just there for their benefit. They are nice only when it will get them somewhere and perfectly willing to betray their grandmothers if they think it will get them what they want. Most of us are not at all like this, but almost all of us have a little bit of Jack in us. Perhaps it is just certain people who we treat this way, or perhaps we are only like this when we are stressed or preoccupied. We can see what is wrong with this behavior. It hurts the people we interact with, and it closes us off to a more involved relationship with them.

Of course, we can't always be involved with everyone we meet. In our busy lives, we sometimes need to have short interactions. We can still do this without treating people as if they existed just to serve us. It begins with thinking about people differently. We try to look at people and imagine the story of their lives. Who are they? What do they think about? Why are they smiling or frowning? You can cultivate this awareness of others during your ordinary routines—as you ride the train in to work or ride the elevator to your floor. In your less-casual relationships, you can do much more. You can ask people what is going on with them and listen attentively to their answers. The awareness of people as having their own stories can affect your interactions with people as they recognize that your interest is genuine. Even your briefest encounters can start with a greeting or eye contact.

The idea of treating people as moral equals is a bit more complex. First of all, it doesn't mean treating people as though they were equal in every way. People have different abilities, different roles, and different histories that make us think they are more or less deserving of respect. So treating people as moral equals does not mean that the VP has to give up her office and share the cubicles with the rest of the staff.

Equality is one of those words with many different meanings, and moral equality is just one of them. We try to describe it this way. Think about why you think you are a valuable person and are entitled to be treated with some degree of respect. Is it because you are the VP? Suppose you are laid off. It is okay for a person to steal from you now or run you over with their car? "Of course not," you say. Well, why not? Maybe it's because of your lovely brown hair, or your nice manners, or the fact that you drive an expensive foreign car. Now, imagine taking these things away. Is it okay to treat you badly now? Eventually, we come down to some things about ourselves that really do seem to explain why we think we should not be treated badly.

Most philosophers who agree with Kant point to our capacity to reason about things. Human beings can think in much more complex ways than other creatures on the planet. In addition to being able to do fairly complex thinking, they are reflective. This means that they are able to think about their own thinking. They also care about how it all comes out. Here's an example. Sam is thinking about a crossword puzzle. He begins to think about the general strategy he is using, and then he realizes that he wants to improve his strategy because he wants to be the kind of person who can do crossword puzzles really well. He has been thinking about his own thinking: That is self-reflection.

Another capacity humans have is that we have an understanding of morality and an ability to reflect on what is right and wrong. Now some people love their dogs and think they are really wonderful. But they may worry that they have not paid enough attention to their dogs. They may resolve to groom them more frequently or to have that canine dental work done that they have been putting off. Or they may resolve to be a better companion to their dogs. The dogs, however, do not think about what their obligations are to their owners or about whether they should rethink them. Unlike dogs, people are capable of thinking about their moral obligations.

Humans also have complex emotions. We can love and hate, or laugh and cry, in ways that no other creatures on earth can. This is another reason why we might think of ourselves as deserving of basic respect.

In short, then, respect seems to be our due because of our humanity. As soon as we notice this, we realize that everyone who shares in humanity is equally entitled to this basic respect. This is the idea of moral equality: the idea that we are equally entitled to basic respect because we are all humans.

Now some people are not too happy with this whole concept of respect because they worry that animals and other creatures get left out of it. They have responded in two ways. Sometimes they point out that other animals have the same capacities as humans to think and feel, although these capacities are not as well developed. The other response has been to say that we have become so fond of our own species that we invented an ethic that just applies to us. We think the best response is to acknowledge that respect really does apply best to human-to-human interaction, though respect is not the only moral idea. Some of the other moral ideas we discuss are much better for dealing with animals.

Back to Jack. We don't expect everyone to become more respectful. For some people, the best strategy is to work around them and try not to promote them to places where they can do real harm. So Jack is probably not going to begin to treat other people as moral equals. However, we could point out to Jack (and to those in a position to influence him) that the people who work with and for Jack are feeling demoralized and undervalued. He might be persuaded to change his style of interaction. Luckily, there aren't too many people like Jack out there. But the important point to note here is that the rest of us can learn from the story about Jack and begin to rethink our own attitudes and behaviors.

▶ **Decision Procedure 1: The Universality Test**

1. Describe morally relevant features of the case.
2. Look for possible principles to govern actions in the case.
3. Ask if the principles are categorical or defensible in terms of the Categorical Imperative.
4. Apply principles that meet the test.

▶ **Decision Procedure 2: The Respect Test**

1. How are persons being treated?
2. Is this treatment consistent with not using people as mere means?
3. Is this treatment consistent with treating them as moral equals?
4. What treatment would be consistent with not using people and treating them as moral equals?

▶ **Exercise 3.4**

Look again at the situation you described in Exercise 3.2 and apply a Kantian perspective. What is the outcome? Does it differ from the one you got when you used Utilitarianism? Use it to defend your decision.

Often, we end up coming to the same decision no matter what approach we take. Sometimes, though, Kant's approach and Utilitarianism would lead to different decisions. It makes sense that there could be a conflict between respecting persons and using consequences to make a decision. We might like to think that we will almost always end up with good long-term consequences when we treat persons with respect, but this won't always be the case. When such a conflict occurs, we must choose what to focus on in the situation at hand. We have to try to strike a balance in the situation.

We leave it to you to decide how to do this. Whatever balance you strike for yourself, you have to be able to communicate effectively with people who would strike a different balance. So even if you think you can make every decision by just focusing on the consequences for all concerned, keep in mind that you will be interacting with people who might not agree with you. Perhaps they will want to focus more on respecting persons, even if doing so does not have obvious good consequences.

Respect for Others: Moral Rights

A contemporary and influential way to talk about respecting persons is the moral rights tradition. Kant was one of the fathers of this tradition. "Moral rights" is often used synonymously with "human rights." They both indicate entitlements that are connected with our status as rational creatures. "Civil rights" are often used to refer to moral rights too, but that term is a bit misleading because it also indicates rights that are bestowed in virtue of our civil (legal) systems. The moral rights tradition is particularly strong in the United States, and it is enthroned in two of our most important political documents, the Declaration of Independence and the Constitution. It is also a common moral appeal internationally, as in the Universal Declaration of Human Rights. Whenever there is a heated debate about a social or political issue in the United States or internationally, you can bet that people on all sides of the debate will claim that they have rights at stake.

Since this tradition is so much a part of our political and moral heritage and because rights are invoked so frequently, it is important to get clear about what a moral right is. Different defenders of moral rights have come up with varying analyses of what a moral right is. In what follows, we offer our own interpretation, drawing on the great body of work done by philosophers on this subject.

Features of Moral Rights

We need to get clear about what moral rights are, and also about what they are not. First, *they are not legal rights*. When we say that people have a legal right, we mean that their legal institutions protect them in having or using something. So we might say that in the United States all citizens who are not convicted felons have a right to vote. This means that if citizens want to vote, no one can prevent them from registering and exercising this right. But legal rights differ from place to place. People in some countries do not have a legal right to vote.

Moral rights differ from legal rights in one important sense. Having a moral right is not a matter of living under a particular legal system. Regardless of what country you live in, if something is a moral right, then you have it whether or not the law protects it.

Second, *moral rights are claims that society should enforce.* What this means is that if we are persuaded that people really have a right, then we recognize that we have to do something to make sure they can exercise the right. That is why people make so many rights claims, and it is why we take them so seriously.

Third, *moral rights imply duties.* This means that if someone has a right to something, somebody else has a duty to see to it that the right is respected. There are two different ways of understanding the correlative duties. The first view is called the negative rights view. On this view, if someone has a right to something, then everyone else has to get out of their way when they want to exercise this right. A more formal definition is: *If P has a right to X, then everyone else is required to refrain from interfering with P's having X.* Let's consider an example. There is some agreement that persons have a right to life. On the negative rights view, this means that one must refrain from killing anyone.

The contrasting view is called the positive rights view. This view grows out of the insight that refraining from interfering is often not sufficient to protect someone's exercise of a right. Here's an example. Suppose a person is visiting someone with small children, and she observes one of them slipping under water in the pool. Suppose further that she is in the pool next to the drowning child and could merely reach out her hand and pull the child to safety, but that she chooses instead to do nothing and watch the child drown. It appears that she has satisfied the negative rights standard with respect to the right to life—she did not kill anyone—and yet many would argue that what she did (or did not do) is the same as killing.

This kind of example has prompted some people to add a further clause to the understanding of a right: Respecting rights involves not interfering, but it also involves helping when help is needed. The formal definition is: *If P has a right to X, then everyone else is required to refrain from interfering with P's having X AND should cooperate, when necessary, in P's having X.*

These two different ways of explaining what it is to respect rights marks a major divide in social and political debates. Libertarians embrace a negative rights view, and liberals embrace a positive rights view.[9]

The fourth feature of moral rights is that *they cannot be waived.* What this means is that if a person has a right, he cannot give it up, even if he wants to. Suppose a woman wants to give up all her choices in a marriage contract. She agrees to stay with her husband until she dies, accept whatever treatment he sees fit to mete out to her, and do whatever he asks of her. Would such a contract be morally enforceable? Defenders of the moral rights tradition say that it would not be because this contract ignores her right to liberty and her right against harm. A formal definition of this condition is: *If P has a right to X, then P cannot give up his/her claim to X.*

There are two more conditions for moral rights. The fifth is that a right takes precedence over all other considerations. The formal way of stating this is that *rights cannot be overridden.* That is: *If P has a right to X, P's claim to X counts more heavily than any other consideration.* What this means is that if one has a right to something, then you cannot take it away even if doing so would create good consequences. You've probably noticed by now that philosophers love to think up examples. Here's an example that illustrates this condition. Suppose that you have a spleen with wonderful properties. Medicine could use your spleen to create endless supplies of blood products that would cure some types of cancers. Is it okay to take your spleen without your permission? Most people would say no. What this suggests is that there is a right here. Philosophers call this right the right to bodily integrity. Let's change the case and make it your heart. This case is even clearer, since taking your heart would kill you. Now we are dealing with two rights: the right to bodily integrity and the right to life. Let's change the example again. Suppose they just want the dandruff that has fallen onto your shoulders. We'll let you think about this one.

The last condition is that rights apply to everyone. You don't have them because you live in a certain country or are a certain gender or social class. The formal way of saying this is that *rights apply universally.* Thus, *if P has a right to X, then anyone else in P's situation would have a legitimate claim to X.*

Who Has Moral Rights?

There are ongoing debates about who has moral rights. Some people have said that only humans have rights, and that they have them regardless of their mental or physical status. Some have wanted to include animals. Whatever your answer is, you have to defend it by showing that members of your group have particular characteristics that make them right-holders. Remember that Kant picked out rationality and moral agency as the two criteria for being a person worthy of respect. Many in the rights tradition would agree with him. Other people would want to add another property: the ability to have appropriate emotions and attachment to others. When we use Kant's criteria, it looks like we would have to say that most humans have rights. People who want to include animals as right-holders either have to show that animals can be rational moral agents with emotions and ties of affection, or that we need a different analysis of what a right-holder is. Since humans are often seen as the paradigm right-holders, the term "moral rights" is often used interchangeably with "human rights."

We are now ready to state a decision procedure for rights.

▶ **Decision Procedure**

1. What possible rights are involved?
2. Are these really rights?
   a. Should society enforce this claim for everyone?
   b. Do we have duties with respect to X?
   c. Can P give up his/her claim to X?
   d. Would it be okay to ignore X if it conflicted with some other consideration?

3. Are the rights being violated?

4. What would respecting these rights require?

5. If rights are coming into conflict, how can we balance them?

▶ Exercise 3.5

There are two important social issues that are talked about in terms of rights: smoking and health care. Do you think we have a right to smoke? To health care? Answer these questions using the decision procedure above.

Character and the Virtuous Person

The other characteristic of integrity we will discuss in this chapter is virtuous character. (For the remaining characteristics from the outline at the beginning of the chapter, see Chapter 4.) "Virtue" is an old-fashioned word nowadays. We are now more likely to describe someone in terms of psychological diagnoses than in terms of their character. However, we think there is much to gain from a return to thinking about persons in terms of their characters.

Aristotle had insightful things to say about character, and philosophers still look to him when they are thinking about virtue.[10] He said that a good person is virtuous, meaning that a good person has the right virtues in the right balance. A virtue is an abiding (not fleeting) trait of a person's character. We say of someone, "Oh, that was so in character," or, "He doesn't usually act that way." For Aristotle, a virtue is the mean between two extremes. For example, it is not good to be greedy, but it is not good to give away so much that you cannot care for yourself. We can balance these two tendencies by being generous and prudent.

Should everyone have the same virtues? Should one's dentist and one's favorite artist have the same kind of character? We think they should to a certain extent, but beyond that we probably want them to be a bit different. For this reason, it makes sense to talk about two different kinds of virtue. These can be called general virtues and special virtues. We define a general virtue in the following way: *A general virtue is an abiding charac-ter trait that makes one a good friend and a good citizen.*

While there are some virtues that all humans should possess regardless of their particular circumstances, there are other virtues that we want only some people to have. We call these special virtues. *A special virtue is an abiding character trait that helps you to fulfill your function in society well.* So one's dentist should share a lot of virtues with one's favorite artist, but be-yond that we would probably want the dentist to be clean, whereas we might not require this of an artist.

We can define vice in terms of virtue. A vice is a character trait that undermines your ability to function as a good friend and a good citizen, and thereby prevents you from fulfilling your function well.

We can now think about some character traits we would want people, es-pecially those who are leaders in some way, to have. One may think *courage* would have to be on the list. Think again of some morally dubious people you have encountered. Like bad families, bad people can be bad in different ways, but one way a person can be bad is if he or she refuses to ever go out on a limb. We don't want our leaders to be foolhardy, but we do want them to stand up for what they think is right even when it is hard to do this. The second virtue we would include is *honesty.* It is hard to work with someone whom you cannot trust, who says one thing and does another. The last virtue we believe is critical is humility. *Humility* is the balance between arro-gance and total self-effacement. We have all had to deal with arrogant peo-ple. They do not listen to anyone, they always think they know best, and they try to force everyone else to go along with them. Self-effacing people, in contrast, are never willing to trust themselves to know anything. They constantly defer to others. Most of us have experienced this kind of leader-ship as well. We call it "leadership-by-who-talked-to-me-last."

There are other possible virtues, and different virtue traditions have fo-cused on different sets of virtues. In what follows, we will mention two traditions: Aristotle and the Christian tradition. We will discuss the Con-fucian virtue tradition in more detail in Chapter 5.

In the *Nichomachean Ethics,* Aristotle gave a fairly comprehensive list of virtues and how they can be shown to be means between extremes (he discusses courage in Book 3, the rest in Book 4; Justice is discussed in Book 5). This list is summarized in Table 3.1.

TABLE 3.1   Aristotle's List of Virtues

Extreme of Too Much	*Mean*	*Extreme of Too Little*
recklessness	courage	cowardice
extravagance	generosity	stinginess
vulgarity	magnificence	miserliness
vanity	high-mindedness	pettiness
short temper	gentleness	apathy
obsequiousness	friendliness	grouchiness
boastfulness	truthfulness	self-depreciation
buffoonery	wittiness	boorishness

It is reasonable to ask what Aristotle meant when he said virtue was a mean between two extremes. He offered two answers. First, a mean is that between too much and too little of a disposition. This is not an arithmetical mean but a mean relative to individuals. He used the example of athletes in training and how much they should eat. The mean will differ for each athlete, depending upon the athlete's size and level of training. An athlete who is expending a large number of calories needs to make sure to eat enough calories. An athlete who is building muscles needs to make sure to eat enough protein. There is no set amount that each of these athletes must eat; we must decide in each case what is too little or too much. Second, hitting the mean with respect to virtue is having a given disposition at the right time, in the right place, toward the right person for the right reason, and in the right way.

It's not clear that these two explanations are compatible. The second characterization suggests that sometimes one ought to be furious and sometimes only slightly angry, depending on the situation, while the mean in the first sense between short temper and apathy is gentleness. Since Aristotle's commentators are still divided on this issue, we suggest you pick the one that makes most sense for you. You could use the following practical strategy for hitting the mean: Keep away from the more dangerous error, and avoid errors you are personally tempted to fall into.

When we look at the list of Aristotelean virtues, it is important to remember that Aristotle had a particular type of person in mind: a person of authority and power in a society where such people were also the warriors who protected the society from outside threats. The list of virtues Aristotle gives allows for a thriving society of this kind. Other traditions have different lists of virtues, in part because they support a different kind of society. Important virtues in the Christian tradition, for example, include faith, hope, charity, chastity, humility, and obedience, and these virtues support the monastic tradition. We will look at a fuller list of Confucian virtues later, but note that they are supposed to provide for flourishing families, which in this tradition are the foundation for a flourishing state. You need to decide for yourself what virtues you think should be cultivated. Begin by thinking about what a good society would look like, and then ask yourself what virtues people would have to have to be good friends and citizens in that society. Then you can catalog special virtues by looking at the roles you think would exist in that society.

Becoming Virtuous

Confucius wrote many insightful and timely things about virtue. We especially like his discussion of how to become virtuous. In the *Analects* he is quoted as saying: "At fifteen my mind was set on learning. At thirty my character had been formed. At forty I had no more perplexities. At fifty I knew the Mandate of Heaven. At sixty I was at ease with whatever I heard. At seventy I could follow my heart's desire without transgressing moral principles."[11] Here is our reading of what Confucius meant:

1: We are taught by our elders what actions are considered virtuous. Most of us are lucky enough to have parents and teachers who taught us the right thing. This raises the question of whether people who missed this part of their early education can ever be virtuous. We think they can, because we all have the ability to reason about what kind of a life we want to live and what kind of a world we want to live in. There are some other people who were damaged in a much more serious way in their early childhood. These people were abused and neglected as children. Some of these people will never be able to develop enough empathy and trust in the world to be virtuous. This is a lesson for all of us. We have a responsibility to make sure that children grow up in a way that makes it possible for them to become virtuous members of society. This is necessary for their happiness and for a flourishing society for the rest of us.

2: When children are well taught, they develop habits of behaving a certain way even though they don't really understand why this is the right way to behave.

3: Much later, we begin to understand what is virtuous. At this point, we have questioned what we've been taught and come to understand it. We have also had the opportunity to reflect on what we should keep and what we should give up. It is now our responsibility to practice the habits of virtue. If we behave in virtuous ways we will stay on the path of virtue.

4: At this point in our lives, we have a pretty good understanding of what is virtuous, and we are trying to stay on the path of virtue. We want to be virtuous, but sometimes we fail because we have not gotten our desires under control.

5: Finally, for those of us who do reach this stage, our desires and the dictates of virtue coincide. We are no longer tempted to behave in a vicious way because we have no desire to do so. Now, it is extremely unlikely that any of us will ever reach this stage. Confucius himself claimed that he never did. Still it is good to keep our eyes on this goal because it will help keep our feet on the path to virtue.

Why Be Virtuous?

Like the shepherd in the fable of Gyges' ring that Plato recounts in *The Republic*, we may wonder whether we should be virtuous when we think no one will notice.[12] This fictional shepherd found a ring that made him invisible. He used it to do all the bad things he'd always wanted to do. Why shouldn't we all do the same thing? There are two answers. The first is that we want others to be virtuous because we value good friends and a good and efficient society. Fairness demands that we ask the same thing of ourselves. Besides, we are "other" to the other people around us. Another answer comes from Plato and Aristotle. We should be virtuous because true human happiness can only be achieved in a virtuous life. Try the deathbed thought experiment again here. Imagine you are on your deathbed. What kind of a person would you want to be? What do you want people to say about you at your funeral?

Though Aristotle and Plato agreed that moral virtue is necessary for happiness, it is not enough. Aristotle thought we would also need a basic level of material well-being, intellectual virtues, and good friends.

We've seen how we can become virtuous. Since none of us is perfectly virtuous yet, we need guidance to help us be virtuous right now. It might help to ask why anyone would fail to be virtuous, since it is part of a happy and complete life. Aristotle distinguished between four types of people: (1) the temperate person—the person who wants to do the right thing and who succeeds without conflict, (2) the continent person—the person who wants to do the right thing and usually does so, but with conflict and struggle, (3) the incontinent person—the person who wants to do the right thing but often doesn't, and (4) the licentious/intemperate person—the person who doesn't want to do the right thing. The first is the truly virtuous person; the second and third are on the way to being virtuous, and the last is the true villain. This division mirrors Confucius' description of becoming virtuous. As adults, we cannot change the way we were raised, but we can change our character nonetheless. We can begin by resolving to become more virtuous. We can then use the following strategy in assessing our everyday conduct.

▶ Decision Procedure

1. What virtues/vices could (did) we display?
2. What role did these virtues/vices play in how we behaved?
3. What will be the effect on our character of behaving this way?

4. What virtues should have been displayed?
5. How would things have turned out differently if these virtues were displayed?
6. How can we become more virtuous in the future?

> **Exercise 3.6**

Spend some time thinking about what you want to be able to say about yourself on your deathbed. What will you want to have accomplished? What kind of a person do you want to be? If you could go to your own funeral, what would you want people to say about you? What kind of a society would you have wanted to live in? What kind of a role would you have wanted to play in that society?

Conclusion

In this chapter, we introduced a model of the person of integrity. We discussed the first three characteristics: the ability to sort out consequences, respect for others, and virtuous character. In the next chapter, we will look at the next three: care, fairness, and understanding of one's professional obligations.

> **Study Questions for Chapter Three**

1. What are the characteristics of people with integrity?
2. What is Act Utilitarianism? How would you use it to make a moral decision?
3. What are the alternative concepts of social utility? How do they differ?
4. What are four major problems for Act Utilitarians? How might they respond?
5. What is Rule Utilitarianism? How would you use it to make a moral decision?

6. How does Rule Utilitarianism differ from Act Utilitarianism?

7. What is Kant's first version of the Categorical Imperative? What does it mean for a principle to be reversible? What does it mean for a principle to be universal?

8. What is Kant's second version of the Categorical Imperative? What does it mean?

9. How might Utilitarianism conflict with Kant's approach?

10. What is a moral right? What are the key features of moral rights? Explain each.

11. Who has moral rights?

12. What is a virtue?

13. What does Aristotle mean when he says that a virtue is a mean between two extremes?

14. Give some examples of Aristotelean virtues. How are these means between extremes?

15. How does Confucius describe how one becomes virtuous?

16. What is weakness of will? What role does it play in Aristotle's virtue theory?

NOTES

1. Jeremy Bentham, *The Principles of Morals and Legislation* (originally published 1789) (Amherst, N.Y.: Prometheus Books, 1988).

2. John Stuart Mill, *Utilitarianism* (originally published 1863), available in *The Basic Writings of John Stuart Mill: On Liberty, The Subjection of Women, Utilitarianism,* edited by J. B. Schneewind (New York: Modern Library, 2002).

3. The contemporary distinction between Act and Rule Utilitarianism was made by Richard Brandt, but some argue that the distinction was originally made by Mill. See Brandt, *Ethical Theory* (Englewood Cliffs, N.J.: Prentice Hall, 1959).

4. See David Lyons, *Forms and Limits of Utilitarianism* (Oxford: Oxford University Press, 1965).

5. Immanuel Kant, *Groundwork of the Metaphysics of Morals* (originally published 1785), translated by Mary J. Gregor (Cambridge: Cambridge University Press, 1998).

6. See the second section of Kant's *Groundwork* for an explication of the three versions of the Categorical Imperative.

7. Kant distinguished between imperatives of prudence—hypothetical imperatives—and imperatives of morality. Hypothetical imperatives apply to you if you have a particular desire. Suppose you desire to buy the safest car you can get. If you think Saabs are safe cars, then you will want to take a look at them. So for you the imperative "Look at Saabs" applies. But if you want the sportiest car you can get, perhaps you will look elsewhere. The imperatives of moral-

ity do not depend on whether one has a particular desire, and thus he called these imperatives categorical. He gave three versions of the Categorical Imperative, though he says that they are all versions of the same idea.

8. Kant, *Groundwork*, 6.

9. For a discussion of Libertarianism, see Robert Nozick, *Anarchy, State, and Utopia* (New York: Basic Books, 1977). For a discussion of Liberalism, see Richard Epstein, *Skepticism and Freedom: A Modern Case for Classical Liberalism* (Chicago: University of Chicago Press, 2003).

10. Aristotle, *Nichomachean Ethics* (originally written circa 335–322 BCE), translated by Terence Irwin (Indianapolis: Hackett Press, 1985).

11. Confucius, *The Analects*.

12. Plato, *The Republic* (originally written circa 380 BCE), translated by G.M.A. Grube (Indianapolis: Hacket Press, 1992).

CHAPTER 4

Moral Perspectives II

Care, Fairness, Professional Codes

One characteristic of people with integrity is their ability to care for others and to foster good relationships. Caring for others is more than having sympathetic feelings for them; it requires that one take concrete action to look after the needs of others. Caring for others and fostering good relationships go together for two reasons. First, humans are essentially social creatures—we live and work in groups, and most of us would be absolutely miserable if we didn't have meaningful relationships. So caring about persons means caring about their relationships. Second, we cannot accomplish many of the tasks we need to undertake unless we can foster good relationships. This includes the task of giving care to others.

Let's start with an example and see how caring works. Doug is concerned with trying to salvage an account and wants to send someone to visit the client. Tuan is the most likely candidate, since he has a good working relationship with the client, but he is scheduled to visit another client on a much bigger account. Susan has some experience with this client and has been known to save accounts in similar situations, so she is Doug's next choice. Carlos is a possibility, but he is not as familiar with the product as Susan. Doug recalls that Susan's father is in the last stages of his battle with congestive heart failure, and he wonders whether it would be fair to ask her to go. He calls her into his office, and Susan says that her father would probably want her to go. Satisfied, Doug sends

Susan on the trip, but the account is lost anyway. Did Doug do the right thing? We can now answer this question by asking whether Doug was sufficiently caring.

Care for Others and Fostering Relationships

Care is a basic human capacity to recognize and respond to the needs of others and to moderate our behavior by appeal to the good or harm it might cause to others. Martin Hoffman is a prominent moral psychologist who sees care as growing out of our natural capacity for empathy.[1] This capacity is evident even in newborns, who cry when they hear another baby cry. Later in their development, children become motivated to help whenever they encounter others in distress. Finally, reflection allows us to build on our basic empathic distress at the suffering of others. We then can generalize beyond our immediate experience of someone's distress and imagine the distress of someone who is distant from us. In both cases, we feel impelled to help.

This impulse to help can be undermined in a number of ways: by blaming the victim for his or her own distress, by feeling overwhelmed by the distress of others, or by consciously avoiding the awareness of the distress of others. Further, we have a natural impulse to prioritize the needs of those who are close to us. Hoffman pointed to the natural, evolutionary basis for empathy, but he suggested that we could use this natural capacity to motivate ourselves to be responsive to distant others as well. In other words, we can make a conscious commitment to being caring persons. Because there is a natural basis for care, care can be both a strong motivation for doing the right thing and a basis for recognizing right actions. In this way, caring for others provides the foundation for a moral perspective.

Moral perspectives can be connected to basic human capacities. But there is another way to think about moral perspectives: We can see them as growing out of ideal ways to respond in a certain context. For example, if one thinks about what is involved in doing one's moral best in the context of a marketplace between relatively independent and self-interested strangers, the value of honesty and trust are central. The care perspective in moral philosophy grew out of looking systematically at what is required to be a responsible member of a flourishing relationship. Sara Ruddick, for instance, looked carefully at what is involved in being a good mother to dependent children.[2] Many contemporary defenders of an ethic of care, and many historical antecedents such as David Hume and Adam Smith, have thought that one can generalize beyond relationships with our intimates. Thus, once we find out what values motivate a person to be an ideal caring person in an intimate relationship, one can apply those values to situations that involve distant strangers. When one understands what practices best allow us to apply these values in intimate relationships, then one can generalize these practices to other situations.

Though not all defenders of an ethic of care see care as a virtue, we think this is the most plausible way to understand it.[3] Like other virtues, care is a general disposition to behave in a particular way. Unlike other virtues, care is what we call a meta-virtue—that is, it provides an organizing principle for all the other virtues. If my overall orientation is to be a caring person, then I will be courageous when what I value is at risk; I will be honest because honesty is usually the best way to care for others; I will want to be prudent because I recognize that I must balance the needs of others with my own needs. So the traditional virtues of courage, honesty, and prudence are organized under the meta-virtue of care.

When Carol Gilligan first described the care orientation, she described it as a typically female moral orientation.[4] However, there is nothing gendered about caring; if it is more prevalent in women than in men, it is because women are socially conditioned to do much of society's caring work—they are more likely to be involved with caring for children and the sick, for example. Care is a basic human capacity and as such it is both possible and important for all of us to be caring persons. Developing our capacity to give care requires that we commit to this ideal and that we practice exercising care. When we truly care about someone or something, we have certain emotions and motivations. If we see someone in dire need, for example, we will feel compassion and will be motivated to do something to respond to the need. Finally, it is not enough to merely have the appropriate emotion and motivation; care involves an appropriate response.

Caring is not just a response to need; it is a response to a variety of other features of moral situations as well: harm, past promises, role relationships, and so on. In the case of need, our obligation to respond in an appropriately caring way arises when we are able to respond to need. A "need" is different from a "desire": A need is something that is basic to survival and to a minimally decent life, whereas a desire is something that we merely want and that is not basic to survival or to a minimally decent life. Things that humans need for their survival include food, water, clothing, shelter, and health care. Things that humans need for a minimally decent life can be debated. Aristotle cited friendship; Mill cited liberty; and Rawls offered self-esteem. Still, there is no universal, cross-cultural understanding of need. Rather, need is mediated by a number of factors, including family, culture, economic class, gender and sexuality, and disability and illness. Finally, as we respond to needs, we should recognize the vast differences in power that exist and shape the recognition and articulation of needs. Sometimes, people are unwilling to express their needs freely because they fear that their needs will not be met. They may even be in such a state of dependence or despair that they are no longer able to identify their needs.

Harm is another feature of moral situations. Most people understand that being the cause of harming someone else creates an obligation to respond. But causation is a complex idea. We can be part of the causal story even when we don't think of ourselves as the primary cause. Suppose, for example, that you are taking an exam, and you notice the young man next to you looking at some notes written on the palm of his hand. You realize that he is cheating on the exam. Suppose further that this is an exam that is designed to demonstrate competence in a skill crucial for a health-care practitioner. Suppose that you simply look the other way, and later you find out that a patient was seriously harmed because the practitioner really did not understand the procedure he should have followed, and that this procedure was the very one he was being tested on when you saw him cheating. Do you have a responsibility here? We would argue that you do, though it's not always clear what you can do after the fact. At the very least, you now know that you shouldn't look the other way when you see similar cheating in the future.

There are two other things that mark the moral dimension of a situation that are worth noting here—past promises and role responsibility. When we make a promise, we commit ourselves to a certain course of action. An ethic of care doesn't say that you are always committed to keeping a promise, because sometimes doing so can be harmful to all concerned. But it does impose a moral obligation to respond. Similarly, being in a particular role (for example, teacher) comes with a set of general obligations.

We've now looked at some of the features of situations that suggest that we have an obligation. In order to see what our obligations are in a particular situation, we need to look at the features of an ethic of care. Though humans have always included features of care in their constructive interactions with each other, it emerged only recently as a systematic moral perspective. Nel Noddings's influential book *Caring: A Feminine Approach to Ethics and Moral Education* was the first contemporary work that described care in some detail as a moral orientation.[5] Virginia Held, who has also been an influential defender of this perspective, has most recently extended the concept to the global arena.[6] There are important differences and similarities in the different descriptions of an ethic of care, but here we will be using the model developed by Rita Manning.[7]

There are four central ideas in an ethic of care: moral attention, sympathetic understanding, relationship awareness, and accomodation and harmony.

Moral Attention

Moral attention is the attention to the situation in all its complexity. When one is morally attentive, one wishes to become aware of all the details that will allow a sympathetic response to the situation. It is not enough to know that this is a case of a particular kind, say a case about lying or cruelty. In order to understand what our obligations are, we have to know all the details that might make a difference in our understanding and response to the particular situation at hand.

Sympathetic Understanding

When one sympathetically understands the situation, one is open to sympathizing and even identifying with the persons in the situation. One tries to be aware of what the others in the situation would want one to do, what would most likely be in their best interests, and how they would like one to carry out their wishes and interests and meet their needs. We call this attention to the best interests of others maternalism. It is done in the context of a special sensitivity to the wishes of the other and with an understanding of the other's interest that is shaped by a deep sympathy and understanding. When it is hard to be sympathetic, one may try several strategies—perhaps imagining others as oneself in an earlier crisis. As one adopts this sympathetic attitude, one often becomes aware of what others want and need. Finally, as we respond to others, we look to satisfy their needs in ways that will preserve their sense of competence and dignity while at the same time addressing their needs or even ameliorating their suffering.

Relationship Awareness

There is a special kind of relationship awareness that characterizes caring. A person recognizes that others are in a relationship with him or her. First there is the most basic relationship, that of fellow creatures. There is the immediate relationship of need and ability to fill the need. Another relationship is created when you are the cause of harm to someone else or have a past history that implies obligations. One might also be in some role relationship with the other that calls for a particular response, such as teacher–student. A caring person is aware of all these relationships as he or she surveys a situation. He or she is aware of the network of relationships that connects humans, and cares about preserving and nurturing these relationships. As caring persons think about what to do, they try not to undermine these relationships and try to nurture and extend the relationships that are supportive of human flourishing.

Accommodation and Harmony

Related to the notion of relationship awareness is accommodation. Oftentimes there are many persons involved in a situation and how best to respond is not obvious. The desire to nurture networks of care requires that one tries to accommodate the needs of all, including oneself. It is not always possible, or wise, to do what everyone wants. But it is often important to do what you think is best while at the same time giving everyone concerned a sense of being involved and considered in the process. When we do this, we have a better chance of preserving harmony. If you do what you think is right without consulting anyone, you risk upsetting the harmony of the group. Of course, not all harmony is worth preserving. The oppressive society may be pretty stable and harmonious, but at the price of ignoring those at the bottom. An ethic of care would be opposed to this type of superficial harmony, since it is dependent on treating some as though they do not deserve the same care as others. Ideally, we should aim for the harmonious society in which all are treated with care.

Putting It All Together

Let's return to Doug and see how he might have thought about the situation with the account that was at risk if he'd been more skillful at caring. Doug did not really think about Susan's situation very carefully. He should have realized that she was upset about her father's illness. Since we are all distracted when something this serious is going on in our lives, she was probably also worried that her concern might put her job performance in jeopardy. Doug should not have taken her words at face value, because it's hard to believe that her father really wanted her to go. Perhaps he was just being a good father and trying to put Susan's needs above his own. Very likely, he was worried about how his illness was affecting her. He might have told her to go to give her some time off or to protect her job.

Doug also did not give much thought to how well Susan would be able to interact with the client while her father was dying miles away. The result of his action was a lost account and considerable discomfort for Susan. This lack of care on his part probably will affect his relationship with Susan and her effectiveness in future negotiations. Whenever she has to go visit a client, she may be reminded of that precious time she lost with her father. Doug should have given more thought to finding other alternatives to sending Susan on the trip during this trying time. It looks like Doug failed at caring in a number of ways. He did not focus moral attention on the situation in all its complexity. He was unsympathetic, because he did not realize how Susan and her father felt at this difficult time. He failed to notice that his decision interfered with Susan's ability to care for someone who was close to her, and he missed the opportunity to make a decision that would have led to harmonious relationships between Susan and her father, between Susan and himself, and between his organization and its clients.

The Care Voice and the Justice Voice

Now that we've seen how the care perspective works, let's turn to a brief history. Carol Gilligan's pioneering work, *In a Different Voice,* was the first systematic attempt to describe the voice of care and to distinguish it from what she called the voice of justice. Since then, psychologists and philosophers have been elucidating the central concepts and testing for various aspects of the two voices.

Gilligan began by responding to the views of Lawrence Kohlberg, who developed a theory about how people reason and develop morally.[8] His theory of moral reasoning posited that people reason morally by applying principles to cases, thus yielding judgments about what they ought to do. Moral development, on Kohlberg's account, is cognitive and proceeds to progressively more general principles, with ideal moral development culminating in principles that are universal and binding on all persons.

Carol Gilligan noted that Kohlberg's subjects, though culturally diverse, were all male. She began to apply his tests to female subjects of various ages. Her conclusion was that some people, notably females, appealed to what she called a care voice, which stood in contrast to the principle-based justice voice of Kohlberg. The care voice involves a thorough understanding of the context of a situation and a willingness to balance the needs of self and others in a way that preserves both. For Gilligan, moral development was thus both cognitive and emotional—it involved growth in one's ability to see a situation from the perspective of self and others and to care about one's self as well as others.

She illustrated the differences in moral reasoning with two eleven-year-olds, Jake and Amy. Jake and Amy are both given Kohlberg's Heinz dilemma to solve. A druggist has invented a drug to combat cancer. A man by the name of Heinz has a wife who needs the drug, but Heinz does not have the money to buy it. The druggist will not give it to him. The children are asked whether Heinz should steal the drug. Jake quickly answers affirmatively and defends his answer by appealing to the relative importance of life over property. Amy begins by saying that it depends. She points out all the things that could go wrong if Heinz steals the drug—perhaps he will get caught and go to jail and his wife will be worse off. She suggests instead that Heinz and the druggist should sit down and work it out to everyone's satisfaction.

Jake fits easily into Kohlberg's schemata: He imagines himself in Heinz's position and applies a principle that quickly yields an answer. He does not need any more information about Heinz, the druggist, Heinz's wife, etc. Amy, in contrast, is virtually impossible to analyze on Kohlberg's scale because she never states or even implies a principle that will yield an answer. Instead, as she imagines herself in Heinz's shoes, she sees the complexity of the situation and realizes that its solution requires that Heinz and the druggist and Heinz's wife recognize their involvement in a relationship and that they honor this awareness by working out a solution that will enable them all to survive and, if possible, flourish. For Jake, the solution is cognitive: Heinz merely reasons about the situation and takes action on the basis of that reasoning. Amy sees a real solution as necessarily involving growth in moral sensitivity and commitment.

There is an additional way to sort out the differences between the care and justice voice, and that is in terms of self-understanding. This was suggested by Nona Lyons, who argued that a particular self-understanding, a "distinct way of seeing and being in relation to others," explains the moral agent's preference for a particular moral voice.[9] Lyons identified two different self-understandings: what she called the separate/objective self and the connected self. Persons who fit the separate/objective self model describe themselves in terms of personal characteristics rather than connections to others. Connected selves describe themselves in terms of connections to others: granddaughter of, friend of, and so on. This suggests that the separate/objective self sees oneself as distinct from others in a more profound sense than the connected self does. The separate/objective self might, for example, see oneself as connected to others only through voluntary agreements. The separate/objective self might value autonomy more highly than good relationships with others.

Lyons described further differences. Separate/objective selves recognize moral dilemmas as those that involve a conflict between their principles and someone else's desires, needs, or demands. Connected selves, in contrast, identify moral dilemmas as those that involve the breakdown of relationships with others. Separate/objective selves fear connection and dependence, and hence value autonomy and independence. Connected selves fear separation and abandonment, and hence value connection and responsiveness.

We can see then how these self-understandings support different moral orientations. Separate selves understand themselves as distinct from others. They conceive moral dilemmas as arising from the conflict between their moral principles and the needs, demands, desires, and principles of others. As such, they must mediate their interaction with others in the voice of justice—in terms of ground rules and procedures that can be accepted by all. This is the only foundation for interaction at all, since ties of affection are not seen as strong enough to provide a basis for interaction, especially in persons who fear connection and dependence. This fear of dependence and attachment also explains why they value the objectivity and impartiality that can stand between themselves and intimates. At the same time, separate/objective selves recognize that interaction with others plays a role in one's satisfaction, so they value community and relationship insofar as these play a role in individual satisfaction.

Connected selves see themselves in terms of others, so relationship is central to self-identity, rather than seen as voluntary and incidental. The problem of interaction is not then conceived of as how to get others to interact on terms that would be acceptable to all, but how to protect the ties of affection and connection that are central to one's very self-identity. Moral dilemmas arise over how to preserve these ties when they are threatened, and these dilemmas are mediated by the voice of care. Since the primary fear is of separation and abandonment, a strong value is placed on community and relationships.

Care and Other Moral Perspectives

At this point in the discussion of an ethic of care, we want to make a meta-ethical point. We are not convinced that in some ethically preferred world, everyone would adopt the same moral theory or the same way of dealing with the moral realities of life. We are certainly not convinced that in this world, everyone can do so. Rather, we think that each moral theory has insights to offer and sheds light on a different aspect of our moral lives. We also think that each of us has a particular history and moral narrative that limits our ability to adopt new moral perspectives, regardless of how we may evaluate one moral theory against another. Finally, we think that when we try to make moral theories guides to action in the rough-and-tumble world of complex and difficult choices, we ought to take comfort where and when we can. If one particular moral theory sheds new light on a difficult and novel issue, then we should comb it for every bit of insight we find useful. It is for these reasons that we prefer to speak of moral perspectives rather than moral theories.

It is also important to distinguish between an ethic of care and an ethical approach to caregiving. One need not subscribe to an ethic of care as a moral perspective to realize that there are special issues that arise for any of us in our various roles as caregivers. We think that an ethic of care will shed light on a range of issues, certainly including the ethics of caregiving, but we are not committed to the view that moral perspectives are necessarily incompatible. They are often complementary. Care and Confucian ethics are similar in some important respects, for example. Ideal Humanness (*jen*) and propriety (*li*) play a central role in Confucian ethics. Jen is analogous in some important respects to care, while li, like accommodation, reminds us that the good society must value harmony among its members.[10]

One helpful way to connect moral theories is to notice that they each focus primarily on a different component of our moral experience. Utilitarianism and other consequential views invite us to be sensitive to the consequences of our decisions and actions. Kant reminds us of two things. First, our motivation and not just the outcomes of our actions are morally significant. Second, persons have a special place in the moral hierarchy. The moral rights view provides a way of understanding the implications of this special place in the moral hierarchy. Virtue theories focus not just on actions, but on the agents who are responsible for these actions. They direct our attention to the character traits that underlie our actions and our commitments. They also focus our attention on how concepts of the good life both anchor our views about the good society and grow out of particular societies.

An ethic of care adds yet another dimension. It reminds us of the importance of human relationships. It places moral value on communities as well as persons and asserts that our actions take place in the context of relationship: Our decisions should consider existing relationships and are often carried out via social action. Doing the right thing and living the morally good life must be understood in the context of trust, reciprocity, and concern for others.

▶ **Decision Procedure**

1. Direct your moral attention to others.
2. Be open to sympathetic understanding.
3. Be aware of the need to sustain and preserve networks of care.
4. Act so as to preserve harmony insofar as you can.
5. Shortcut to action: What would my ideal caring self do?

> ► Exercise 4.1

Suppose you were just hired as the manager of a technical writing group. You are told that one of your first tasks will be to lay someone off. The technical writers all write documents for a group of project managers. One of the writers is a single mother who has a child with a fairly serious disability. The project managers all give her unfavorable reviews. Another writer is a single young woman who is independently wealthy and works just to keep herself busy. She gets strong reviews. A third writer is a married man whose wife is a well-paid lawyer. He is the life of every party and is largely responsible for the wonderful cohesion of the group. The fourth is a quiet and industrious former engineer who knows the technical details of the product better than anyone else. He was unemployed and homeless for several years because of problems with alcohol. Now, using the perspective of care, what should you do, and how should you do it? Look at this example again from the point of view of respect for persons. Finally, look at it from the perspective of Utilitarianism.

Fairness: Social Contract Views

It is hard to be a good person and an effective leader if you are seen as unfair. Fairness is an important value in the United States. We learn to resent unfairness at an early age, though most of us are not really sure about what fairness is. For example, coauthor Rita Manning's daughter made the honor role at school. Children on the honor role are supposed to be able to buy lunch before the other kids. This is an important reward when you go to the typical junior high in California—like most of the other California schools, this one is huge and overcrowded. When Rita asked her daughter how that was going, she said that the teachers were not doing it all the time because they wanted to be fair. Rita asked her what she meant by fair, and her daughter said it meant treating all the kids equally. The author suggested that being fair might mean following the rules. Who is right? Philosophers have had wonderful arguments about this question for over 2,000 years, and it is a good exercise to think about this type of situation for yourself and see what you think. What we will offer here is a way to think about how to be fair that has a history in the West dating back to Thomas Hobbes, John Locke, and Jean-Jacques Rousseau. John Rawls is a contemporary defender of this tradition, which is called Social Contract Theory.[11]

Social Contract theories differ from one another, but they share a common insight. Basically they state that the right moral rules are those that would be chosen by rational persons under the right circumstances. We can use a thought experiment to see what is involved in being a rational person and what the right circumstances would be. Suppose you found yourself shipwrecked on a deserted island with fifteen other people, and that five of you were injured and unable to help gather food and build shelter. Suppose further that one of the five was exhibiting extreme mental confusion. Imagine that seven of the uninjured people were so strong that they could impose their will on the rest of you if they wanted to do so. Now let's suppose that you have a meeting to decide what rules to adopt to increase the odds of survival until you are rescued. Would you be willing to go along with the suggestion that everyone should go it alone? How about the suggestion that things be decided by unanimous vote and that everyone should have an equal vote, even the person who was extremely confused? Would you be willing to give an equal voice to people who refused to be informed about what the problems were? Would you be willing to let all the strong people take what they needed regardless of whether there was enough left for everyone else? Suppose that some of the people in the meeting said they would be willing to talk about rules, but that they would decide from day to day whether or not they wanted to follow them.

Now think about your answers and see if you don't agree that any such meeting would have to meet the following conditions. First, you would have to find a way to keep people from simply voting for whatever was in their self-interest. Second, you would not want anyone to be able to coerce the rest of you into doing things their way. Third, you'd probably want people to be willing to live by the rules. Finally, you would probably want everyone who could vote to be informed about what the issues were and to be able to make a clear and rational decision.

These insights are what prompted John Rawls to come up with his version of the Social Contract: The right moral rules are those which would be chosen by rational bargainers, in the Original Position, behind the Veil of Ignorance.[12] He uses a bit of interesting jargon in this definition, so let's take it piece by piece. First, rational bargainers are people who are mentally competent and aware of the relevant facts. The Original Position (OP) is an imaginary bargaining situation where we all commit ourselves to live by whatever rules are chosen. The Veil of Ignorance (VI) is like a veil that falls across our eyes that makes us forget those things we know about ourselves that would allow us to act in our self-interest. It serves as a device to make sure that bargainers don't know enough about themselves to bring self-interest to bear. We think it is useful to think in terms of a forgetting pill. We imagine that when we take this pill, we no longer know whether we are male or female, strong or weak, hurt or healthy.

We use this whole picture to decide on moral rules. This is how it works. First, we imagine that we really are in a position to make the moral rules and that we would really be willing to live by them. Second, we assume that everyone involved in the rule-making process is rational and fully informed. Third, we imagine that we've all taken a pill that causes us to forget all those things about ourselves that would allow us to bring our self-interest into the discussion.

Rawls made some interesting assumptions about this imaginary bargaining session. One important assumption is that we would all be averse to exposing ourselves to catastrophic risk. Rawls thinks we would protect ourselves by imagining how each rule would affect us if we turned out to be the least well off person in the situation. He used the notion of the least-well-off person a bit differently from the way we will use it here, but we think that our use is a bit less controversial. We encourage you to read Rawls and see if you agree with us.

Since these rules must make it possible for us to live together in a relatively stable society, and since we could each be one of the least well off once the Veil of Ignorance is lifted, the rules chosen must be acceptable to the least well off. This doesn't mean that the rules will automatically benefit the least well off. We might turn out to be one of the best off. But just in case we are the least well off, we want to make sure that we could live with the rules. Now that we have the whole picture in mind, we can summarize the decision procedure.

> **Decision Procedure**

1. What are the possible rules?
2. For each rule:
   a. Would it be chosen by rational bargainers in the OP behind the VI?
   b. Would it be acceptable to the least well off?

> **Exercise 4.2**

You are on the school board and have to make substantial cuts in the budget. The only reasonable options are: (1) cut the budget for students with special needs, or (2) cut the music and art budget. Assuming that there are no legal restrictions on what you can do (such as state laws mandating a special-needs program, or a music and art curriculum), use the Social Contract model to decide what to do.

Professional Codes of Ethics

Another characteristic a person with integrity needs is a familiarity with and respect for relevant professional codes of ethics.[13] These are rules of conduct for members of particular professions; they are often written down, but sometimes they are merely implicit. One of coauthor Rita Manning's friends, a plumber, used to say there were only two things a plumber needed to know: that sewage doesn't flow uphill, and that payday is Friday. Of course he was joking. There really are norms of professional conduct for the building trades, though they may not always be written down. Other professions have explicit codes of ethical conduct, some of them, like the Hippocratic Oath for physicians, dating back over 2,000 years.

One preliminary question is, What is a profession? Why do we describe some activities as professions and some as mere careers, or even jobs? The traditional view of the professions is that they involve individuals who each have a high degree of autonomy. They are personally responsible for their decisions because they are not in a position in which they are expected to follow orders that they had no part in creating. Second, the professions themselves are described as dedicated to the common good. Third, members of professions collectively assign moral responsibility to their members and articulate that responsibility in the form of professional codes of ethics.

Professional codes are designed to summarize a shared view of moral standards for particular professions, to provide a standard for teaching and discipline, and to guide the behavior of members in difficult situations. They must be sensitive to the possible harm that particular professions can cause and the temptations to do the wrong thing that face professionals. Engineers, for example, have a code that makes protecting the public from harm a central concern. This makes sense when we recognize that civil engineers are responsible for projects like building bridges. Health-care professionals are privy to personal information about patients and thus have codes that make confidentiality a prime obligation.

Like all moral rules, professional codes of ethics must be defended. The defense can be made by appeal to their centrality to the furtherance of a particular institution and the utility of that institution, or on other moral grounds (for example, respect, care, virtue). Let's see how this works. In the United States, lawyers are obligated to zealously defend the interests of their clients. Criminal lawyers must defend their clients regardless of their personal opinions about any particular client's guilt or innocence. This obligation is defended in terms of our legal system, which is an adversarial system that assumes people are innocent until proven guilty. The adversarial system of justice is in turn defended as the best possible way of seeing that justice is done, and the presumption of innocence is defended in terms of the Constitution. Both the adversarial system and the Constitution can be defended in terms of rights, utility, or care. So although an individual lawyer may at times be a bit uncomfortable with her clients, she can be comfortable that in defending them she is defending the adversarial system and the Constitution.

But notice that professional codes are not absolute. We needn't assume that every professional code was carefully drafted or that it should be followed in every possible case. When we have some concerns about a particular professional code, we need to look to see what institution it is protecting and what moral views provide its justification. There are other codes adopted by organizations besides professional codes. The same procedures used to evaluate professional codes can be used to evaluate these organizational codes.

Sometimes, members of organizations are called upon to help develop an organizational code of ethics. Whether the organization is a professional group or some other type of group, it may be helpful to answer a few questions before deciding how to set up the code. Is there a professional code that governs some of the activities of the organization or profession? What is the purpose of the organization or profession, and is this a worthy goal? Is the organization or profession organized maximally to achieve this goal? Can the proposed organizational or professional code be defended in terms of moral values? A decision procedure can be summarized as follows:

▶ Decision Procedure

1. Describe the morally relevant features of the situation.
2. List the professional codes involved.
3. Evaluate the professional codes, or clauses of codes, involved.
4. Describe the action required by the appropriate code.

▶ Exercise 4.3

Find out if there is a professional code that governs your work-life. If there is, get a copy of it. Review each clause carefully and assess the entire document. Do the same for any organization that you belong to.

▶ Hints for Developing Integrity

1. Remember that developing integrity is a life-long project.
2. Integrity has three components: deciding what is right, being motivated to do what is right, and having the appropriate emotional re-

sponse. Work on each of these components. You will improve your ability to decide what is right by using the decision procedures in this chapter and Chapter 3. Working on your motivation will be the hard part, but remember, practicing integrity gets easier as it becomes a habit. Notice what your emotional response is in moral situations. Now compare your emotions with what you think would be the right thing to do. Since emotion has a large cognitive component, thinking things through will help to reinforce appropriate emotional responses.

3. Seek out a support group of like-minded people and stay in touch.
4. Finally, remember that it is not just what you do, but how you do it that counts.

Conclusion

We have now sketched the most common Western strategies for making moral decisions. In the next chapter, we will turn to perspectives from around the world. Many, if not most, of these world perspectives will have a great deal in common with the perspectives we have outlined so far, so at this point, we think we've given you a fairly broad picture of what is involved in living a life of integrity.

▶ Study Questions for Chapter Four

1. What are the central features of care?
2. What are the four central ideas in an ethic of care? How would you use this ethic to make a moral decision?
3. List some ways in which the care voice differs from the justice voice.
4. What is the common insight that all Social Contract theories share?
5. Describe John Rawls's version of Social Contract Theory. Make sure you include the following: *original position, veil of ignorance, least well off.*
6. How can you use Rawls's theory to make moral decisions?

7. What is a professional code of ethics? How should you use a professional code of ethics to make moral decisions?

8. How does a professional code differ from an organizational code of
   ethics?

NOTES

1. Martin Hoffman, *Empathy and Moral Development* (Cambridge: Cambridge University Press, 2000).

2. Sara Ruddick, *Maternal Thinking: Toward a Politics of Peace* (Boston: Beacon Press, 1989).

3. Michael Slote is a virtue theorist who also sees care as a virtue. See *Morals from Motives* (Oxford: Oxford University Press, 2001).

4. Carol Gilligan, *In a Different Voice* (Cambridge: Harvard University Press, 1982).

5. Nel Noddings, *Caring: A Feminine Approach to Ethics and Moral Education* (Berkeley: University of California Press, 1986; 2d ed., 2003).

6. Virginia Held, *The Ethics of Care: Personal, Political and Global* (Oxford: Oxford University Press, 2005).

7. Rita Manning, *Caring: A Feminist Perspective on Ethics* (Lanham, Md.: Rowman and Littlefield, 1992).

8. Lawrence Kohlberg, *The Philosophy of Moral Development* (New York: Harper and Row, 1981).

9. Nona Lyons, "Two Perspectives on Self, Relationship, and Morality," *Harvard Educational Review* 53 (1983), 125–145.

10. For a comparison of Confucian ethics and care, see Julia Po-Wah Lai Tao, "Two Perspectives of Care: Confucian *Ren* and Feminist *Care*," *Journal of Chinese Philosophy*, 27, no. 2 (June 2000), 215–240.

11. John Rawls, *A Theory of Justice*, rev. ed. (Cambridge: Belknap Press of Harvard University Press, 1999).

12. In our discussion of Rawls, we are simplifying to a certain extent in order to get the main points across. We invite you to take a look at *A Theory of Justice* for the important and interesting details.

13. For a very comprehensive list of codes of ethics, see http://www.ethicsweb.ca/resources/professional/codes-of-ethics.html.

CHAPTER 5

Ethics around the World

So far, we've looked at a number of moral perspectives: Utilitarianism, respect for persons (Kant, moral rights), virtue theory, Social Contract Theory, and care. Professional codes, when they can be justified, offer an additional way to think about one's moral obligations. While these views are not exclusively Western, they tend to capture much of moral theorizing in the West. But we live in an increasingly global world, and there is certainly no reason to think that the best insights come from the West. Even if you feel comfortable with this particular mix of moral perspectives, it is important to broaden your horizons so that you can work with people who share different moral orientations.

There are three things to keep in mind as we venture beyond the West to see what other cultures have to say about living a moral life. The first is that we needn't leave the West to find other moral orientations. In the West, many people have made critiques of some of the views we've looked at and offered alternatives of their own. We will return to a discussion of some of these views following our look at different traditions.

The second thing is that there are tremendous differences in moral orientation within cultures. We've already seen differences in "Western" perspectives: Utilitarianism and Kantianism have very different views of individual persons; virtue theorists may have very different ideas of the good society and consequently what virtues people should cultivate. The same multiplicity of perspectives exists around the world. In what follows, we will be painting with a broad stroke, but keep in mind that within these perspectives, there is a great deal of disagreement. There are countless moral traditions and strategies for moral life. There will be common strands in all of them, and some important and interesting differences. This discussion will just only scratch the surface, looking briefly at just a few perspectives.

Third, when we talked about Western perspectives, we did not look at religious views, but we will be looking at some religious views when we look beyond the West. There is a pragmatic argument for looking at secular rather than religious perspectives: People with diverse religious perspectives can agree about secular ethical perspectives even when they disagree about religious commitments. The Western theories we looked at include insights from religion but in a secular fashion. When we look at other traditions, it is often not easy to separate religion and ethics. Thus, in this chapter we will sometimes be looking at ethical perspectives that are embedded in religious perspectives.

Confucianism

We've already talked a bit about Confucius. In this section we will elaborate on his ideas and introduce Mencius, another important voice in the Confucian tradition. We will begin with some quotes from Confucius recorded in the *Analects*.[1]

The Morally Superior Person (chun-tzu)

The morally superior person has many characteristics, said Confucius. For example, he or she

1. has moral equals as friends (because this is beneficial to one's own virtue) (1:8, 1:14, 16:4);
2. is not concerned with fulfilling desire (appetite) but with duty, learning, and careful speech (1:14);
3. "acts before he speaks and then speaks according to his action" (2:13);
4. always acts in accord with "moral principles," but "never abandons humanity" (4:5);

5. thinks of virtue and sanctions (4:14) and seeks improvement in self but not others (15:20);
6. in establishing his or her own character, "also establishes the character of others" (6:28);
7. becomes prominent "by helping others to be prominent" (6:28).

Some of the items in this list can be stated in terms of virtues, but in addition, the morally superior person has the following virtues: broadmindedness (2:12, 2:14); benevolence (12:16); dignity (13:26); wisdom, humanity, and courage (14:30). He or she is also "strong, resolute, simple, and slow to speak" (13:27), and, above all, has righteousness, which is the most important virtue (17:23).

The morally superior person is not perfectly virtuous, but wants to be, and the "nine wishes" keep the morally superior person on the right track. The nine wishes are to "see clearly"; "hear distinctly"; have "warm expression," "respectful appearance," and "sincere speech"; to be "serious in handling affairs"; and to be one who "asks when in doubt"; "thinks of consequences when angry"; and "thinks of righteousness" (16:10).

Central Virtues

Confucius named three central virtues: *jen* (humanity), *li* (propriety), and *hsiao* (filial piety). He also mentioned two other virtues: loyalty and justice. Let's look in more detail at jen, li, and hsiao.

Humanity (*jen*). Jen is described as "to master oneself and return to propriety" (12:1) and "to love men" (12:22). The person with jen is "naturally at ease with humanity" (4:2). You can come to have jen if you practice five things: "earnestness, liberality, truthfulness, diligence and generosity" (17:6). Confucius seems to endorse these virtues not for their own sake but because they allow one to have good relationships with others. Wisdom and jen are complementary, as is the mountain to the water flowing below (6:21).

Propriety (*li*). Li is sometimes translated as "principle." It is not defined, but it probably refers to the established rules of a society (as long as these are the rules which are compatible with the other virtues and as long as these rules create harmony). The rules of propriety establish harmony and this is their most important function (1:12). If rulers lead with virtue and rule with li, the people "will have a sense of shame and will set themselves right" (2:3). But li must be tempered by jen (3:3).

Filial Piety (*hsiao*).   *Hsiao* is described as supporting one's parents with a feeling of reverence (2:7, 4:18). Some examples of it are staying close to parents (4:19), who are both a source of joy and anxiety (4:21). Because our relationship with our parents is such a source of moral sentiment, hsiao and brotherly respect are the root of jen (1:2).

Confucius tells us that we can sort out virtues from vices in two ways. One way is to seek moderation "to go neither too far nor not far enough" (11:15, 11:21). This is very similar to Aristotle's golden mean. One other way is to follow the golden rule: "Do not do to others what you do not want them to do to you" (12:2, 15:23).

Becoming Virtuous

According to Confucius, we are born upright (6:17), though through practice we can become better or worse (17:2). To become better, he said, it helps to have good parents and do what they say (1:11). But we should also have the right friends (1:8, 1:14, 16:4). We should constantly think about virtue, study virtue, and work at becoming virtuous (4:5, 4:14, 15:20, 16:10, 19:6). We should follow the rules of propriety (1:12). He described his own development (2:4). If we take this as a pattern for becoming virtuous, it involves this progression:

1. You commit yourself to learning about virtue (age fifteen).
2. Your character will be formed (age thirty).
3. You come to know what is virtuous (age forty).
4. You come to know why it is virtuous (age fifty).
5. You accept virtue and act accordingly, though perhaps with a conflict between your inclinations and your beliefs about what virtue requires (age sixty).

6. Finally, you act virtuously, and your actions and your inclinations are in harmony (age seventy).

Confucius and Mencius

Confucius was the first in a long and important tradition in China and the Far East. Mencius was another important figure in this tradition.[2] Mencius agreed with Confucius that we are born good, and indeed, he made much of this in his writings (*The Book of Mencius*, 7A:15). He also said we can become worse (6A:8), and we do this by not thinking about our behavior (6A:15) or by being distracted by our desire for material things (2A:6).

Mencius believed that the foundation of morality was sentiment, our feelings of sympathy for others (jen), shame and dislike, respect and reverence, and right and wrong (li) (6A:6). Virtue involved noting our relation to others and responding with the proper sentiment and/or behavior. The most important five relations were:

father and son—affection
ruler and minister—righteousness
husband and wife—attention to separate functions
old and young—proper order
friends—faithfulness (3A:4)

In addition, he noted four basic virtues: benevolence, righteousness, propriety, and wisdom. Benevolence was for him the primary virtue and it was based on natural empathy. He saw the flourishing of this capacity in the superior person ("the sage"), and he believed that the evil person (the characters mean "small person") was stunted.

One might ask whether Confucius and Mencius were defending a genuine virtue ethic or an ethic of principle. We see Confucius defending acting from principle while never abandoning humanity. He also gave us two strategies for acting virtuously: the golden rule and moderation. The first has a Kantian ring and supports the view that principles are prior. The second is a clear virtue strategy (Aristotle adopted a similar strategy).

Confucius has been criticized for being too willing to defend conventional moral norms and practices (for instance, in regard to his discussions of propriety). But he also says that propriety needs humanity. This suggests that propriety should give way when it conflicts with humanity. His insistence that propriety creates harmony prescribes a particular sort of propriety, one that will succeed in doing so. He also broke with convention in his insistence that education should be open to everyone, no matter what class, and in his own life, he actively sought occasions to influence convention by being a teacher of rulers.

Confucianism and Western Traditions

Confucius, Mencius, and Aristotle. Virtues are the traits that enable humans to live the best kind of human life, where the best kind of human life is defined in terms of attributes not shared with other creatures. For Aristotle, the essential attribute of humans was rationality, whereas for Confucius the essential attribute was the capacity for morality where this is fleshed out in terms of relationships grounded in compassion and respect. The Chinese word for humanity, jen, the primary virtue for Confucius, is composed of two characters: the character for "person" and the character for "two."

For both Aristotle and Confucius:

Human happiness is to be achieved through fulfillment of uniquely human capacities.

Virtue is constitutive of the good life and not merely the means to a good life.

Virtue is not just having a good heart, but acting well.

Virtue is having right feelings and knowing how to act on them (practical wisdom).

Virtue can only be learned, hence the emphasis on moral education.

Confucianism and Christianity. Christianity defends the idea of love for all humanity. Both Confucius and Mencius denied that we should love all others equally. Rather, they stressed the obligations we have to particular persons, including the obligation to have a particular sentiment, or at least to behave in the fashion that special relationships require.

Confucianism and the Ideal of Autonomy.   There is another important way in which Confucianism differs from Western ideals. In the United States, autonomy is a cultural ideal. We populate our films and popular fiction with characters who ride off into the sunset after they set things right. Related to this is the idea that as adults we should separate from our families and define ourselves through our own separate values, activities, and relationships. We tend to see obligation to family as one-dimensional—parents have obligations to children who, as adults, will have obligations only to their own children.

In Confucianism, independence of this sort is not seen as an ideal but as a failure to be virtuous. A good parent is one who behaves appropriately in terms of the duties of holding that role, or the duties that accompany that relationship. The moral development of the individual begins by learning to love your family, and it progresses until the individual can extend this benevolence to everyone (in the proper fashion, as dictated by the relationship involved). For this reason, and because virtue can only be learned in the family, Confucius puts an emphasis on family (the virtues for children are love and respect, and for parents, nurturance).

Hinduism

Hinduism is an incredibly diverse and prolific religious tradition originating in India. No book could ever hope to encompass all of the perspectives on ethics and integrity that this tradition holds; this section, however, attempts to give the reader a taste of Hindu ethics and a distinctive perspective from the ancient text, the *Bhagavad Gita*. This text, still popular in current Hindu traditions, is a didactic dialogue inserted approximately in the middle of an immensely long Indian epic entitled the *Mahabharata*. The focus of this larger work was an epic power struggle between two factions of a warring family, the Kurus and the Pandavas. When the Pandavas and the Kurus are drawn to war, the scene is set for the conversation recounted in the *Bhagavad Gita* between Arjuna and Krishna. Arjuna begins to question whether he should fight his own family, even if the war appears to be for a just cause. Krishna, his charioteer, counsels the mighty warrior, and the dialogue focuses on this interaction.

The *Bhagavad Gita* is a significant Hindu philosophical work because it synthetically combines many previous themes into its narrative.[3] Some of these include the illusory nature of the phenomenal world, the self, and issues of *dharma* (duty) that are prevalent in Hinduism. While extending the ideas of speculation from the *Upanishads,* the *Bhagavad Gita* does not emphasize personal salvation through thought alone; instead, issues of duty, metaphysics, and ethics are all intertwined around personal action and intention.[4] The *Bhagavad Gita* itself is relatively short compared to the immense bulk of its parent text. The text is composed of short verses, arranged into eighteen chapters, that convey the dialogue between Arjuna and Krishna.

Ethical Themes in the Bhagavad Gita

Concerning the metaphysical theme of the relation between the everyday notions one has of self (the physical individual, usually) and the ultimate source of all things (*Brahman,* or ultimate Self), Krishna has much to say. While Arjuna fears the evil that lies within killing his own relations and friends, Krishna implores him to uphold his duty as a warrior. Krishna argues that the physical self is merely an illusion, and that the ultimate Self within does not die:

> He who thinks that this (soul) is a slayer, and he who thinks that this (soul) is slain; both of them are ignorant. This (soul) neither slays nor is slain. It is never born, nor does it die, nor having once been, will it again cease to be. It is unborn, eternal and everlasting. This primeval one is not slain when the body is slain. He who knows that it (the soul) is indestructible and eternal, unborn and unchanging, how can that man slay, O Partha (Arjuna), or cause another to slay? (2:19–21)

Here the idea is introduced that the world and the self (or soul) that we typically think of as being "real" are ultimately illusions; the actions that one takes in this world really do not affect one's true personality. The real meaning of one's "self" is in relation to the ultimate Self, personified by Krishna in human guise. It is this Self that is described as "the Self of all beings" (2:30).

Even the multiplicity of forms and ways of being one observes in everyday life have their basis in ultimate Self: "Non-injury, equanimity, contentment, austerity, generosity, fame and ill-fame, are the different states of being which arise from Me alone" (10:5). Worldly creatures (including humans) are all fundamentally united with the ultimate Self: "I am the Self seated in the hearts of all beings, O Gudakesha [Arjuna]; I am the beginning, the middle, and also the end of all beings" (10:20). Arjuna eventually acknowledges that Krishna as ultimate Self "penetratest all and therefore . . . art all" (11:40). Thus, the typical individuation that we intuitively sense about our existence is an illusion; Brahman, or ultimate Self, is the true reality.

The second theme in the *Bhagavad Gita* deals with how one is to act upon becoming enlightened about the true nature of ultimate Self. Since one's empirical self is an illusion, how is one to act? What is the goal of action? Initially, Krishna points out that "no one can remain, even for a moment, without performing some action" (3:5). Thus, Arjuna must act in the situation he finds himself in; retreat and inaction are not options. The true sense of being that Arjuna aims for is enlightenment, and Krishna indicates that he should "seek refuge in intelligence; pitiful are those whose motive is the fruit (of action)" (2:49). This attitude of detachment comes from the dispelling of the empirical self: "When a man abandons all the desires of his mind, O Partha (Arjuna), and is satisfied in his self by the self alone, then he is called a man of steady mind" (2:55).

The fundamental impetus for action is the recognition that action is unavoidable and that the individual self is an illusion. Given these two claims, one must try to act in such a way as to not deny the reality of ultimate Self. Krishna describes the attributes of an enlightened person to Arjuna: "His intelligence is firmly established whose senses are completely withdrawn from the objects of sense" (2:68). By equating your self with the ultimate Self in all beings, the rewards are immense: "He who abandons all desires and acts without longing, without self-interest or

egoism, he attains peace" (2:71). Finally, this peace is the ultimate liberation from personal confinement in the body: "This is the eternal state, O
Partha (Arjuna); having attained it, one is no longer confused. Fixed in it
even at the time of death, one attains to the bliss of Brahman" (2:72).

The overarching theme is that action (in this case, Arjuna taking part
in a war) should be performed with the realization that ego is an illusion;
selfless action leads to liberation from the trap of ego attachment. Arjuna
is told to "perform thy allotted work . . . perform thy action free from attachment" (3:8–9), and "being free from desire and selfishness, fight freed
from thy sorrow" (3:30).

Implications for Ethics and Integrity

The *Bhagavad Gita*, while telling us something about how Indian culture
conceptualizes issues of action and ethical integrity, can also be used to illustrate new ways of acting for a Western audience. The first theme of the
ultimate unity of all beings initially seems remote from the ethical import
of the workplace and from the Western world in general. However, the
goal-oriented and success-driven nature that many of us possess can be
tempered by the ethical implications of this claim. In a similar fashion to
Kant's Formula of Humanity, Krishna's counsel advises that all beings
should be treated with compassion and respect because they are an essential extension of one's Self. Ethical concerns in medicine and general
business often include issues of personal worth and value; if we do not
value others as respected entities in the interaction, they will feel margin-
alized and react negatively. Thus, the *Bhagavad Gita* allows Western individuals to see what the metaphysical basis is for one of the perennial
views of the East.

A second implication for our understanding of ethics is the unique
reading on action provided in the *Bhagavad Gita*. Crispin Sartwell's
analysis of the *Gita's* conception of action illuminates the ethical significance of this text.[5] He argued that even inaction is considered action by
the *Bhagavad Gita*, pointing to Krishna's statement that "there is no one
who rests for even an instant; every creature is driven to action by his own
nature" (3:5). For Sartwell, Krishna was not suggesting that "we act

wholly and always without ends" because "that would make human action impossible." "Rather," he wrote, "we ought to reconstrue the *relation* of means to ends in our actions. . . . Our action should not be performed *merely* for the sake of the end; the end must not absorb or expunge the means in our deliberation."[6] Discussing our sole focus on ends in action, Sartwell said:

> If we could achieve the end by sheer force of will, if we could realize it without performing the means, we would. Krsna [Krishna] asks us, not to renounce all desire and thus all action, but to desire the means as intrinsically valuable as *well* as valuable in service of the end. The means are not to be absorbed in the end; the time and energy devoted to the means are not wasted. Rather, this time and energy are to be *consecrated*.[7]

Human action, far from being a stranger to goal-orientation, must be seen as a holy, worthy undertaking that also gives us value. Valuing action only so far as it achieves a certain end transforms that spent time into *wasted* time if the goal is not achieved.

This text can provide an Eastern answer to the goal-oriented ethics of Western businesses. Too often, ethics becomes widespread and en vogue because it offers the chance for "better business success in the long term" and for more congenial community relations. Instead of rereading the meaning of action in the workplace or community, these two views seem to aim at maximizing the desired consequences. Both of these goals, while admirable, can be challenged by the deontological or duty-based view of the *Bhagavad Gita*. Instead of assuming that one acts in a vocational capacity simply for money or for advancement, the text seems to draw one's attention toward the relational aspects of working and the value in a job well done. One's job often involves many individuals; instead of ethics attempting to maximize the utility of either these people or your relationship with them, attention can be directed to the value that these others have intrinsically. Indeed, Eastern communicative practices generally emphasize the relational aspects over task-oriented goals.[8]

Additionally, duty and occupational demands often play a large role, according to the *Bhagavad Gita*, in what one is bound to do. Normatively,

Arjuna is compelled to fight against his own relatives in a war that has been building in force for hundreds of pages in the *Mahabharata*. Though violence is not encouraged wholesale by Krishna, the duties of the various castes are quite binding; thus, Arjuna can slay his uncle, Bhishma (who is also the commander of the opposing army), after the *Bhagavad Gita* section of text, because it is their duty to fight against each other in this war. Although they are not happy about this confrontation, both realize that their positions compel them to fight. Their feelings, however, compel them not to hate each other or revel in the bloodshed. Western individuals can see in this text this seemingly foreign notion of caste-based duty, in which one must uphold the duty of their station.

Of course, other factors influence what one's duty is in any given situation. For instance, the human demands of wealth, pleasure, life-position, religion, and so on also factor in. One's occupational demands, however, can often override personal concerns or relations to others in a more formal sense. Thus, a police officer may be morally obliged by the demands of his occupation to arrest a close friend for an offense that a stranger would also get arrested for. While one must have sympathy for all, this text espouses the view that occupational codes must override many other interpersonal obligations. The personal aspect of the self is distanced from the caste-grounded (occupational) duty inherent in one's position. It is this distancing that allows for and necessitates selfless action on the part of the occupational person. Though concerns for one's selfish desires do motivate one to work, one should hold as primary the motivation to work hard (that is, to fulfill the demands and duties of one's position) in order to sanctify the time spent in this action.

Islamic Ethics

Ethical thought in much of the Islamic world is dominated by the holy *Qur'ān*, a text of approximately 6,252 Arabic verses revealed through the prophet Muhammad. This work is the heart of the Islamic tradition, a 1,300-year-old religion that shares theological affinities with Judaism and Christianity. Those familiar with the ethical milieu surrounding Judaism and Christianity, however, often misunderstand the religion of Islam and its implications in practical ethics. This short section cannot attempt to convey the richness that Islam holds in all of its manifestations around the world. Instead, we will attempt to lay the groundwork for understanding Islam's place in business situations by looking at some of the basic tenets of the *Qur'ān* itself, and then provide a summary of the thought of two important ancient Islamic philosophers—al-Fārābī (d. 950 CE) and al-Ghazzāli (1058–1111 CE).

Basics of the Qur'ān

The *Qur'ān* is said to have been formulated in its present form in the years 650–655 CE as revealed through the mouth of the prophet Muhammad. This text is not a unified story, but is instead composed of didactic verses that sometimes cluster around common issues. Muhammad is supposed to be the last of a long line of prophets, and as such, no following revelations are to supersede his words. What he reveals in the *Qur'ān* forms the basis for Islamic ethics and also for much of Islamic philosophical speculation.[9]

It is important to realize that like Christianity and Judaism, Islam is a monotheistic religion that begins with an important separation between God (Allah) the creator, on the one hand, and the created, human beings (and the world, etc.), on the other. God is the basis for the world, and as such is the one that humans should serve and submit to—even the word "Islam" comes from the root "slm" which means "wholeness and peace."[10] This submission to God leads the follower down the correct path to salvation. Such a salvation is predicated on the mercifulness of God. Most of the suras composing the *Qur'ān* begin with the Basmala, "In the name of God, Most Merciful, Most Compassionate." The creation of the world, its sustenance, and maintenance are all overseen by God and are a sign of his compassion.

Free will at some level is assumed by the *Qur'ān* ; every human is given the ultimate choice to follow God's commands or to be an unbeliever. It is important to note that the *Qur'ān* does not demand forcible conversion of nonbelievers in the pursuit of honor or power; instead, the nonbelievers are simply looked upon as those that "wander blindly" through the world. True nobility comes from a submission to the word of God—*muslim* itself linguistically implies submission, but this submission is tempered by justice and love for one's fellow humans. Indeed, Muhammad wanted a true focus on both the afterlife and the form and function of society in the here and now. In the days of Muhammad's life, the average society (such as that of the Bedouin tribes) was violent and focused primarily on maintaining power for one's own gain. Through the *Qur'ān*, human laws and God's laws are brought together to treat all of humanity with respect, as they are all equally created by God. Thus, the ethics of Islam tend to focus on compassion for the weak and on how to form a society to best instantiate revealed law.

Indeed, in the *Hadith* (other sayings of the Prophet), Muhammad is quoted as saying that warfare conducted on behalf of Islamic societies is to be conducted humanely, as a religious act, and should not include harming women and children. Even slavery, a condition allowed by most ancient scriptures, is treated with some concern—slaves are encouraged to buy their freedom from their master, and the master is supposed to allow such an opportunity. Additionally, slaves are to be well cared for by their masters, as they are also a part of God's creation. The *Qur'ān*, the foundation of Islamic thought, is predicated on humanity's separation from an all-powerful divine being who allows redemption through belief and good deeds. It is from such a basis that later philosophers in the Islamic tradition evolved.

Al-Fārābī

Al-Fārābī was an influential Islamic philosopher, and an overview of some of his ethical thought can show one direction that Islamic ethics has taken. Al-Fārābī believed that philosophical thought should come first, followed by religious instruction. The philosopher should deduce the truths of ethics and morality from his or her own divinely granted reason, and then allow religion to use holy scriptures to disseminate these ideas to the masses. His thought was influenced by Neoplatonic and Aristotelian philosophy, which led to him to describe the world as a series of emanated levels of reality flowing forth from a perfect, necessary God. Thus, the world is pictured as unified, but essential separations still remain. For instance, humans partake in both the activities of the nonintellectual lower world (such as plants and animals), but they also take part in the intellectual and abstract realms of the higher worlds (culminated by God).

As with preceding Neoplatonic philosophy, the higher levels of the world are correspondingly more perfect, until absolute perfection is reached in God. This notion of perfection plays an important role in al-Fārābī's ethical and political work, as the individual person and the community must act so as to increase the perfection of each. "Good" holds a dual meaning—it applies both to the creation of God (thus all things) and to that which assists in the further perfection of these creatures. "Evil" is the privation of this perfection. From the perspective of human existence, the good is that which emphasizes and develops our intellectual abilities. The Islamic society envisioned by al-Fārābī thus operates on an ethic of creating conditions to foster social virtues (such as justice, temperance, and the like) and other intellectual attributes that allow for humans to reach the highest level of perfection. This level of being will also correspond to the highest level of happiness that an individual can achieve. Similar to Aristotle, al-Fārābī found that happiness is that which is pursued for its own sake; such a pursuit requires individual and communal assistance.

Al-Fārābī said not only that the individual must use reason to attain a state such as that of the Prophet, but also that society should be arranged such that harmony is achieved. Like the rest of the universe, human society has a state in which it functions most perfectly. In one work, he divided society into five main classes—the philosophers, the interpreters, the assessors, the fighters, and the rich. In other texts, he simply pointed out that each part of society had a part to play in its maintenance and flourishing. Harmony in these situations is achieved by doing one's duty in regard to one's role in society. A harmonious society can be attained through effective, rational leadership as well as through a populace that is taught allegorical lessons by the use of religion. Either way, the end is the same—the instantiation of a harmonious social setting that allows all their due portion of happiness in this life as well as a chance for happiness in the afterlife.[11]

Al-Ghazzāli

The Islamic thinker al-Ghazzāli is important in that he resisted the urge to demote religious thought to a place lower than human reason. And yet he made this point through reasoned argument. While al-Ghazzāli's works are too complex to summarize here, what can be emphasized is his concern with the power of reason in relation to God. Al-Ghazzāli argued that ethical thought must be permeated by theological concepts, as human reason cannot reach a level of certainty that would completely describe God and ultimate reality.

For instance, God's actions must be beyond good and evil, as God creates all things that can be judged to be good or evil. Al-Ghazzāli found that good and evil in ethical discussion are dependent upon which viewpoint is occupied. He was not advocating a shallow relativism; rather, he was arguing that God and humans occupy fundamentally different levels of reality (viewpoints), and as such, human reason cannot be said to accurately describe things as God may see them. From God's viewpoint, all actions and events are good, since they are causally necessitated by his divine will. From humanity's viewpoint, the good is that which is pleasant, useful, and beautiful, whereas the evil lacks these qualities.[12] Unlike al-Fārābī, al-Ghazzāli said that human reason is not the last word in matters of morality, as there are other realms of existence that transcend such a faculty of our thought.

Al-Ghazzāli emphasized dominant trends in Islamic ethical thought that continue up to the present day. The individual must to some extent recognize the limits of reason and submit to the revelation of God. Though he prized wisdom and intellect, al-Ghazzāli believed that the important functions of society and morality were instructed by the Qur'ān and religious doctrine. For him, ultimate happiness lies in the afterlife, which necessitates religious doctrines of resurrection and immortality of the body. Though such topics may seem more a concern of religion than of philosophy, it is important to realize that the line separating these two areas of thought is often murky and disputed. Al-Ghazzāli's work shows that even one arguing for the fallibility of reason concerning matters of God should be able to engage in reasoned opposition. Simple appeals to religious dogma are, for the most part, absent in his work. Instead, reason can be used to acknowledge its own limitations, by, for example, acknowledging that God's perspective transcends human vantage points.

▶ **Exercise 5.1**

Think about someone you have known who comes from a religious, ethnic, or national group different from your own. Now think of instances where you and this individual thought differently on some topic of importance. Was it because of your different backgrounds? How exactly did this difference in traditions affect your moral reasoning, if at all? Do you recognize any of the themes or traditions just discussed?

Feminism

To return to the realm of Western ethics, we find that feminists offer a number of critiques of traditional Western views. Feminists are committed to taking women's experience seriously, and they contend that many traditional ethical theories merely expound on the experiences of men. One criticism along this line is that autonomy as an ideal is not possible for most women, nor is it possible for entire societies.

In most societies, women do the bulk of caring work. They spend a great deal of their time providing both material and emotional comfort to their families and friends. Many taking a feminist view feel this is not a fair division of labor. If we are serious about autonomy, we must notice this disparity and address it in our theorizing. But even if we gave equal access to autonomy to women and men, some feminists would still reject this as an ideal. Imagine what our society would look like if everyone were focused on his or her own personal autonomy. Who would care for the sick, the very young, and the very old? Who would care for any of us, since even the strongest among us sometimes need help?

An ethic of care is in part a response to the concern that women's experience be taken seriously, since it had its beginnings in Carol Gilligan's work on the moral voice of women.[13] Some feminists are critical of an ethic of care because it violates the feminist goal of confronting oppression. In an ideal world, it might make sense to advocate for an ethic of care, but we live in a world where women care too much and men too little. In addition, there are other important differences between people. Some people are barely able to care for themselves, while others are able to hire a virtual army of caregivers for themselves and their families. In this world, care is all too often delegated to the poor, the female, and the disenfranchised.

This critique can be extended to ethics in general. Why should such oppressed people take ethics seriously? Some suggest that perhaps they should instead fight for their own liberation using whatever means necessary. This focus on oppression raises a number of issues for any ethical perspective. First, an adequate discussion of any issue must take oppression and its effects into consideration. Second, ethical perspectives must include overcoming oppression as a goal. Third, ethical perspectives must consider the possibility that people have different sets of obligations and entitlements based on their relative advantage or disadvantage. This focus on oppression is shared by other critiques to which we shall now turn.

Postcolonial Morality

Postcolonial Theory is an emerging interdisciplinary and global intellectual field. There are a great number of postcolonial views about morality, but we can make some generalizations. First, there is a strong focus in Postcolonial Theory on the experience of colonized peoples. Second, there is a critique of universalism as a cover for the imposition of Western ideas and interests.[14] The variety and sheer number of postcolonial works is so vast that here we will only mention a few, but we encourage you to explore further on your own.

There have been a number of responses to the shared experience of colonial occupation. Martin Luther King Jr. embraced many traditional Western moral views while at the same time criticizing the West for not honoring them. Mahatma Gandhi effectively used a similar strategy. There is a story, perhaps apocryphal, about Gandhi. When asked what he thought of Western civilization, he is said to have replied, "I think it would be a good idea." Both Gandhi and King adopted nonviolence and in so doing appealed to both Western and non-Western ideas. Gandhi, inspired by themes in his Hindu tradition, appealed to the basic principle of *ahimsa*—holding the lives of your enemies "as sacred as those of our own dear ones." King was influenced, in turn, by Gandhi and by Christian ideals of brotherly love, as well as by African ideals of community.

Franz Fanon, an important Algerian theorist and activist, in contrast, argued that civil disobedience would not liberate colonized peoples.[15] Instead he advocated violent overthrow. He didn't say this because he liked violence but because he thought it was the only way to achieve important goals. He argued that decolonization (replacing those in power with those at the bottom) required violence because colonization was maintained by pure force and would only yield to violence. He also thought that colonized peoples needed to regain their sense of respect and that it was only through violent struggle that the colonized could regain their humanity, be released from despair and inaction, and have their fear transformed into fearlessness.

In Latin America, colonization was a brutal and lengthy process that introduced European and Catholic elements into the culture. It also provided the fertile ground for postcolonial opposition to these new elements. We see this blend of traditions in liberation theology, a powerful critique of inequality that draws on Christian notions of human rights. Paulo Friere's *The Pedagogy of the Oppressed,* which describes the role education plays in both maintaining oppression and in furthering individual attainment of freedom and justice, has continued to be an influential work for more than thirty years.[16]

Karl Marx continues to be an important influence in many countries in the world and plays an important role in some postcolonial critiques.[17] Many Marxists believe that moral values, like virtually all ideas, are inextricably linked with the economic system. A capitalist economy requires that people have a certain amount of liberty to engage in economic activity. Property relations must be recognized in order to have something to exchange with others. Contracts must be honored, and most things must have a price. Those of us who grew up in a capitalist economy take many of these things for granted, but ask yourself these questions: Are there prices in heaven? Private property? Economic activity of any kind?

These same Marxists are critical of the way values are defended in a capitalist society. Marx himself wrote about the worth of liberty to someone who lived under a bridge. Liberty may be valuable for someone with the time and money to use it productively, but virtually useless to someone who lacks either the time or the money to exercise liberty in any meaningful way. If we take this critique seriously, we will be suspicious of all moral perspectives. After all, if moral perspectives exist just to protect the status quo, and the status quo really isn't very fair to all of us, why should we take moral perspectives seriously?

There are other Marxists who interpret Marx in a different way. They focus on his discussion of human nature (which emphasizes meaningful work and happiness) and his critique of capitalism. Marx objected to capitalism because he believed it was an economic system that made people unhappy. Workers, he said, are exploited, underpaid, and alienated from their own creativity. Capitalists are alienated from their workers and from their own human nature, and even relatively secure and well-paid workers feel so alienated that they try to buy happiness by purchasing more and more consumer goods.

This second interpretation of Marx gives us a reason for objecting to capitalist exploitation. For those taking this view, one can object because humans are suffering under capitalism. If we accept the first interpretation, we have no way to critique capitalism. If values are a mere reflection of the status quo, then we can't appeal to them in criticizing the status quo. If we live in a capitalist system, we do not even have any values that would allow us to critique our social world. We think there is a middle ground here. One can agree with the first group of Marxists that much of what passes for morality is a justification of the status quo while also agreeing with the second group that some moral values are defensible.

Cultural Conflict

Now that we've had a chance to survey many different moral perspectives around the world, we turn to the important question of how to navigate among these different perspectives. In spite of all the differences, we are inclined to think that there may well be more commonality in human moral perspectives and ways of life than it may at first appear. There are two main reasons for thinking this. First, we have a great deal in common as humans. We have similar needs, desires, and abilities; and we face similar challenges. Second, differences that seem great may often disappear on analysis.

Take the following example. In most states in the United States, marriage between first cousins is not allowed. In many other parts of the world, marriage between first cousins is perfectly acceptable. On a superficial reading, it looks like we have a conflict about incest. But on a deeper reading the conflict disappears. The conflict depends on the shared idea that incest should be discouraged. The only difference is how incest is defined. If we look even deeper, we may find another commonality. Incest is discouraged in virtually every human society because it is seen as damaging to the people involved. This suggests that we have an important shared commitment to not harming persons. We may have different understandings of what counts as harm and even what counts as a person, but the commonality is strong nonetheless.

Still, not all conflicts will disappear on closer inspection. So what do you do when you have a conflict? First, recognize that you are not really in a position to negotiate the conflict until you adequately understand the other's point of view. Be patient and respectful in trying to come to an understanding about another person's position on a moral issue. Second, decide for yourself what is negotiable and what is not. You cannot maintain your own moral integrity if all your values are up for grabs. Third, consider what is at stake and what the options for compromise are. Finally, you will either be able to compromise, walk away from the situation, or stand and fight, depending on what is at stake, what is negotiable, and what compromises are possible.

▶ **Exercise 5.2**

Now that you have been exposed to some different traditions of ethical reasoning from Western and non-Western sources, revisit the issue of cultural relativism. Do the traditions discussed in this chapter lead you to be sympathetic toward relativism? Consider again the criticisms of this position from earlier chapters. Do you think that the traditions discussed in this chapter add new reasons to object to the relativist position?

Conclusion

This chapter provided a brief look at some other perspectives, both from within and outside of the Western tradition. There are many other places to look for inspiration and insight. If you want to be an effective advocate for your moral point of view, it is important to recognize that your audience may come from a different point of view. One way to educate yourself about other points of view is simply to ask about them. Keep in mind, though, that when someone is one of the few members of their race, gender, culture, religion, sexual orientation, disability community, age, and so forth in a particular setting, they may be constantly barraged by questions about how their group thinks. Walk softly here and try to be open about gaining understanding without making someone feel that they are a spokesperson for an entire group.

▶ Study Questions for Chapter Five

1. What are the main characteristics of the "morally superior person" in Confucian thought?
2. According to Confucius, what are the three central virtues?
3. What are Mencius's "five relations," and why are they important to moral improvement?
4. What does the *Bhagavad Gita,* through the character of Krishna, say about the nature of the self? How should one do their duty?
5. What is the Islamic philosopher al-Fārābī's view of the relation of reason to religious insight? How does al-Ghazzāli's view differ from al-Fārābī's?
6. What are some major criticisms of traditional Western moral theory from feminist and postcolonial thought?

NOTES
1. All citations for Confucius are from *The Analects.*
2. All citations for Mencius are from *The Book of Mencius.*

3. Eliot Deutsch, *The Bhagavad Gita: Translated, with Introduction and Critical Essays* (New York: University Press of America, 1968); H. Zimmer, *Philosophies of India* (New York: Princeton University Press, 1989).

4. W. T. De Bary, *Sources of Indian Tradition,* vol. 1 (New York: Columbia University Press, 1958).

5. C. Sartwell, "Art and War: Paradox of the Bhagavad Gita," *Asian Philosophy* 3 (1993), 95–102.

6. Ibid., 97.

7. Ibid., 97–98.

8. N. C. Jain, "World View and Cultural Patterns of India," in L. A. Samovar and R. E. Porter, eds., *Intercultural Communication: A Reader* (Belmont, Calif.: Wadsworth, 1991), 78–86; J. C. McCroskey and V. P. Richmond, "Human Communication Theory and Research: Traditions and Models," in M. B. Salwen and D. W. Stacks, eds., *An Integrated Approach to Communication Theory and Research* (Mahwah, N.J.: Lawrence Erlbaum Associates, 1996), 233–242).

9. Joseph Puig Montada, "Reality and Divinity in Islamic Philosophy," in E. Deutsch and R. Bonteko, eds., *A Companion to World Philosophies* (Oxford: Blackwell, 1997).

10. Ian P. McGreal, *Great Literature of the Eastern World* (New York: Harper Collins, 1996).

11. Harry Bone, "Al-Fārābī," in B. Carr and I. Mahalingam, eds., *Companion Encyclopedia of Asian Philosophy* (London: Routledge, 1997).

12. Mourad Wahba, "The Concept of the Good in Islamic Philosophy," in E. Deutsch and R. Bonteko, eds., *A Companion to World Philosophies* (Oxford: Blackwell, 1997).

13. Carol Gilligan, *In a Different Voice: Psychological Theory and Women's Development* (Cambridge: Harvard University Press, 1982).

14. Edward Said, for example, offered a very influential critique of Western-centered views. See *Orientalism* (New York: Vintage Books, 1979).

15. Franz Fanon, *The Wretched of the Earth* (New York: Grove Press, 1963).

16. Paulo Friere, *The Pedagogy of the Oppressed* (New York: Continuum International, 2000).

17. See *The Communist Manifesto* for a brief and accessible account of the views of Marx and Engels.

CHAPTER 6

Justice

By now you may be thinking that this model of integrity sounds just wonderful, but it won't work in our imperfect world. We hope we have given you confidence that striving for integrity can indeed make you a better person, but you are right to worry about how to do this in your everyday life. Don't give up, because you have much more power to make a difference than you may realize. You can make a difference by acting with integrity, and you can make a difference by helping to change things. You needn't try to change the world; just start working on your little corner of it.

It's easy to get discouraged about your own power, but keep in mind that the world is changing all the time and it is ordinary people like you who are changing it. You might as well join them, and the changes you begin to make might as well be changes for the better. But maybe we're getting ahead of ourselves here. Before you start changing your part of the world, you need to think about how you would like to change it. We're going to focus in this chapter on one crucial part of the good society—justice. Justice is one facet of good leadership that is mentioned again and again, and it is an essential part of any good society.

The Just Society

In the just society, everyone has to be committed to being just, but this is just the beginning. A just society would not work very well if everyone had a different notion of justice. Instead, in the just society everyone must accept roughly the same principles of justice. There are two different dimensions of justice: procedural justice and substantive justice. In a just society, all the basic social institutions conform to these widely shared principles of justice. In addition, in a just society all these principles must be public. This means that everyone who is reasonably attentive knows what the principles are, and it means that the principles are available in some way so that people can refer to them. Any changes must be made with ample time for publicity about the nature of the changes.

There are three basic parts of procedural justice: (1) All decisions are made impartially; (2) rules and procedures are public and applied consistently; and (3) no arbitrary distinctions are made between people. So if someone is a just judge, he or she won't favor friends over strangers, but will apply the law impartially to all. If the judge uses a standard of decorum in her courtroom, for example, he or she will apply it in the same way to everyone who appears in the courtroom. Finally, the judge won't favor some people over others on the basis of some arbitrary standard, such as whether they are tall or short.

So far what we've said about the just society is relatively uncontroversial. There are other areas of justice that people disagree about. Here we will touch on just three: democracy, power, and equality. We will not be arguing for any particular position on these (although we certainly have positions), but we will describe the options and arguments that you need to consider in order to decide for yourself what should be included in the just society.

Many people in the United States simply assume that the just society must be democratic, but not everyone would agree with that assumption. Plato made an interesting case for a quite different society in his dialogue *The Republic.*[1] There he argued for philosopher kings and queens. He began by pointing out that not everyone is equally wise or virtuous, and since these qualities are requirements for a good ruler, we should find a way to exclude some people from positions of power. Second, not everyone is motivated by a desire to nurture the common good. Too many people are focused on what is good for themselves and their friends.

Plato suggested that if we wanted good rulers, we would have to set up a system of education and socialization that would produce such leaders.

He thought that we should begin by choosing intelligent young people and then consciously educating them for leadership. Plato called these people "the Guardians." He was unusual for his time in explicitly saying that we would find the qualities we wanted for leadership in both men and women. To make sure they were wise and morally upright, we should give them an excellent education, including a strong background in philosophy. To further mold their moral characters, we would pay attention to every aspect of their lives, including the music they listened to. To make sure they had the common good at heart, Plato devised a unique family organization. Guardians would get together on special feast days and mate with each other. The children born of this mating would be taken from their mothers and raised communally, and in such a way that none of the Guardians would know who his or her children were. Thus they would feel an obligation to all children, any one of whom might be their biological child. Except for the mating plan—a controversial part of Plato's idea—his program was part of the blueprint for education at the United States Military Academy at West Point, and this blueprint still informs much of the education of the cadets there.[2]

The Guardians would spend their time furthering their education and protecting their society in battle. The wisest and most virtuous Guardians would be eligible for positions of leadership in their society, and the best of these would become the philosopher kings and queens who would govern.

Even if you find democracy a better blueprint for society than Plato's, you still need to address some questions about democracy. First, it is worth noting that there are different types of democracy. We can have direct or representative democracy. In a direct democracy, each citizen has an individual say in every important discussion. Rousseau thought this was the best type of government because it would best protect the interests of the citizens, but he noted that it could only work in small societies.[3] He argued that the ideal number of citizens was the number of people who could gather under a large spreading oak tree. Though direct democracy might fit better with the moral ideals we discussed in earlier chapters, efficiency provides the impetus for representative government, where we elect people to make decisions for us. In the United States, through the Bill of Rights, which is designed to protect individuals in a representative democracy, we've struck a compromise between respecting all persons and efficiency.

The second question to ask is whether the just society is thoroughly democratic, or just democratic in its political life. Most people do not think about democracy as applying in the workplace, for example, but there are interesting arguments that a commitment to democracy must be extended in this direction.[4]

Now that we've gotten you to think about democracy, we turn to our next issue: how power is distributed and justified. Philosophers have thought a lot about how governmental power can be justified. Thomas Hobbes is one of the founders of what is known as the Social Contract tradition.[5] In *The Leviathan*, he described the world before humans organized themselves into societies with institutions charged with maintaining order. In such a world of "war of all against all," life would be "solitary, poor, nasty, brutish and short." In such a world, he argued, we would choose to give up part of our liberty in exchange for protection. In other words, we would form a social contract to obey the laws that provided protection for all.

Now, none of us ever had the chance to be in on that first negotiation, so why are we obligated to obey the law? And are there limits to what the law may demand of us? Many philosophers have weighed in on these questions. John Locke argued that the law cannot violate our moral rights.[6] This Lockean insight was adopted by the Founding Fathers of the United States when they stated that we all have the right to life, liberty, and the pursuit of happiness. As you decide what rights you think the government ought not infringe on, recall our earlier discussion of moral rights.

But the government is not the only body that exercises power over us. John Stuart Mill worried about the "tyranny of the majority."[7] In his famous essay "On Liberty," he argued that no one, not even the government or one's neighbors, may interfere with an individual as long as the individual is not harming someone else. Further, he argued that individuals have the right to make their own decisions about whether to engage in behavior that harms only themselves. Present-day libertarians adopt much of this view and use it to argue for such things as the repeal of drug laws.

Michel Foucault, an influential twentieth-century French philosopher, pointed out that power is something that is exercised in different ways by all of us, and resistance to power is possible for even the weakest among us.[8] Here he was reminiscent of the famous French philosopher Jean Paul Sartre, who was perhaps the most influential expositor of Existentialism.[9]

If power is such a broad phenomenon, then the question of the role of power in a just society is a complex one. We cannot possibly discuss all the nuances here, but we can point out a couple of relatively uncontroversial limitations on power. First, in a just society, power must not be excessive, and power must not be exercised arbitrarily. We see the limitation on excessive exercise of power in the prohibition of cruel and unusual punishment in the US Constitution. The widespread practice of evaluation and notification before termination of employment is an example of a restriction on the exercise of arbitrary power.

The final issue we will raise is equality. Most people think that there should be some equality in a just society, even if it does not mean equality in all things. But what is equality? Here we will distinguish between four different notions of equality.

Aristotle defended equality among equals.[10] This means that if you are in a certain category, you should be treated the same as everyone else in that category. So, for example, if you're a captain in the army, you should have the same rights, privileges, and responsibilities as all the other captains, but you shouldn't expect to have the same status as a major.

Equality can also be interpreted as treating everyone exactly the same way. Critics of the Equal Rights Amendment often appealed to this idea. They raised concerns about unisex bathrooms, for example. But this is not a plausible way to interpret equality. The basic idea of equality is the Kantian notion that we are all moral equals, entitled to be treated as ends in ourselves and never merely as means. This doesn't seem to commit us to unisex bathrooms.

Equality of outcome is perhaps the most thoroughgoing notion of equality. This view says that we should end up with an equal share of the benefits that society has to offer. Critics have wondered whether this is fair, and they have worried about the effect of this kind of equality on motivation. But if we commit ourselves to the Kantian idea of moral equality, it does seem that some things should be equal. If we don't have decent schools and health care, for example, it's hard to see how we can achieve any of the goals we set for ourselves.

The last notion of equality, and the least controversial, is equality of opportunity. This means that we start out equally and achieve our goals on the basis of our abilities and hard work. There is a great deal of debate about what it means to start out equally, however. Liberals like Amy Gutman argue that this principle requires the same excellent quality of education for all.[11] Susan Okin argued that it even requires making sure that families do not limit the options of their children through overly doctrinaire education and socialization.[12]

Now that you have some idea of the different notions of equality, you can decide for yourself to what extent the just society should be committed to it. You can also decide how democratic the just society must be and how power ought to be exercised and limited.

We cannot talk about a just society without saying something about the citizens of a just society. We can use some notions borrowed from Social Contract Theory here. The citizens of a just society must be well informed, willing to negotiate over differences, and willing to balance self-interest with the common good. We can see intuitively how these principles work. Let's suppose that you belong to a softball league and you need to find practice times to fit people's schedules. The first thing you would want is some idea of what schedules people have and when the fields are available for practice. Next, you would want people to be willing to negotiate. If one of the teams was sponsored by a company that had given large donations to the town to maintain the fields, its members could throw their weight around and insist that if they don't get what they want, the company would stop contributing. This kind of behavior is familiar to all of us, but most people would agree that it is not fair. Finally, we would want everyone to be flexible so that we could continue to have a league. If the players insisted on satisfying their own narrow self-interest, we wouldn't be able to satisfy all of them, and the league could fall apart.

We can now put all these ideas together and come up with a list of questions to ask when we want to know if a society is basically just.

▶ Decision Procedure for Basic Justice

1. Are the procedures for making decisions consistent, impartial, and nonarbitrary?
2. Is the society appropriately democratic?
3. Is the exercise of power neither arbitrary nor excessive?
4. Is the society appropriately equal?
5. Are the citizens well informed, willing to negotiate, and willing to balance their own self-interest against the common good?

▶ Exercise 6.1

Describe your workplace in terms of the characteristics of a just society. Does it qualify as a just society? If not, what are its problems? Draft a memo describing the problems. Share it with someone outside of your workplace. If you think it would be helpful and appropriate, share it with someone in your workplace. What was the reaction?

Three Dimensions of Justice

Now that we've talked about basic justice, we can look at three important types of justice—retributive justice, compensatory justice, and distributive justice. There are roughly three views of retributive justice, which covers the issue of punishment for crimes and other offenses. These views roughly correspond to Kant, Utilitarianism, and virtue theory. The Kantian version is called retributivism. This view says that punishment should be meted out because a crime was committed and we need to restore the balance in some way. For a retributivist, we restore the balance by making the punishment fit the crimes. The biblical injunction "An eye for an eye" is an example of a retributivist view. The second important view is the deterrence view. This view says that punishment should be sufficient to deter people from committing crime. There are two kinds of deterrence: special deterrence and general deterrence. Special deterrence means that we punish a person who has committed a crime so that this particular person will be less likely to commit another crime in the future. General deterrence says that we should punish someone enough to deter others from committing a similar crime. This is the view behind the idea of making an example of someone. Rehabilitation is the view that is most compatible with the virtue perspective. Here, both the justification for punishment and the practice of punishing are focused on reforming character and bringing offenders back into a proper balance with their society.[13]

It is interesting to consider how these types of justice would apply to specific types of crimes. Take the current debate about disparate penalties for crack versus powder cocaine, for example. First of all, there is a great debate about whether we are justified in punishing anyone for so-called victimless crimes. As we've seen, John Stuart Mill would argue that we should never interfere when a person is harming only himself. But even if we thought that punishment was justified in such cases, it's not clear how we would defend meting out different punishments for crack versus powder cocaine. Does retributive justice warrant different punishments for these two crimes? Or is deterrence the reason for the difference? How would the rehabilitation view affect the way we deal with drug crimes?

Compensatory justice deals with the issue of compensating someone who has been the victim of an injustice of some kind. How do we decide how to compensate the victims of a defective automobile, for example? Often we will want to do two things—we will want to punish the wrongdoer and compensate the victim. This is why civil judgments are of two kinds: Punitive damages are assessed to punish the wrongdoer, whereas compensatory damages are given to compensate the victim for the harm suffered. Compensatory justice is an area that cannot be avoided. You may never serve on a jury in a civil matter, but you will often have to decide how to compensate someone for past mischief. This is an issue that comes up in our personal as well as civic lives.

Distributive justice is concerned with principles that govern the distribution of benefits and burdens in a society. It presents a special challenge to leaders, who are often in a position to delegate tasks and distribute rewards of various sorts. Next, let's take a closer look at principles of distributive justice—that is, different methods that have been proposed for determining how these benefits and burdens should be distributed.

Principles of Distributive Justice

Distributive justice is probably the first dimension of justice that children experience. "How come she got a bigger piece of cake than I did?" "Why did he get to stay up late?" Philosophers have defended a number of different ways to answer these perennial questions.

Numerous principles of distributive justice have been defended by philosophers and others. Some people argue that their principle is so compelling that we should use it as our only guide every time there are benefits or burdens to be distributed. It can also be useful to think about applying different principles to different kinds of things. For example, you may want to distribute basic necessities equally while other things are distributed by some other means. Sometimes you will want to combine two principles. You might, for example, begin by giving everyone health benefits, but have add-ons for hard-to-recruit employees.

Equality Principle

On this view, benefits and burdens should be distributed equally. In other words, everyone gets an equal share of all benefits and burdens. There are two interesting complications here. The first is deciding what is an equal share. Suppose we are giving out bonuses and want to do so equally. Should everyone get the same dollar amount, or should everyone get the same percentage? At first glance, the same dollar amount looks like the most equal amount, but let's look again. Suppose the dollar amount is $4,000. This would be pocket change to the top execs and a great deal of money to the entry-level employees. If we wanted to have an equal effect on people's pocketbooks, we might want to give them a sum that had a similar effect on all. This is an argument for percentages.

Some people at this point in the discussion might suggest that we distribute the bonuses on the basis of contribution. But if we did that, we would not be following the equality principle at all; instead, we would be following a contribution principle (discussed below). One thing to keep in mind here is that the equality principle is not concerned with merit. The principle of equality says we always distribute things equally.

The second complication is that there are two quite different understandings of equality at work here. The first is equality of opportunity, and the second is equality of outcome. Under the first view, we should distribute opportunities equally, and the end product will be influenced by equal opportunity as well as other factors, such as hard work and luck. The second principle says that what matters is how we end up. Luck, for example, is not something that we can control and hence something for which we cannot take credit. Thus luck should not be a factor in how we distribute goods. These are very different views, and you must decide for yourself which version you think is more plausible. Keep in mind that you do not have to use the same principle for all cases. You might, for example, decide that it makes more sense to use equality of outcome for the distribution of basic survival goods, and equality of opportunity for all other goods.

This principle, like all other principles of justice, can be justified in terms of some of the other moral perspectives we discussed earlier. Respect for persons is a natural one. When we recall that persons are moral equals—entitled to be treated equally as persons—we can see how Kant's view could justify the equality principle of distributive justice. Utilitarianism would justify the equality principle in those cases where an equal distribution would maximize utility. Some would argue that this principle should always apply; others think it is best suited for basic needs.

Contribution Principle

The contribution principle says that we should distribute benefits and burdens based on the contributions that individuals have made toward a common task. Some defenders of this view would also want to include the contributions a person might reasonably be expected to make in the future. The difficulty in applying this principle is trying to figure out what counts as a contribution. There is another difficulty as well. Sometimes people have different ideas of what the common task should be. We can see this difference in health care, for example. Some nurses have argued eloquently that part of their job (perhaps a major part) should be comforting patients and families. This picture of nursing is not shared by everyone in the health-care field, especially not health-care executives. They may think that nurses are too expensive to be doing such pedestrian tasks. Indeed, if you look at the average hospital in the United States, you'll see fewer and fewer RNs, and they will mostly be charged with passing out meds and doing other highly skilled tasks.

There are lots of ways to justify this principle, but Utilitarianism seems like the most likely strategy. Defenders of this principle argue that if we distribute on the basis of contribution, then people will contribute more. You might also defend the principle on the basis of fairness, the idea that each of us deserves to be recognized and compensated for the contributions we make.

Need Principle

Some people are more able to do certain tasks, while others have difficulty doing even the simplest task. Some of us are healthy and relatively well off, while others struggle to secure food and shelter. For these reasons, some have suggested that we distribute benefits and burdens on the basis of two factors: need and ability. This principle says that everyone should work to the level of their ability, and everyone should get their needs met. This principle can be defended in many ways. A Utilitarian defense might be that this kind of a distribution would result in an efficient society in which all were getting their basic needs met. You could also appeal to respect for persons—if we followed this principle, we would be treating everyone as moral equals entitled to respect. The concern for others would be expressed in terms of treating all people as individuals with special abilities and needs. Again, if this principle sounds right to you, you still must decide whether to use it in every case or only in those cases where basic needs are concerned.

Membership Principle

There are some things that seem to belong to us by virtue of our membership in a particular community. In such cases, benefits and burdens are distributed on the basis of that membership. For example, you might work at a place where everyone gets to use the gym, the dining room, and the employee parking lot. We can justify this principle in terms of care: We provide certain things to all the members of a community because this is how we build and maintain stable, flourishing communities. We can also appeal to utility considerations: The companies that offer benefits like this will be able to recruit more effectively. But how do we distribute membership in the community? Consider the question of immigration. Everyone who is a US citizen is entitled to certain benefits and is assessed certain burdens. But there are many people who very much want to be members, in large part because they want the benefits and are willing to shoulder the burdens.

There is a related difficulty. Suppose that basic needs are distributed only to members of a particular community. Those outside the community might well claim that this is unjust, since basic needs seem to be things that all humans need. We might meet this objection by limiting the membership principle to cases where we are distributing benefits that go beyond basic needs. Think back to our softball example. Playing softball is not something we need to do, but softball players think of it as a benefit. It seems permissible to distribute practice times only to teams that are in the league. But suppose the league is overly restrictive and will not allow new teams to join even if there are practice and playing times available. This suggests the need for another rule—there should be no arbitrary restrictions on membership.

Market Principle

This principle is the backbone of the political movement called Libertarianism.[14] Libertarians base the market principle on the rights tradition: People have a right to their liberty and the fruits of their labor. No one, including, especially, the government, has a right to anything that anyone else acquired through hard work. What this means is that it is wrong to impose a burden (such as taxes) on some people to provide benefits for others. If you have very little, you will either have to work harder or find some private charity.

Many people accept a less radical version of this principle, and everyone can embrace a modest version of it: Some things shouldn't be distributed at all. You should be able to collect some benefits in whatever way you choose, and some burdens should be strictly self-imposed.

Rawls's Approach

According to John Rawls, everyone has a right to the most extensive liberty compatible with everyone else having a like amount. Social inequalities are to be arranged so that they can reasonably be expected to be to everyone's advantage, and they should be attached to positions open to all.[15]

This is the most complex principle of distributive justice, and Rawls appeals to respect for persons in justifying it. Many people have pointed out that the second part of his principle is most readily defended in Utilitarian terms, however. Basically, what he is saying is that everyone is entitled to equality with respect to basic liberties. So we should all be accommodated when it comes to voting, for example. But when it comes to other things, like jobs and salaries, we should distribute them in such a way that everyone as a whole is better off. Let's look at an example. Suppose Luis is your top salesperson. His sales are benefiting the entire company. If we pay him a large commission, he will continue to work for the company, and everyone else will continue to have a job, benefiting from the overall prosperity of the firm. Rawls would say that we should go ahead and pay Luis what it will take to keep him on board, as long as everyone else has the opportunity to achieve the position Luis has, and as long as Luis having the benefits he does doesn't make anyone else worse off.

Motivation and Principles of Distributive Justice

Some people worry that certain ways of distributing things will undermine motivation. This is a serious concern for leaders, who often find that the most acrimonious discussions center around who got what. This same concern is often heard in discussions of merit pay. We think that it is important to examine an important underlying assumption in the argument that people are motivated primarily by salary and other compensation. We are not convinced that this is true. We think that many people place a high value on being happy with their work, and they need only enough compensation to be comfortable and feel valued. These people are interested in how interesting and challenging the work is, the match between their skills and the tasks involved in the job, the working conditions, the sense of camaraderie among workers, good leadership, and recognition of one's contribution. They are motivated to work because they enjoy the work, feel a sense of accomplishment, and like their coworkers. Consider the example in Exercise 6.2.

> ### ▶ Exercise 6.2

Suppose that you need surgery and your doctor gives you a choice between two surgeons who are equally skilled. Dr. Interested is fascinated by surgery and by patients and makes a point of taking patients first on the basis of their medical needs and then on a first-come-first-served basis. Dr. Bucks is only in it for the money and looks first at how much the surgery will cost and what kind of insurance the patient has. Assuming their skills are roughly equal, which surgeon would you choose, and which surgeon would you want to be?

Many people choose or stay in relatively low-paying jobs in spite of high educational attainments and the availability of other options. Teachers certainly come to mind here. We do have a shortage of credentialed teachers in this country, but considering the level of education needed to be a teacher, the level of stress, and the relatively low pay, it's surprising that we have as many teachers as we do. Teacher education programs are filled with aspiring teachers who walked away from relatively high-paying jobs because they wanted to do something they found meaningful and socially productive. This is not to say that pay and benefits are irrelevant; the looming teacher shortage and the rapid burnout of new teachers is clear evidence that we cannot ignore pay even when we think the primary motivation is not related to pay.

The flip side of the concern about motivation is the effect of distributions on morale and camaraderie. Sometimes any unequal distribution will create hard feelings, and sometimes an equal one will have this same effect, if the parties feel that not everyone is making the kind of contribution they are capable of. One should consider morale in distributing benefits, and Utilitarians would argue that this is an important factor. However, it is also important to remember that distributing the burdens fairly is just as important as distributing benefits to improve morale.

Whenever you have to decide how to distribute benefits and burdens, you must think about many factors, including motivation and morale. But keep in mind that good leaders do not just debate about what to do; they are skilled at knowing how to do things. If you are acting with integrity, you have already done a lot of work to create a motivated team whose members trust each other. In this atmosphere, questions of distribution are less volatile.

▶ **Applying Principles of Distributive Justice**

1. First decide which principle you want to defend. Keep in mind that you can adopt one principle for all cases, or one principle for one type of case (for example, basic needs) and another principle for other types of cases.
2. Apply the principle to the case.

▶ **Exercise 6.3**

Think about your workplace or community organization. What benefit causes the most conflict? What burden? Describe how you would distribute these benefits and burdens by using all of the principles above. Which seems like the best way to distribute the benefit? The burden? Draw up a memo defending your choice and share it with someone in your organization. Finally, use this principle when you have the opportunity to distribute a benefit or burden and reflect on how the method worked.

▶ Exercise 6.4

Suppose that you were told that you had to layoff 10 employees in your group of 100, and further suppose that you had already laid off the worst performers. Which principle of justice would you use to make your decision? Why? (Hint: One way to use the equality principle is a lottery. This way everyone has an equal chance of being laid off or retained.)

Conclusion

In this chapter, we've covered a lot of territory. We began by distinguishing between procedural justice (the process we use to gain just outcomes) and substantive justice (the principle of justice that would be accepted by a just process). We then described a just society as one in which everyone knows and accepts principles of justice, and the basic social institutions reflect this understanding. We distinguished between retributive justice (justice with respect to punishing), compensatory justice (justice with respect to compensating victims), and distributive justice (justice in distributing social benefits and burdens). Since how we distribute benefits and burdens is such a complex and controversial subject, we spent the bulk of our discussion here, outlining various principles.

There are many decisions you have to make as you bring all this material to bear. First, decide what you think the just society would be like. This is not a task that you can do overnight. It is a life-long endeavor. You might start by reading about other societies and paying attention to what life is like in places you visit. Get familiar with the great works on justice. Think about what things cause conflict in communities and how they could be avoided or resolved. Think about the principles of distributive justice and try them out whenever you have something to distribute.

Remember that change is very slow, but that it will come with you or without you. Every little thing you do will influence the future. Decide what you want the future to be like and act accordingly. Become an active leader in your community. Have ideas, voice them, listen to others, and be willing to follow through.

> ▶ Study Questions for Chapter Six

1. What are the central features of a just society?
2. What is the difference between procedural and substantive justice?
3. What are the different forms of democracy? How might each fit in a just society?
4. Why did Plato think that we wouldn't need democracy in a just society?
5. What is power? How might limitations on power fit in a just society?
6. What are the four different notions of equality?
7. What are the three dimensions of justice?
8. What are the six basic principles of distributive justice? How would each work in making decisions about just distribution? What are some of the strengths and weaknesses of each?

NOTES

1. Plato, *The Republic* (originally written circa 360 BCE), translated by C.D.C. Reeve (Indianapolis: Hackett, 2004). (Many works in the history of philosophy are also available online.)

2. When Rita Manning taught at the U.S. Military Academy at West Point, she read *The Republic* in her ancient philosophy class. The cadets were fascinated to see the ways in which West Point is modeled on this text, and one of the cadets jokingly asked, "You mean Plato invented drill?"

3. For a collection of much of Rousseau's political work (*Social Contract* was originally published in 1762), see Victor Gourevitch, ed., *Rousseau: "The Social Contract" and Other Later Political Writings* (Cambridge: Cambridge University Press, 1997).

4. See, for example, Chapter 10 of Carol Gould, *Globalizing Democracy and Human Rights* (Cambridge: Cambridge University Press, 2004).

5. Thomas Hobbes, *The Leviathan* (originally published 1651) (New York: Penguin Classics, 1982).

6. John Locke, *Two Treatises on Government* (originally published 1690) (New Haven, Conn.: Yale University Press, 2003).

7. John Stuart Mill, *On Liberty* (originally published 1869) (New York: Penguin, 1982).

8. Michel Foucault made this point in much of his work, but a good place to start might be *Discipline and Punish: The Birth of the Prison* (New York: Pantheon Books, 1977).

9. Again, we see this insight in much of Sartre's work, but a clear introduction is found in "Existentialism Is a Humanism," a lecture given in 1946. Reprinted in *Existentialism from Dostoyevsky to Sartre*, edited by Walter Kaufman (New York: Meridian, 1989).

10. Aristotle, *Politics* (originally written circa 350 BCE) (New York: Penguin, 1981).

11. Amy Gutman, *Democratic Education* (Princeton, N.J.: Princeton University Press, 1999).

12. Susan Moller Okin, *Justice, Gender and the Family* (New York: Basic Books, 1989).

13. For an example of this approach to punishment, see Herbert Morris, *Guilt and Shame* (Belmont, Calif.: Wadsworth, 1971).

14. See Robert Nozick, *Anarchy, State and Utopia* (originally published 1974) (New York: Perseus Books, 2007), for a full discussion and defense of this view.

15. John Rawls, *A Theory of Justice* (originally published 1971) (Cambridge: Belknap Press of Harvard University Press, 2005).

CHAPTER 7

Communicating with Integrity

One aspect of integrity that people often overlook is communication. Most people know that communication is a key part of an *effective* person's repertoire, but few consider the *ethical* dimensions of communication.[1] Being able to make your point in any given interaction is an important skill, but having the right orientation toward that communicative situation is what truly instills integrity and moral worth into that action. It is said that Mussolini was a violent dictator, but that he made the trains run on time—effective and ethical are two qualities that obviously do not always go together. In this chapter, we hope to introduce you to the ethical aspects of communication: that is, how we can communicate with integrity.

There are two things involved with ethical communication. First, in communicating with others you must respect them as persons with moral value. Second, in order to transform your environment into one that is more ethical, you must be able to communicate your values to others in an articulate and persuasive way. Part of communication is getting your own ideas across. The other part of it is listening, reading, and learning from others.

Though we all pay lip service to the idea of communication as a two-way street, we too often see only our side of it. This is so pervasive that in English we don't even have a word that captures two-way communication. Instead we speak of "speakers," "listeners," "audience," "writers," "readers." It's always important to keep in mind that communication is a complex activity; we listen and we speak.

Doing Things with Words

Deborah Tannen has described a difficulty that often arises in conversations between men and women.[2] If a woman tries to talk to her partner about something that is upsetting, he typically responds in one of three ways: by staring at her with a blank expression on his face, by giving advice, or by asking what he should do about it. The woman may feel frustrated by this response, because she really just wanted someone to understand what she was feeling and to sympathize. What is happening here is that men and women often do not have the same idea of the purpose of the communication. Such misunderstandings are common, and they frustrate many attempts to communicate. It stands to reason that in order to communicate with integrity, it is necessary to become more aware of some of the things we can do with communication.

One of the things we can do with communication is inform. I give you information that you did not previously have. This is a pretty straightforward interaction. Other types of communication are usually more complex.

The second thing we can do is misinform. There are two ways to misinform. First, I might want to give you accurate information, and I give you information that I think is accurate, but it turns out that my information is incorrect. The second way to misinform is to make what looks like an informing communication, but with the intention to mislead the listener. In either case, I succeed at misinforming if my listener believes what I say.

We can also use words to inquire. My inquiry is successful if I ask for information and you understand my request. You can then choose whether to inform or misinform me, and I can choose whether to accept or reject what you say.

We can use communication to build relationships. We can seek reassurance, and we can reassure. We can seek understanding, and we can convey that we do understand. Or we can use language to torpedo relationships. We can criticize, alienate, and create unhealthy competition.

Good leaders understand the power of language to sustain good relationships and they use it consciously.

Relationships are not simply dyadic—that is, they are not just between two people—but we will start with this type of relationship to illustrate how we can use language to build up a relationship. Georg Hegel was a nineteenth-century German philosopher who described relationships as crucial factors in our self-understanding.[3] As Aristotle pointed out, humans are essentially social creatures. We develop our sense of self through interactions with others. No matter how healthy your sense of self is, it will be nurtured or damaged in your interactions with others. If you are constantly criticized, you will begin to doubt yourself. If you are excessively praised, you will begin to distrust the messenger. Hegel's great insight was to see that this dynamic goes both ways, even when there is a great disparity of power. An example will help to make this clear. Let's consider the relationship between Jay and Howard.

Jay is Howard's employee. Howard is very hard on Jay. He expects Jay to always be available and to anticipate his every whim. Jay manages to keep his job because he satisfies Howard's expectations, even though Howard never acknowledges this. Indeed, Howard only comments on Jay's work when Jay has made a mistake. We can see how Howard is damaging Jay. The lack of recognition for a job well done diminishes Jay's sense of accomplishment, and Howard's criticism damages Jay's self-esteem. Because of the unreasonable expectations, Jay is much more aware of Howard's needs than his own. As Hegel would point out, Howard is also diminished by their interaction. Howard's sense of self-mastery is undermined by his continued reliance on Jay. Since Jay feels no sense of joy in their interactions, Howard never gets a sense of himself as a pleasant human being. The longer they are locked in this interaction, the worse their own self-understandings will be.

Let's look at another case. Sara is an administrative assistant who works for Roberto. Roberto makes a point of respecting boundaries. He never asks Sara to do more than her job description requires, and he stays on top of his own tasks. He is quick to complement her on a job well done, and he is sensitive to her life outside the company. Sara feels valued, and Roberto feels competent and fair.

There are two important things to keep in mind here. The first is that we all influence and are influenced by the people with whom we interact. The second is that relationships are not static. They will continue to grow either negatively or positively. If you want to be an effective and ethical leader and a healthy and happy person, you must reflect on your relationships. Try to establish and nurture positive interactions and limit negative ones. Think about the enormous power of words to create and sustain relationships, for good or ill.

Just about everyone has been to a family get-together or a class reunion where all those in attendance seem committed to outshining each other. While on the surface it seems as though people are just trading information about their lives, they are really trying to one-up each other. Everyone has the most accomplished kids, the best job, and the highest compensation package. Here we see the power of communication to express hidden agendas. Some of the most common hidden agendas are displays of status and displays of emotion. When we use communication to display status, we are often trying to show power over and contempt for others. Conversely, we might be showing our submission to others or trying to assert our equality in the face of a challenge. We can also use communication to display emotion. We raise our voices and use criticism to display anger; we lower our voice and our eyes to express disinterest.

Communication in Leadership

Human communication is amazingly fluid and effective at doing many things. If you want to be an effective and ethical leader, you must first notice what you can do with words and then communicate thoughtfully and deliberately. Ethical leadership is more effective leadership because it embraces honest, informative, and supportive communication.

Communication must be honest because it is not possible for us to continue in dishonest communication. You might think you are not going to speak out about what you view as unfair treatment, but you will communicate this in other ways if you don't communicate it in a clear, deliberate manner. You will communicate it to the wrong person, at the wrong time, or in an inappropriate way. Communication for leaders must involve sharing information because leaders cannot succeed without loyal and committed followers who are able to carry out their tasks, and the followers cannot carry out their tasks if they are burdened by incomplete and inaccurate information. Finally, communication for leaders must build trust. No team activity can succeed without the full and generous cooperation of all members of the team, and this full and generous cooperation cannot take place without an atmosphere of trust.

Orientation in Communication

When one is in a role of leadership, one has ample opportunities to communicate with other people. Indeed, communication seems to be necessitated not so much by leadership, but by human nature itself. As Aristotle noted long ago, humans are social animals. It is through our community and communication that we define others, the world, and ourselves. Language, and the ways we use it, have a world-shaping power in that they let us manipulate the world or offer a way for our social world to change us. For instance, the skin color of an individual can become the grounds for radical hate—simply because of hateful stories and narratives that locate that "group" of people as lower in the "chain of being" than the individual making the judgment.[4]

What is of importance at this early stage of discussion is to draw attention to how our communication *orients* us to the world. Besides pointing out what is of importance, the way we use words also tells something about how we approach the world. In the world, leaders must communicate. The choice that remains deals with what type of *orientation* that person in the role of leadership brings to his or her communicative activities with other people. Each person has a particular orientation to how he or she views the use of language in communication. Such an orientation answers such questions as:

How is the other person to be treated?
What is the goal of communication?
How are the participants in communication related to each other?

This orientation exists in all who communicate, though the answers to these questions may be more unconscious than overt. For instance, say Tom goes into a business meeting to convince others that a particular plan of action would be beneficial. Tom makes a powerful presentation about why this plan should be adopted by the company, and the others leave thinking he is correct in his assessment of the merits of the plan. What was the purpose of Tom's speech, and how did he interact with the other participants in this instance of communication? Perhaps Tom felt that his overriding goal was to get the others to believe him. This, however, betrays his orientation toward this instance of communication—the goal of the communication was to get what he wanted.

Although it may seem like Tom was treating others with respect, this foundational orientation toward achieving the desired end of persuasion may have compromised the value he placed on the other participants. To extend the example, imagine a situation where the listeners do not find the speech compelling. To what extent would the speaker go to get them to agree with his or her view? What would provide limits to this quest to get others to agree with one's ideas, wishes, or proposals? As you can see, one's orientation toward communication, and toward the other participants involved, is crucial in an interaction, and understanding orientation is crucial to examining issues of integrity in leadership. While a variety of ethical guidelines have been given, two competing orientations will be described below to help illustrate the foundation that a leader with integrity carries into communicative situations.

Persuasion-Centered Orientation.   One extremely prevalent approach to communication in Western society can be labeled the "persuasion-centered" orientation. This is the orientation that most individuals are exposed to and the one they often unknowingly assimilate. This conception of communication comes from a long line of theories that owe allegiance to Aristotle, who stated that rhetoric (communication) was "the power to observe the persuasiveness of which any particular matter admits."[5] According to this orientation, the purpose of communication is to achieve something *the communicator* wants—thus, it becomes a tool, as in Aristotle's formulation.

This orientation, however, is not without its flaws. It can easily lead to an unethical focus on the self at the exclusion of other people and their interests; it can also lead to denying the intrinsic worth of communication. How these two limitations become evident will be illustrated in a moment. What is of importance now is to unearth the presuppositions behind this view of communication. We will assume that those who hold the persuasion-centered view are committed to the idea of persuasion, even if they are not aware of it.

The persuasion-centered view is based upon some key presuppositions about how the world works and how people relate to each other.[6] First, it assumes that communication is composed of *atomic individuals pursuing their own desires and goals*. When one speaks, one is trying to get what one wants, and each individual is portrayed as separate from each other individual in terms of what each wants and how it is to be achieved. Often these individuals are seen as competing in communication. For example, say that in Tom's business meeting, there was some disagreement about the appropriate course of action. The communicators can be seen as each pursuing his or her own desires and employing the communicative tools needed to achieve them (for instance, a polished presentation/speech).

In addition, under this orientation, *ethical norms must recognize this separate and competitive nature of reality*. The audience and the speaker are ultimately separate, so what is often termed as "ethical" communication is that which avoids negative reactions from these separate individuals— ethics becomes tied to effectively achieving one's goals. As our intuitions tell us in the case of the Mussolini example, effectiveness and achieving one's goals do not always translate into ethical behavior or integrity of leadership.

Third, the goal of communication under this orientation *is to affect the world—to adapt it to one's desires*. Under the persuasion-centered orientation, the speaker is an individual who sets out to change the actions or behaviors of some audience. He or she may want to make the audience believe a message, agree with certain ideas, feel particular emotions, have a good impression of the speaker, and so on. Communication is conceived of as a tool for "fixing" the world; what is "broken" about the world, of course, is everything that is not in line with the speaker's desires, wants, and needs.

Lastly, this orientation toward communication holds that *actions that are not effective in reaching one's goal are not rationally advisable.* One speaks solely to accomplish a specific purpose, and this goal must be realized in order for the speech to be valuable; otherwise, one would do something else. With this view, if Tom in the previous example knew that his speech would not be successful in changing the minds of the other people present, he would have chosen another tactic to achieve the goal (to get a certain plan put into action), or may not even have proposed the plan at all.

▶ **Exercise 7.1**

Think about a time when you were treated badly by another person in the way that he or she communicated with you. How were you treated? Did you feel valued? Why or why not? What could the other person have done to make you feel more valued? What was the other person's goal in the interaction with you?

Invitational Orientation.   Another orientation to communication is labeled the "invitational orientation."[7] In contrast to persuasion-centered communication, which involves domination and control, invitational communication draws upon fundamental values such as "equality, immanent value, and self-determination"[8] in informing theoretical commitments. This orientation is predicated on *openness* by the speaker. The invitational communicator does not see communication as a tool to bend others to one's will, but as a way of *presenting* oneself through communicating one's experiences, opinions, and views, and of *inviting* the responses of the other participants in the communication. This fundamental openness to others seeks to *invite,* not force; it welcomes the transformation of both the audience member and the speaker but does not try to force any transformation upon one party or the other.

Invitational rhetoric also holds certain presuppositions, many of which are opposed to the persuasion-centered view. Initially, this perspective holds that *individuals are interrelated and interdependent.* Each person resides in a complex web of relationships and dependencies that cannot be escaped. For instance, one depends on others for the production, packaging, safety, and quality of one's food. Additionally, the choices that a farmer makes concerning his or her livelihood affects other people in important ways—those who work on the farm, those who compete against it in the market, and those who end up consuming the food it produces. Thus, the invitational perspective recognizes that individuals are not separate entities trying to achieve their own goals, but interdependent beings pursuing complementary goals, common objectives, and similar interests.

This linkage of individuals also means that *individuals involved in communication have intrinsic worth.* Many ethical systems have laid out guidelines and justifications for why people should be treated with respect in instances of communication. The newest twist on this idea comes from feminist theorists, who often find that individuals are radically different and unique and that as such they hold intrinsic value that is separate from any value they may have in achieving certain goals, ends, and the like.[9] But this view has a long and respected history. Some deontological (duty-based) systems find that humans are intrinsically valuable because of essential similarities—for instance, Immanuel Kant found that individuals all have the same faculties of reason and the moral law which derives from it.[10] Eastern texts, such as the *Bhagavad Gita* and the *Astavakra Gita,* postulate that all humans are valuable because they are all part of one big Self, or consciousness.[11] The point behind all of these theories is that humans have a value that goes above and beyond their usefulness to any person or purpose. Thus, in communication, participants are equals and not "pawns" to be moved around as if they were game pieces.

The invitational orientation also holds that *the goal of communication is to increase free interaction and transformative opportunities.* Persuasion as coercion is not seen as allowable in this view—communication that relies on tactics to scare or cower participants into siding with the communicator are not methods of communication that respect others as equals.

Instead, the participants in communication should see a discussion or speech as a way of inviting transformation in others as they offer their perspectives, views, personal experiences, and so on. The speaker is not trying to control or change the other person. The offering that he or she gives to the others in the form of a speech includes openness to the experiences and views of other people and does not assume that other people are objects to be manipulated. Because the same type of openness is hoped for in the audience, certain external conditions are looked upon as favorable, since they can facilitate audience offerings. External conditions for audience openness are optimal when the speaker creates a *safe* environment for interaction, recognizes the intrinsic *value* of the audience members, and makes all parties feel *free* to interact.[12]

These conditions, if fostered by the rhetor, can *invite* audience transformation through open interaction—in other words, by not being treated as objects to be manipulated, the audience members feel valued as individuals and can open up to the views of the speaker and of the other audience members. It is this open flow of ideas that affirms the self-worth of all involved, preempts defensive reactions to differing messages, and clears the way for actual change to occur—change that the participants agree with and freely choose.

One last commitment can be added to this picture of the invitational orientation—*the value of communication is not contained solely in its consequences.* The moral issues surrounding consequences and intentions in actions are examined at other points in this book. Here it suffices to say that "ineffective" communication is often morally praiseworthy. There will be times in one's life when duty, position, or hope may compel one to take a stand, to speak out on a certain issue to individuals who probably will not listen or change. The invitational orientation recognizes that leaders will often have to stand *against* overwhelming odds, and they will not always be assured of achieving desired results.

You may be alone, facing a hostile audience, but you may feel that you *need* to speak your mind and oppose what you find is a grievous harm to tolerance, diversity, or some other principle you believe in. You deliver your perspective eloquently, and with respect for others who hold opposite opinions. If the crowd heeds your invitation to temper their actions, so much the better for you and your desires. If they do not, your action still exhibited integrity and honor. Part of this integrity comes from the fact that you did not silence yourself as someone who was not equal in "voice" to the others.

▶ **Exercise 7.2**

Recall a situation where you felt valued as a person through the way another person talked with you. What did that person do that made you feel valued and important? How did that person see you as a participant in the conversation? What was his or her goal in that conversation?

▶ **Exercise 7.3**

Recall a time when you spoke to a boss, a fellow employee, or a group of colleagues in a work-related situation that could have called for either the persuasion-centered approach or the invitational approach to communication. Which orientation did you choose? What choices and strategies did you use in the way that you spoke? How would these have been different if you had picked the other orientation?

Communicating at Full Potential

If one believes that the invitational orientation is superior to the persuasion-centered orientation (because it recognizes the worth of individuals, allows for the interrelations between individuals, and gives actions values even when they may not be successful), does that mean that one need not work hard at preparing and delivering a persuasive or compelling message or speech?

The answer is simple. With the construction of a message, one should attempt to honor or value one's audience, one's ideas, and oneself. If you truly care about an *audience,* or group of people to be addressed, then the way you prepare and construct that message should reflect this respect. Honoring the audience means presenting them with the best message or speech you can muster. When you are faced with a decision about whether to present the audience with a worthy, polished message or not, this is an ethical choice, since it highlights the issue of the respect you give to your audience and the value that you place on them. In addition, if you truly care about your *ideas*, then you will place them in the most compelling light possible and present a strong argument. If you care about these ideas enough to share them, why slight them with shoddy wording or distracting delivery? Honoring the ideas means preparing a speech worthy of their importance both to you and to the audience. You can also honor *yourself* in and through your message. If you construct a speech on important ideas and you do not do the ideas justice, you not only fail to respect the ideas but also demonstrate that you do not care much about how committed you seem toward those ideas.

The section that follows provides some guidance about how to fulfill your obligation to communicate your ideas at "full potential." The way you go about writing, delivering, and even listening to prepared speeches is part of what makes you a leader with integrity. Each person literally can have a "voice" in our society, but it takes practice to express that voice to your fullest potential. The ability to stand and speak up for what you believe is important merits communication that is eloquent, prepared, and worthy of the ideas presented. Not every kind of speech is formal, or on serious topics. But even in more conversational settings, one's communication can be carried out with integrity. In both serious and more ordinary contexts, communication involves respecting yourself, respecting important ideas and values, and listening attentively and respectfully to others. Thus, *effective* communication and *ethical* communication join in actual practice.

Formal Communication: Speeches and Presentations

For the purposes of this discussion, we will begin with the prepared "speech," since an overview of the skills used in formal settings will actually help to lay the groundwork for describing the skills used in everyday conversational interactions. Prepared speeches are important in a wide range of situations, from those involving government and professional organizations to those bringing together the members of a religious, educational, or nonprofit group. Knowing how to use strategies for success in preparing a speech and delivering it will give you the power not only to invite transformation in others, but also to do justice to yourself and your ideas. It is also the form of communication that causes more sweaty palms than any other—so we may as well dive in and get started. After that, we will turn to more conversational communication.

Preparing Your Speech

When you are called upon to address some sort of crowd larger than four or five people, and you are expected to deliver a presentation or introduce and lead a discussion, you have entered the realm of public speaking. This presentation of ideas usually involves some preparation time, whether that means the minute available for gathering your thoughts before you give a toast at a reception, or the days or weeks you have to prepare for a crucial business meeting or speech before a large audience. The advice that follows can serve you well in both of these situations, although the more time you have to prepare, the better you can carry out these procedures in a thoughtful way. Regardless of the time factor, all of the components of a good speech given below should be considered, as they will help you hone and polish any message and ensure that it does justice to the ideas, audience, and speaker in its construction and delivery.

Find Your Purpose.   The first thing you must do in preparing a speech is to decide what the purpose of the talk is to be. Classical rhetoric finds that most speeches fulfill one of three general purposes—a speech can be to *entertain,* to *inform,* or to *persuade.*[13] These purposes can be chosen by the speaker, or they may be placed upon the speaker by the occasion, the organizers of the speaking context, and/or audience expectations.

When the president of a company gives a speech after a company dinner, for example, then the general purpose of the speech will probably be to *entertain.* The audience is not expecting or desiring a complex oration after a tense day and a great meal. The company president may attempt to evoke certain emotions in the audience, not for any educational purpose, but for comedic or dramatic effect. The type of speaking done by professional comedians is also typical of this category. Although the co-median may engage in some social commentary, his or her overriding purpose is to entertain the audience.

If the purpose of a speech is to inform, in contrast, then the speaker will aim to teach the audience about some topic (event, process, object, people, place, and so on) that they do not already know much about. This type of speech will use facts, sources, and information to clarify, explain, and discuss new ideas and topics so that the audience will leave the speaking context knowing something new. This type of speech is preva-lent not only at schools and colleges but also in professional contexts, where one is often called upon to give a presentation about, say, a status report, about how something works, about company policies or proce-dures, about what may lie ahead for the company, or about some other as-pect of the company's activities or direction.

A speech that seeks to persuade invites the listeners in the audience to change or modify their values, beliefs, attitudes, or behaviors in some way, or to reinforce those things, if the audience already agrees with the per-spective offered. Thus, one may have to give a speech where the purpose is to change a supervisor's attitudes toward a certain new policy, or make a presentation that invites a customer to change his or her behaviors and purchase a new type of product. The audience members presumably al-ready hold a position on the topic covered, but the speaker is seeking to change, modify, or reinforce that position. The speech then serves as a rea-soned case as to why the audience should accept the speaker's view or plan.

When you give a formal speech, you must be aware of what your pur-pose is and what is expected of you. You would not want to show up to speak before a high school assembly thinking that the purpose of your presentation was to persuade the students to apply for employment with your company, when the principal (and possibly the audience) wanted you to deliver an informative presentation on the new technology your company was using. If you gave a recruitment pitch instead of an educa-tional talk about technology, your audience would be disappointed, and your relationship with the principal would be damaged. Whenever you are invited to speak, think carefully about why you are giving the speech—is it to entertain, to inform, or to persuade?

Central Ideas and Organization.   After you have determined the general purpose of your presentation, you need to formulate your basic position on the subject. This entails constructing the central idea of your speech, which is usually a single, declarative sentence that summarizes what you want to say. If the audience leaves with only one thing on their minds, this one sentence should be it. For instance, say you were to give a presentation to the city council against a proposed new housing development in an agriculture-rich suburban zone. An effective central idea might be, "This proposed housing development threatens not only our agricultural resources but also the long-term interests of this town." This central idea would most likely be for a speech to persuade, although, if the council was simply collecting information on the proposal, it could fit a speech to inform. At any rate, the central idea should be written early so as to guide you in constructing the speech as a whole. When you deliver your speech, it should come early in the presentation, preferably as part of your introduction. Finally, some people find that working out the central idea is more easily done before they have done much of the research and writing. However, be open to going back and changing the central statement if you find out things during your research that change your views.

After figuring out what your central idea is, determine how your presentation will be organized. Ideally, you should divide it into two or three main points (more are allowable for presentations over thirty minutes in length). This simple division helps the audience remember your central idea, and it helps them recall the primary sources of support for that idea and the explanations that you gave. For instance, you would want the town council members to remember not only that you opposed the new development, but also two or three of the main points you made when discussing your opposition. A speaker is not like a book or a tape that can be reviewed at leisure—instead, the audience sees a real-time presentation of the speech and must remember as many of its details as possible. Take this into account when preparing your message.

Most sources on oratory agree on six basic patterns of organization.[14] The first is a chronological pattern. In this case, the two or three main points one wishes to discuss are arranged by some time-based logic—for instance, past-present-future. If you were giving a speech to inform about business practices in a certain country—say, Brazil—your central idea might be, "Business practices in Brazil are extremely dependent upon macro-political sentiment among the populace." You could discuss political sentiment in Brazil in the past and its effects on past business practices, current sentiment and its current effects, and then possible future sentiments and practices. You would want to avoid rambling on about various events in Brazil that were unrelated to this main theme, and instead leave the listeners with a clear central idea. The simple, chronological division would help the listeners remember your main points.

Another organizational layout is the spatial pattern. The main points in a speech employing this pattern would have to do with space or location. For instance, a discussion about the brain could be organized around the functions of the left brain and the right brain. Or you could divide up the speech on business practices in Brazil by area—thus, the first part of the speech could address business practices in northern Brazil, and the second could discuss practices in southern Brazil. Again, dividing one's speech into easily recallable main points that fit together logically helps the audience comprehend your message, making it more likely they will learn something new and remember it in a meaningful way, or accept its invitation to grow or change in thought or action.

The third way to organize a speech is according to a topical pattern. This type of organization presents two or three topics that are discussed individually. For instance, the speech on Brazil and business practices could go into agricultural practices in Brazil first, then move on to discuss financial practices, and then finish with the practices of small business owners. Each main point would relate the subtopic to the central idea about business practices in Brazil. This pattern of organization is ideal when one wishes to present a series of reasons why the central idea is true. For example, say you were testifying in front of a congressional subcommittee on doctor-assisted euthanasia (mercy-killing), and you wanted your central idea to be, "Active euthanasia should not be condoned by state or federal law." Suppose further that you wanted to persuade the members of the subcommittee that your view was the correct way of looking at this contentious issue. You could organize your presentation topically by giving reasons in support of this central idea. Thus, you might address the legal precedents against euthanasia, then discuss the moral reasons for opposing it. The evidence and arguments you would muster in support of the central idea could be logically distributed to fall under these two main points.

A fourth organizational plan is the cause-effect pattern, in which the speaker separates all the main points into the two general categories of causes and effects. In an informative speech about global warming, for example, you could first describe the causes of this environmental phenomenon, using scientific data and the like, and then address its effects on humans, wildlife, the environment, and so on. Thus, the audience would hear a presentation that broke the complex issue of global warming down into manageable blocks of information, and chances would be high that the audience would remember your main points about the topic.

The fifth method of organization is the problem-solution pattern. In this arrangement of information, you first identify and describe a particular problem, and then you discuss what can be done or what has been done to address the problem. For instance, if you found yourself addressing fellow workers at a meeting dealing with falling productivity levels, you could divide the presentation into a discussion of the problem and what caused it, and a discussion about what could be done about the problem. If you wanted to convince the workers or the managers to implement your solution, it would be a speech to persuade; but not all problem-solution speeches are aiming to persuade. If you were giving a speech to inform about a product that your company was producing, you could talk about the engineering obstacles that confronted earlier designs and then describe the solution that the company found and incorporated into the product under discussion. You could even make a hybrid pattern from the cause-effect pattern and this one, organizing the main points by problem-cause-solution. Once again, the audience is more likely to comprehend this material because it is logically laid out in a few simple points, not randomly thrown together as different details pop into the speaker's mind.

The last traditional form of organization is the refutation pattern. This pattern is effective for persuasive speeches that seek to change audience members' minds on a topic they may feel strongly about. If the audience holds an opinion for a few major reasons, then this pattern is an ideal way to systematically "refute" each of their reasons (or a selection thereof). Say you were giving a speech favoring the use of marijuana for medical reasons. For your first point, you could show how marijuana in medical contexts does not lead to higher usage rates among the general public; second, you could explain that it does not function as a gateway drug for patients; and third, you could point out that a medical-use law would not render other drug laws unenforceable. All of the evidence you wished to present would be clearly sequestered into these distinct points, which would make up the body of the speech. The audience would follow your argument point by point and may be more likely to agree with your message.

Once you have chosen some logical pattern for your speech to follow, you must consider how to start and end that eloquent presentation.

▶ Exercise 7.4

What was your instructor's general purpose in the last lecture that he or she gave to your class? Was it to entertain, to inform, or to persuade? What led you to this conclusion?

▶ Exercise 7.5

Think of a topic that you could be called upon to speak about in a formal presentation. It could relate to your job, or it could be something you might want to speak about in a local government meeting, a student government meeting, or some other situation. What might the purpose of the speech be—to entertain, inform, or persuade? Write this purpose down, and then write out a single, clear central idea for the speech. Next, using one of the six patterns of organization described above, write two or three sentences to summarize each main point of your speech.

Introductions and Conclusions.   First impressions are important, especially for anyone who wishes to inspire and lead others. Thus, the beginning of a speech is crucial for establishing your credibility, introducing the topic, getting the audience's attention, and giving the audience a reason to listen. As a general rule, your introduction should be, at most, one-tenth the total length of your speech. For a speech of around ten minutes, an ideal introduction would take no longer than one minute; for a twenty-minute speech, the speaker may take around two minutes to introduce the topic and his or her position on it.

The first part of your introduction is called an opening device. It can use a quotation, some surprising statistics or notable facts, an anecdote, a joke, a hypothetical situation, or some similar technique to get the audience to listen to what you have to say. Thus, in a speech addressed to a particular client about why the client should buy a certain brand of brake pad for their business vehicles, a speaker might begin with a grabbing statistic about the number of automobile accidents due to faulty brakes, the increases in insurance costs to businesses when their company vehicles are involved in accidents, and so on. This approach may get the client's attention, as he or she is likely to be attuned to the financial interests of his or her company, and it gives the client a reason to listen, since he or she will want to save on insurance costs.

After the opening device, the speaker should state his or her central idea and then preview the main points of the speech. Taking the same example, after gaining the client's attention and drawing him or her into the general topic of brake pads and safety, the speaker should state the central idea ("Buying Brand X brake pads will protect your investments and your employees"). Then the speaker should preview the main points of the speech so that the overall organization will be easier to remember (for example, "I'm going to show you some typical problems with ordinary brake pads, and then illustrate how Brand X brake pads avoid these safety problems"). The client now knows the "angle" of the speech and is aware of the general division of the supporting explanation.

The speaker must also give some thought to how best to end the speech, as final impressions can have a lasting effect on what the audience thinks of a speaker and a presentation later, well after the speech is over. A good conclusion ends on a note of finality. Instead of just stopping when the information has been presented, an effective speaker reviews the main points and the central idea of the speech. When you do this, you are helping your audience organize their new knowledge or understanding and reinforcing the main divisions of information for them. Our brake salesperson may conclude with, "So, I hope you have a better understanding of how brake pads can lead to safety and financial problems and how Brand X's pads can avoid these common problems. Buying Brand X pads will safeguard your employees and investments." The main points have been restated, and the central idea has been reemphasized.

But the conclusion does not end there. After reviewing the main points, you should end with a closing device. This can be a story, a statistic, a quotation, a call to action, a reference back to the opening device, or some other method of ending eloquently and on a note of finality. "Bring the speech home" with an ending that leaves the audience thinking about your message and feeling as if they have gained something from listening attentively to your speech and your ideas. Perhaps the brake salesperson can end by talking about an unfortunate, fatal accident involving cheap brake pads, and imploring the client to think carefully about the measures he or she will take to avoid such a tragedy.

So the skeleton outline of the speech would be as follows:

   I. Introduction
      A. Opening Device
      B. Central Idea
      C. Preview of Main Points
  II. Body
      A. Main Point 1
      B. Main Point 2
      C. Main Point 3 (if applicable)
 III. Conclusion
      A. Review of Main Points and Central Idea
      B. Closing Device

But to fill in the details of this outline, you will need to conduct some research and gather ideas and arguments.

Research.   During the research stage of your preparation, you will uncover most of the evidence you will need to make your argument, develop your explanations, fine-tune the arguments themselves, and so on. You will, in short, figure out how to support your main points, thus creating a speech that supports or explains your central idea. Consult sources such as newspapers, magazines, books, journals, and websites to gather information that supports and explains your points.

When researching, keep an eye out for bias in the evidence and arguments you read about, and be cautious about using information from biased sources. If a website, book, or article is written by an author or group that may have a vested interest in a particular position, their support of one side or the other may be "preordained." For instance, you know what "side of the story" the Democratic Party (or the Republican Party) website is going to present on a given political topic, so do not rely on a political party website as an unbiased source of information for that sort of issue. Search for other sources that are accountable and that may not be selectively presenting evidence and information on the topic in question.

Make sure sources are *accountable*—a website, blog, or conservative magazine may not have as much oversight as major newspapers do. In addition, well-documented books and articles are generally more reliable than those that do not name their own sources of facts and statistics. If no sources are cited or referred to, then a particular article or book is probably not a reliable source for your speech. If you want to be a person of integrity, which is the whole point of this discussion about communication, then you do not want to spread misinformation or give a biased view that cannot hold up under scrutiny. Take the extra time to check reliable sources such as serious books on the topic, professional journals, and even qualified experts in the field.

In addition, make sure that the sources you consult are recent—many items in the library and on the Internet are extremely dated and should not be used as current sources of information. Sadly, anyone can put anything on the Internet at basically any time, and dates are often difficult to find on Web pages. Thus, while the Internet is a great source of information, it is also a great source of old, unreliable information. Make sure you know how current something is before you present it to your audience as evidence for your points.

Although much more could be said about research, we will forgo that presentation and instead make a few comments about the nature of persuasion and the types of evidence. According to Aristotle, there are three types of appeals one can make to an audience to support a claim or argument. One can try to persuade others based on one's character, or *ethos.* This is what you are doing when you are counting on the idea that you have enough credibility that others will trust what you say and adjust their beliefs or actions accordingly. Your credibility depends on your knowledge of the subject at hand, your trustworthiness, and your dynamism. Thus, speakers attempt to appear as knowledgeable as possible. They also want to be perceived as honest and sincere by the audience. Sincerity, like dynamism, is integrally linked to the way one delivers his or her message. We'll go into more detail about this shortly; first, we'll look at Aristotle's other two appeals.

Aristotle also said that a speaker can appeal to *logos* in his or her speech. Such an appeal is based on logic and reasoning, hence the importance of evidence and its use in speeches. For instance, antismoking commercials in the 1980s and 1990s gave a straightforward presentation of statistics and studies to discourage smoking; given information about the large percentage of smokers who ended up with certain diseases, viewers were expected to understand the risk that he or she would be taking by starting to smoke or continuing to smoke. By relying on statistics and the reasoning that followed from generalizing from them, these ads used an appeal to logos. Assuming that the sample size and methodology of these studies were sound, viewers could accurately generalize these risks and harms and make a decision not to smoke.

Another type of appeal that Aristotle said can be constructed is an appeal to *pathos,* or emotion. This type of appeal invites the audience to change by allowing them to experience certain emotions. For instance, a recent television advertisement against smoking displays a woman discussing the duplicity of the tobacco companies—through a tracheotomy-induced hole in her throat. This raspy image of what smoking can do to a person is an emotional shock to the audience and can help the viewers experience the more "human" side of this issue. Statistics and studies show the risk and size of a problem, but individual examples can cause the audience to empathize with someone and understand the problem in a new light—in other words, unlike numbers, such examples can let the audience know about a different way of existing (for example, with a hole in one's throat due to smoking). Although one must be careful in using such examples, as they may not be representative of all members of the group in question, they can be effective complements to a speech that is full of logical appeals. It is a good idea to take some time to construct a diverse message that provides not only statistics and facts but also personal, descriptive examples. Both approaches play a part in convincing an audience to accept a speaker's invitation to listen and change.

▶ **Exercise 7.6**

Discuss some examples of commercials that appeal to ethos, pathos, or logos in trying to persuade the consumer to buy certain products or services. How do these short persuasive messages go about constructing these appeals?

▶ **Exercise 7.7**

Pick a topic that one may be persuaded on, such as smoking or not smoking, or saving for retirement. Construct two short strategies for inviting audience members to change their views on this topic, first by appealing to logos, and then to pathos.

Communication as Performance

Giving a presentation or speech in class or in the world of work is more than simply sharing ideas—it is a performance using one's body, voice, and mind in a concerted effort to invite the audience to take that message with all its seriousness and even to transform by considering its views and attitudes. Consequently, preparing a great speech is only half the battle, so to speak. To honor one's ideas, self, and audience, a speaker must go all the way and practice the speech performance with the goal of producing the best possible communicative presentation. This section will provide some tips for practicing effectively, which also entails attention to the nonverbal elements of one's delivery, such as voice, body, eyes, and so on.

Practice.   One cannot write a speech and assume it will come across as brilliant if one simply reads it. Instead, the performance of that message should seek to capture all the inspiration, energy, and effort you put into the creation of that message; if the ideas are truly moving, inspiring, and powerful, then you owe it to them and your audience to convey these ideas as such in your performance of your speech. Thus, as you begin to prepare your speech, you need to make a choice: Will you write out the entire speech, or deliver it from an outline?

The first option entails performing the speech off of a manuscript, which can be useful if you think it is important not to change even the slightest bit of your presentation. This performance, however, will look dry and sterile unless the speaker makes an extra effort to look at the audience and add emphasis and inflection at key points. Delivering a speech without notes, or from a very basic outline that contains only key ideas, is called extemporaneous delivery, and it is the best method to use when a speaker wants to engage the audience in a conversational manner. In most speeches one can alter minor things like word choice, so delivery from an outline is recommended. An outline allows the speaker to make eye contact with the audience while having ample reminders about what comes next in the presentation. A good outline will keep you from simply rambling on about a topic without a clear direction.

Once you've chosen your style of delivery, you must practice your speech. This is an extremely important part of the act of communicating, especially for those who are new to public speaking. In everyday communication and conversation, we often get away with "um's" and "ah's" and lackluster vocal performances, but when one is giving any type of formal presentation, the audience expects to hear something that transcends the type of banter one hears around the water cooler. Thus, practice ahead of time. When practicing, do your utmost to simulate the speaking environment. You will probably be standing when the presentation occurs, for example, so you should stand when practicing. Practice your speech from beginning to end, and time it if length will be a consideration. Check out the speaking location beforehand, and look for anything in the way of lighting, seating arrangement, noises, and other elements of the space that may throw you off when you are making your speech.

The point is that you should be prepared. The better you know the speech, the less nervous you will be and the more powerful your speech will be. When practicing, try to become conscious of how you are using your voice and body language. This awareness will help you learn to use nonverbal elements of communication effectively, and it is the topic to which we now turn. Although there are many forms of nonverbal communication—the use of the hands, for example—we will cover only the effective use of voice and eye contact in more detail.

Effective Use of Voice.   The way you use your body, including your voice, in delivering a speech is absolutely crucial. While the verbal elements of the speech are important in conveying the ideas and thoughts behind certain words, the nonverbal elements of the delivery are important in conveying emotions, invoking emotions, seeming authoritative, seeming interested in the topic, and the like. Think about it—if a speaker does not seem to care about the ideas he or she is discussing, why should you? A speaker who respects his or her own ideas and respects the audience will do both justice and work on using nonverbal elements to complement the message.

Most speakers do not put much thought into how they are using their voices. True, the voice is used in most speeches to convey the ideas and thoughts, but is it used well? Does it show how important some ideas are, how awful some statistics are, or how much the speaker believes in the ideas being presented? Here we will provide some guidance about how to use your voice to complement your message.

One of the most important uses of the voice is to highlight the emotional undertones of the speech. For example, you can emphasize important points. If you simply wrote a document, you could highlight important ideas with italics. For instance, you could write, "Over *70 percent of all employees* will find themselves facing this crucial decision." The reader knows that one part of this sentence is more important than others. Read this sentence aloud, and use your voice to emphasize the highlighted phrase. In a speech, instead of italics, you can use your voice to show emphasis. Say you report this same statistic to your audience. Try reading the sentence aloud two times. The first time, say it in a monotone, without any emphasis. The second time, emphasize the phrase "70 percent of all employees" as you read the sentence. Notice any difference? If you do your job as a speaker, you will draw the audience's attention to important facts and ideas through the emphasis in your voice. Your voice indicates the emotional valence behind the words and the emotional reaction expected in the audience.

What exactly can you do to add emphasis with your voice? Such emphasis can be accomplished by varying the three main qualities of the voice: its volume, its pitch, and its rate.[15] Each of these three should be varied over the course of your presentation. We all naturally use such variation and emphasis in our daily conversations, but most of us suddenly lose the ability to do this when facing an audience. Part of the reason is that most of us are under a lot of stress when we must speak to an audience; we are also concentrating very hard on everything we want to remember to say. To overcome this problem, learn to consciously manipulate the nonverbal characteristics of your delivery while you are practicing your speech. Try videotaping yourself to see if your delivery is captivating, inspiring, or just plain boring. If it is painful for you to watch yourself on the video, then go back to practicing. Work on making the important parts stand out, for the audience's sake.

The volume of your voice can be altered to complement the verbal message your words are conveying. If an idea or fact is important, you can set it off from the other ideas by slightly increasing your volume at that point in the sentence. For a good example of this tactic, watch Martin Luther King Jr.'s "I Have a Dream" oration, in which the volume crescendos over the powerful repeated phrase. Thus, audiences hear "I HAVE A DREam," with a burst of volume-induced energy followed by a decrease in volume until the next repetition. Oddly enough, using a very low volume can also provide emphasis. If you were reporting some awful mortality figures in a speech, for example, you could use a louder volume to convey the importance of the figures; but you could also use a softer volume, to show the sadness behind such figures and convey a pensive tone. Sometimes when a speaker uses this strategy at a key point in a speech, the room becomes so quiet that you could hear a pin drop. This is very effective. Take the following sentence, for example: "Today, over *75 percent* of the American populace will face this *daunting* illness." Try saying it twice, first using a loud volume for emphasis, and then with a very low volume for emphasis. Using volume at strategic points helps convey the emotion behind a sentence; an audience is more likely to remember the point because they also understand its emotional context and importance.

You can also use the pitch of your voice to add emphasis to important points. In everyday conversation, a rising pitch is used to indicate questions and a descending pitch is used to give a note of finality to the end of a sentence or speech. Say the phrase, "and you," both ways to see how your pitch can turn it into either a question ("And you?") or an accusation ("And you!"). We can also vary pitch to make important points of a sentence stand out more. For instance, when volume is added to an emphasized number, pitch can be raised slightly at the same time, thus setting it off further. Thus, one could use both pitch and volume in saying, "In terms of expenditures, *90 percent* of our funds go to this project." Tail off the pitch and end at a slightly lower note than you began with, and the audience will know this sentence and its accompanying thought have ended.

Pitch can also be used productively to add impact to powerful literary quotations that you employ in a speech. For instance, if a quotation from Fyodor Dostoevsky's *Crime and Punishment* were added to a speech, the speaker would want to distinguish the words of Dostoevsky from his or her own words, and would emphasize the quotation so as to maximize its emotive impact on the audience. Thus, the speaker might say, "When we consider these pressing political concerns, it is wise to heed the counsel of Fyodor Dostoevsky, who wrote '*It would be interesting to know what man is most afraid of; perhaps it is taking a new step that he fears the most.*' When we confront this problem, we must not be afraid of such new steps." The speaker can set off the italicized portion (the quotation) from his own words by lowering the voice slightly, and then lowering the pitch even more just before the semicolon and again at the end of the quotation to convey a sense of finality. These are just a few of the many ways that we can use pitch to add emphasis and variety to our speech. By practicing and experimenting further with pitch, you can make your performances better and more effective.

The last vocal characteristic that can be altered is the rate of speech. Speech that is too fast or too slow can be distracting. It can become monotonous, confuse the audience, and cause the audience to make unfavorable judgments about the speaker. Instead, aim for a medium rate of speaking, then vary this speed at points to complement your message. You could increase the rate a bit to convey urgency, for instance. Take the following statement: "In this century, this disease has cost over *300 million dollars, killed over 1 million adults,* and *killed some 500,000 children.*" In this example, the speaker could increase the rate effectively to give the impression of a barrage of harms. By slowing down a bit for the last few words of the quotation (and perhaps tailing off in pitch), this speaker can let the audience think about all of these awful numbers. Throwing in a pause after this sentence, a second or less of silence, would also be an effective way of allowing the audience to digest these statistics.

You can use pauses whenever you want the audience to really think about something important. Here's an example of the usefulness of a pause: "Each and every one of us in this room will have to make up his or her mind on this life-defining issue. [*Pause.*] There is no escaping our responsibility as a citizen. [*Pause.*]" Or for another example, try placing pauses in Patrick Henry's famous quotation: "Give me liberty [*pause*] or give me death [*pause*]." Pauses are stops in rate that allow the audience to mull over what has been said, although too many pauses make the delivery seem choppy and reduce the effectiveness of any particular pause.

We use volume, pitch, and rate every day to convey emphasis, outrage, significance, excitement, and the like, so surely we can learn to use them consciously, with practice, to communicate in formal situations such as speeches. Practice combining these three qualities and varying them—

you can even mark or highlight your outline to provide a reminder about the words or phrases to be emphasized. When adding emphasis, though, do not use too much; use emphasis so that the audience can tell the important facts and ideas from the less important ones. When students highlight important parts of a text, they choose carefully; if you highlighted an entire page in yellow ink, what then would stand out as important? The same principle works with speech: If everything is emphasized, nothing is emphasized. Use these vocal characteristics only on the important points, and they will help your audience grasp the emotional content behind your words. One easy place to add emphasis is in statistics, since these are often used to show how big or small a problem is. If you feel strongly about an idea or phrase, then say it in a way that conveys that conviction and power—the sincerity in your delivery will act as an invitation to your audience to react to your message with an equal amount of concern and engagement.

Effective Use of Eye Contact.   Eye contact is an extremely important aspect of nonverbal communication. Although some cultures do not encourage direct eye contact, North American and most European nations think highly of it and use it in judging speakers as credible, trustworthy, and knowledgeable.[16] When speaking, it is therefore absolutely essential that you give strong, steady eye contact to many different members of the audience, not just to people in the front row or in a particular section. Eye contact should be strong and not fleeting; to make eye contact, look up from any notes you may have and look at the audience for a sentence or two, not just for one or two words. Look at a person in the audience for a sentence or phrase, then shift your gaze to another audience member. This way, everyone in the audience feels as if you are talking to them and that their presence is an important part of the speech.

The more you practice, the more you will be able to make eye contact with your audience during your speech. This is beneficial: Research shows that when you look at your audience, the members of the audience are more likely to be interested in your message, more likely to retain the information for a longer period, and more likely to judge you as knowledgeable about your topic.[17] When you use eye contact with all parts of the audience, you draw everyone into your presentation; when you look someone in the eyes, you are proclaiming that you care about them and want to interact with them in this speech. This is why people often avoid eye contact with people they do not want to interact with. If eye contact is avoided, no conversation is initiated and no contact between the two parties is likely to occur. In speeches, the opposite goal is desired: The speaker wants the audience to be actively involved in the speech. By providing strong eye contact, the speaker initiates the conversation and makes each person feel like they are an important part of the speaking event and message.

Nonverbal elements of a presentation, such as voice and eye contact, are important parts of the *performance* of a speech. The golden rule of delivery is to make your nonverbal actions complement your message, and never let them distract or detract from your message. Nonverbal cues can also be helpful in telling the speaker about the audience—if it looks like they are going to fall asleep, or have failing eye contact, then you may be able to adjust your speech midstream to "liven" it up a bit. If your audience's faces seem alive and interested in the speech, this is a good sign; an angry audience is still an interested, attentive audience. The way you comport yourself in the performance of your speech, however, is invaluable in helping to get your audience interested in your message and keeping them that way.

Taking time in writing, researching, and organizing a speech can bring honor to your message and your audience, but not as much as when these things are coupled with a powerful and inspired style of delivery. Practice your public speaking, and think about how your nonverbal delivery can emphasize key points, emotions, and modes within your message. Above all, remember, if you don't seem to care about your message, why should your audience?

▶ Exercise 7.8

Say the following quotations out loud using the volume, pitch, and rate of your voice to make the quotations sound important and inspiring.

"Nothing is as exhausting as indecision, and nothing is so futile."

Bertrand Russell

"Terrible lies are often believed; terrible truths rarely are."

Leon Trotsky

"That is man's one privilege over all creation—from error he learns the truth."

Fyodor Dostoevsky

"Two things fill the mind with an ever new and increasing admiration and awe the more steadily we reflect upon them: the starry heavens above me, and the moral law within me."

Immanuel Kant

▶ **Exercise 7.9**

Say the following statistics out loud, using your voice (especially volume and pitch) to show that they mean something important.

Over *65 percent* of one's communication is through nonverbal cues.
The US population has swelled to *260 million* citizens.
Approximately *1 million* lives were lost in the fighting that took place in Rwanda.
The US economy grew over *3 percent* last year.
The hero hit *three* home runs in one game last week.

Effective Informal Communication

We've already talked about the most formal type of communication—a speech or presentation. Though this is the type of communication that causes more sweaty palms than any other, it is also important to think about our less formal communication. How do we communicate with integrity in everyday conversations or in situations that may be very special but more personal and private than a public speaking event? Here we will make some suggestions about how to be more effective in informal and more personal interactions.

Context is important in informal communication. One type of communication that we all must engage in from time to time—and that often has a moral component—is the apology, for example. In 1997, King Hussein of Jordan apologized to the parents of seven Israeli schoolgirls who were shot and killed by a deranged Jordanian soldier. There are many ways to make an apology. One can write a note; send a telegram; send an envoy. One can make the apology in person, make it on our home turf, apologize shortly after the offending event, or apologize many years later. King Hussein chose to make his apology in person, by traveling to the victims' homes. When he arrived, he found the families sitting on the floor in a Jewish mourning tradition. He sank to his knees, took each of the mother's hands in his, comforted them, and took personal responsibility for the soldier's actions.

There are various possible interpretations of his motives; some people might think he did the right thing, while others may judge his actions with more skepticism. But whatever we think of King Hussein's apology, this example makes clear the importance of the context of a situation in communicating effectively. How we communicate expresses a great deal, so we need to be sensitive in choosing things like the place, time, and style of our communications.

Communicating in a Clear and Organized Manner

First, we must be careful with words. Philosophers are noted for the extreme care they take with language. When you take a philosophy course, you may find yourself spending weeks reading one text. We don't always have time for this kind of attention to detail in our daily interactions, but we can learn from philosophers here.

Begin by making clarity your most important goal and striving for it in your communication. Don't be afraid to use a dictionary, and don't be afraid to ask someone what they mean when you don't understand what they are trying to say. Don't use words just to sound intelligent. Watch your listeners to gauge their comprehension and reactions. Never send a written communication without proofreading it. If it is important, get someone else to read it and give you feedback before you send it. If all else fails, hire a professional copy editor.

Self-Confidence and Respect for Others

The best way to project self-confidence in communication is to first reflect about what it is you want to convey. Before communicating something important to someone, you might want to talk it over with a friend, write in a journal, or read something that will help you decide what you really believe about a situation and what you want to say. These are all effective ways to get clear about your own ideas.

Go into your communicative interactions with confidence in your own ideas and respect for your partners. They have probably thought about their ideas with the same care that you have, and you may learn from what they have to say. Treating others with respect deepens the trust they have in you, and successful relationships require mutual trust. Self-confidence and respect for others go hand in hand. Once we are confident about our own ideas, it will be easier to be respectful to our partners in communication.

Appropriate Tone

If you have trouble with your tone of voice, see if you can learn to modify the tone you are using. It may take practice to use a voice that conveys gentleness, for example, or patience, particularly if you are not used to speaking in that way. Work with a speech therapist to correct problems with pitch, accent, and articulation. Tone can be difficult to get right in writing as well, especially since the reader cannot hear your tone of voice or make eye contact with you. If you are joking, for example, the reader cannot see that twinkle in your eye to figure this out, and could take something the wrong way. Proof everything you write, even short e-mails. If you feel uncomfortable about your writing and/or oral presentation style, take a course or two.

Nonverbal Cues

When you are speaking, pay attention to what your conversational partner is doing. If his or her eyes are glazing over, perhaps you are doing all the talking, or talking about something that does not interest this individual. Stop and find a way to involve him or her in the conversation. For example, you can ask what he or she thinks about the topic.

Anticipating Responses

Communication is a fluid and spontaneous thing. Even when you are giving a formal presentation, it's amazing how the conversation can move into directions you did not expect. If you want to communicate effectively, try to anticipate what your audience will say. One way to do this is to research the issue and see what different people have written about it. Turn off that TV and computer and practice the old-fashioned art of communication.

Incorporating Responses

There are a number of ways to incorporate your audience's comments in a formal presentation. You can refer to people by name ("As Angela suggested . . . "), for example. The same principle is true for informal communication. You can make a point of saying that you agree with someone. You can thank someone for his or her valuable input. And don't be afraid to change your mind in response to a penetrating criticism. You lose face when you become argumentative when you know that you've been proven wrong.

Try not to think about communication as a fight with only one victor. Instead, think about it as a collective enterprise where we all become better informed. You won't lose face if you respond in the right spirit ("I appreciate your feedback, and I'm going to find a way to incorporate it as I think further about this").

Developing Common Ground

When we feel strongly about something, it's easy to get drawn into a shouting match or to dash off a poison-pen letter. Instead, try to find common ground. Even on the most controversial issues, there is often a lot that people can agree about. Begin with this common ground and see how much you can build on it.

Giving Others Time to Reflect

One of the things that any new teacher quickly learns is that if you want a response, you have to give people plenty of time to respond. If you really want a communication and not just a one-way presentation, place your watch where you can see it and be prepared to wait to give people time to respond. You might try to use the two-minute rule. That is, you decide that when you want a response, you will wait for two minutes for your conversational partner to respond.

This seems like an incredibly long time, and in reality you probably won't ever need to go beyond a minute or so; but giving yourself a rule like this to follow will remind you to really give people time. Most people cannot bear silence, so they jump in and fill it themselves, and the people around them can become progressively more tuned out. If you begin to wait for responses, people might be slow to respond at first, but when they see that you really want to initiate a dialogue they will become progressively more willing to keep up their end.

Effective Listening

Communication is not just about talking; it's also about listening. And effective listening, like effective speaking, is a learned skill. It involves the following.

Hearing What Is Said

We seem to have a tendency to hear what we want to hear and to screen out what we don't want to hear. This gets in the way of effective communication. If we don't hear what is being said, we will not respond appropriately. One way to make sure you are hearing what is being said is to practice reflective listening. Repeat what your partner says to make sure you understand it.

Hearing What Is Not Said

In addition to hearing what is being said, it's also instructive to "listen" for what is unsaid. Ask yourself what kind of a message is being sent. See if you can figure out your partner's unstated assumptions and unasked questions. Look to see what kind of emotion an individual is bringing to the exchange. Finally, look for hidden agendas. Be careful not to jump to conclusions, though; it can be easy to make the wrong assumption about what is not being said.

Communicating Respect

If you want to have powerful and effective communication, find ways to let people know that you want to understand, that you respect them, and that you think what they have to say is important.

Reading Nonverbal Cues

Note your partner's body language while you are engaged in conversation. What is this body language telling you? If someone is avoiding eye contact, for example, this might be significant.

Asking the Right Questions

You can use questions to indicate that you are interested in understanding what someone is saying, to elicit further information, and to check to see if your understanding of what is being said is correct.

Conclusion

In this chapter, we've described the central importance of communication in our moral lives. In the next chapter, we will look at the role of work in our moral lives. Effective and ethical communication is both required and necessary for smooth sailing in the often troubled waters of the world of work. After that, we will look at ourselves as family members and friends.

Communication in these intimate settings is every bit as important as it is in less intimate interactions, and while one would like to think that intimacy makes communication easier, experience suggests that this is often not the case. So keep the insights from this chapter in mind as we go on to think about our moral lives in family and friendship. In our final chapter, we will look at global citizenship. Here language and cultural barriers complicate our efforts at communication, but again, the insights from this chapter will help inform our efforts at global understanding.

▶ Study Questions for Chapter Seven

1. What is the persuasion-centered orientation in communication? What moral assumptions does it make?
2. What is the invitational orientation in communication? What moral assumptions does it make?
3. What basic steps should you follow in formal communication?
4. What are the basic steps in communication as performance?
5. What are the basic steps in informal communication?

NOTES

1. For an empirical report on the importance of communication in the world of business, see Jerry L. Winsor, Dan B. Curtis, and Ronald D. Stephens, "National Preferences in Business and Communication Education: A Survey Update," *Journal of the Association for Communication Administration* 3 (1997), 174.

2. Deborah Tannen, *You Just Don't Understand: Women and Men in Communication* (New York: Harper, 2001).

3. G.W.F. Hegel, "B: Self Consciousness," in *The Phenomenology of Spirit* (originally published 1807) (Oxford: Oxford University Press, 1979).

4. Much of the power that hate groups have derives from their use of religious and secular stories (involving language) that include the receptive listener as a member; thus, some individuals see themselves as fulfilling certain prophecies, avidly defending themselves against a conspiratorial government, etc.

5. Aristotle, *The Art of Rhetoric,* translated by H. C. Lawson-Tancred (New York: Penguin Books, 1991), 74.

6. The ideas in what follows can be seen in a slightly different form in Scott R. Stroud, "Tempering Public Speaking Pedagogy with Insights from the *Bhagavad Gita,*" *Journal of the Wisconsin Communication Association* 32 (2001), 56–64.

7. S. K. Foss, and C. L. Griffin, "Beyond Persuasion: A Proposal for an Invitational Rhetoric," *Communication Monographs* 62 (1995), 2–18; S. K. Foss and K. A. Foss, *Inviting*

Transformation: Presentational Speaking for a Changing World (Prospect Heights, Ill.: Waveland, 1994); S. K. Foss and K. A. Foss, *Instructor's Manual to Accompany Inviting Transformation: Presentational Speaking for a Changing World* (Prospect Heights, Ill.: Waveland, 2000).

8. Foss and Griffin, *Beyond Persuasion*, 4.

9. Ibid.; K. A. Foss, S. K. Foss, and C. L. Griffin, *Feminist Rhetorical Theories* (Thousand Oaks, Calif.: Sage Publications, 1999).

10. See Immanuel Kant, *Foundations of the Metaphysics of Morals*, translated by L. W. Beck (New York: Macmillan, 1985); Immanuel Kant, *Critique of Practical Reason*, translated by L. W. Beck (Upper Saddle River, N.J.: Prentice Hall, 1993).

11. Eliot Deutsch, *The Bhagavad Gita: Translated, with Introduction and Critical Essays*. (New York: University Press of America, 1968); S. Nityaswarupananda, trans., *Astavakra Samhita*, 10th ed. (Calcutta, India: Trio Process, 1998).

12. Foss and Griffin, "Beyond Persuasion."

13. For this and other topics in the practice of public speaking, consult S. A. Beebe, and S. J. Beebe, *Public Speaking: An Audience-Centered Approach*, 4th ed. (Boston: Allyn and Bacon, 2000); C. Jaffe, *Public Speaking: Concepts and Skills for a Diverse Society*, 3rd ed. (Ontario, Canada: Thomson Learning, 2001).

14. Beebe and Beebe, *Public Speaking*.

15. For a more detailed discussion of nonverbal elements, see S. E. Lucas, *The Art of Public Speaking*, 6th ed., Annotated Instructor's Edition (New York: McGraw-Hill, 1998); and R. B. Adler and G. Rodman, *Understanding Human Communication*, 7th ed. (New York: Harcourt College, 2000).

16. L. A. Samovar and R. E. Porter, *Intercultural Communication: A Reader*, 6th ed. (Belmont, Calif.: Wadsworth, 1991); and S. Trenholm and A. Jensen, *Interpersonal Communication*, 3rd ed. (Belmont, Calif.: Wadsworth, 1996).

17. Beebe and Beebe, *Public Speaking*.

CHAPTER 8

The World of Work

Humans have labored in the vineyard since we first lived on earth, and the work we do and the setting in which we do it defines us in significant ways. Though important work is done in many settings, we will be focusing on the paid workplace. Traditions as diverse as those found in Plato, the *Bhagavad Gita*, and Islamic philosophy give importance to one's place in society as constituting what, in general terms, one ought to do in one's interactions with others. One of our most important roles comes in what we do to earn our living. Many philosophers through history have noted a strong link between human happiness and meaningful work. And working conditions can have a profound impact on health and general satisfaction in life.

If work is so important in determining our place in society, our interactions with others, and our happiness and sense of fulfillment, is work a social benefit that everyone is entitled to? What obligations do we have in choosing work? What obligations do we have as workers? What entitlements do we have as workers? Finally, what would a workplace look like if everyone treated everyone else with integrity, and what can we all do to create this kind of work environment?

Worker Entitlements, Part One

We begin our discussion by thinking about the things that make our working lives difficult. This is the easy part. It is more difficult to think about what would be both morally best and possible in our increasingly fragile global environment.

Describe the worst job you ever had. See if you can say why it was such an awful job. Now describe your dream job. What features would your dream job have? Would you describe your dream job as meaningful work? Are you doing this job or training for it? If not, why not?

Your worst-ever job most likely has a number of things in common with the worst jobs that other people usually mention. We can divide these features into two categories. First, there are things about specific work activities that can be unpleasant for workers. Second, there are aspects of working conditions at some companies that people particularly hate.

Let's start with the working conditions. Many people, in talking about their worst job, note low pay, repetitive activity, an unpleasant atmosphere, unsafe conditions, unfriendly and perhaps even hostile colleagues, and cruel and abusive management as things they did not like. We can characterize these failings in moral terms: The worker was not treated with respect, but rather like a machine that produces a product. The worker was not treated with care, and harmony did not exist in the workplace.

But even if working conditions are good, there are some jobs that just won't be very pleasant for us because the activity just doesn't reflect our passions. A worker just may not enjoy doing the activity he or she was hired to do. We all have different passions and abilities, and when the activity we are asked to do does not match up with these passions and abilities, the work lacks meaning for us. When we do these jobs, we have to consciously "put on a role"; we have to pretend to be someone we really aren't. In some cases, such occupations put us in a position that we really do not want to be in. For instance, Arjuna (from the *Bhagavad Gita*) was put into the unenviable position of having to fight a war for his subjects that pitted him against members of his own family and some of his respected teachers. Such a position can hardly be described as the most ideal job one could hold!

We have found that when we talk to people about work, it is easy for people to describe their ideal job in terms of working conditions, but much more difficult to describe it in terms of the activity they would be engaged in. We encourage you to give yourself some time and a quiet place to think about what your dream job would be.

▶ **Exercise 8.2**

What would you be doing if money were no object? Some people would say that they would do nothing, but doing nothing gets rather boring after a while. What would you do after you caught up on all your sleep?

Meaningful Work

In his early work, Karl Marx defined humans as creatures who could be happy only if engaged in socially useful activity that they found personally meaningful.[1] He cited the difference between a bird building a nest and a person building a dwelling. A bird can be creative in the use of construction materials, incorporating found objects such as Styrofoam, but in the design the bird simply follows instinct. Humans are seldom happy to build the same type of house their ancestors built. Instead we create new designs and aim for individual accents that mark a dwelling as our home. As we create for ourselves, we also want to be recognized for our achievements. We want others to admire our nests. At a certain point, feathering our own nest just doesn't seem meaningful, and we look around for activity that helps to create and sustain flourishing human communities.

Marx was following Aristotle in his views about the connection between work and human happiness.[2] This is not surprising, since Marx was trained as a philosopher and wrote his doctoral dissertation on Greek philosophy. Aristotle understood happiness as including achieving our full potential. It's hard to see how someone can do this if they are either at the office or tethered to the laptop and cell phone eighty hours a week.

If Marx and Aristotle are right about this, then work becomes a subject with deep moral implications. We simply cannot live a reasonably happy life without it. Many of us don't find this kind of meaning in our working lives, but look for it in our non-work lives. This is difficult for us, as our working lives begin to take up more and more of our time. Marx thought that we try to make up for the unhappiness caused by the lack of meaningful work by consuming. We think there is something right about this. You need only look at the malls on the weekend or the cars in the parking lots of companies where the lights burn at all hours to see how we have come to define ourselves more by our consumption than by our meaningful activity.

This unhealthy pattern has a number of disturbing effects. First, many people find it hard to be happy. As soon as we acquire one fancy new toy, it loses it luster and we are pining for the next one. As we engage in this endless cycle, we are using up the earth's resources at an alarming rate and leaving our descendents a garbage heap instead of the clean and pristine place we could pass down to them. Meanwhile, much socially useful work is undervalued, underpaid, and undone.

Robert Bellah wrote about this in *Habits of the Heart*.[3] There he distinguished between a career and a vocation. You have a career if you have reasonable working conditions and you can plot a more or less upward path from your first job to your retirement. You have a vocation if you have a work life that allows you to express your personal passions and use your abilities fully and creatively. One could add a third thing to the description of a vocation: It allows you to do something that is socially useful. We agree with Marx that you wouldn't take a sense of pride in work if it expressed your personal passion but was not recognized by others as socially useful. This doesn't mean that we all have to be cancer researchers; there are a lot of ways that we can create good for our societies. We also would add one other category to Bellah's—a job. You have a job if your working conditions are not great and you don't find any personal meaning in the activity.

Many people do not have much of a choice with respect to the work they do. They may be poor in an economy that offers few alternatives. They may live in a country with little social mobility. But many people do have a choice. They needn't settle for a job, but can aspire to have a vocation. Take a good look at the work you are doing or training to do. Will it make the world a better place? Do you find it personally fulfilling? Are your creative juices flowing? Many of us find ourselves stuck in a rut, lacking the courage to change. But remember two things. First, courage is a virtue that you have to practice. Either you will become more coura-geous, or you will become more cowardly. It is your choice. Second, you will likely spend most of your adult life working. Many people put aside their own happiness in the hope for a big payoff later. They dream of re-tiring on their stock options at forty. If this sounds like you, ask yourself these questions. How realistic is your dream? Are you making the world a better or a worse place through your work? Are you happy now? How is your health?

The political question is much more difficult. If one's entire society is locked into a work-consume-work-consume cycle, it is hard to opt out. If your society does not value meaningful work, such work is likely to be underpaid. But remember that social transformation *will* take place, and it will do so through the personal decisions of millions of people just like you.

Work as a Social Benefit

Unless you have a tidy trust fund, you will be unable to have a minimally decent life unless you have a reasonably well-paying job. And unless you have meaningful work, you will find it difficult to be happy. This sug-gests that work is important enough to require just distribution. Let's sort out the various items involved. First are the basic needs that must be filled if anyone is to have a minimally decent life. Second are the jobs that are the route to filling these basic needs in a capitalist economy. Third are the jobs that provide people with meaningful work. We can then ask whether society has an obligation to provide its members with each of these things.

We can begin with basic needs. All of the moral perspectives we looked at in earlier chapters assume that humans have moral worth. The moral rights perspective assumes that we all have a right to life. Utilitar-ians assume that we must all be counted in any utility calculation. This suggests that we do have an obligation to see that each one of us has his or her basic needs met. But providing everyone with a job is not the only option. There are people who will be unable to hold a job, and there are some negative effects on the economy of providing jobs for all. For these reasons, in the United States we have usually chosen to give everyone a basic safety net. The Works Progress Administration provided jobs during the Depression. Social Security was created to protect widows, orphans, and the elderly. Welfare was enacted to protect families with minor children. One of the reasons that the Welfare Reform Act of 1996 was so controversial was that it seemed to violate this basic social contract. In a flourishing economy, it might be possible for every welfare recipient to get and keep a job, but what happens when the economy stalls? What will we do when a parent with minor children uses up all the family's welfare eligibility? Will we let this family go hungry? It would be hard to argue that we have no moral obligation to meet basic needs, but as we've seen, there are other ways to do this. Let's see what the principles of distributive justice tell us about meeting basic needs.

The principle of equality would endorse practices for making sure that everyone's basic needs were met. The principle of contribution would need to be supplemented by some notion of what would count as a contribution. We could look at past contribution, as we often seem to when we discuss the needs of the elderly, or we could look at future contributions, as we do when we look at the needs of children. The principle of need would have the same result as the principle of equality in this case, since we are talking about distributing the means to fill basic needs, and we all have the same basic needs for food, clothing, and shelter. The principle of membership suggests that we meet the basic needs of those who belong to the same group as we do. In the United States, this is construed in two ways—as citizens of the United States we have certain entitlements, and as citizens of individual states we have others. The principle of the market is really just another way of saying that we shouldn't distribute the means to fill basic needs at all. Persons must find ways to fill their own needs. The final principle comes from Rawls, who indicated that we should distribute liberty equally and everything else by appeal to the consequences of various distributive schemes. Notice that basic needs needn't be distributed equally, but it is hard to imagine that a relatively wealthy society with people homeless and starving would be one with greater utility than one that met its citizens' basic needs.

The question of meaningful work is much more problematic for several reasons. First, there is no consensus about what would count as socially useful and personally meaningful work. Second, meaning can be found outside of work. Third, the search for meaning seems by its nature to be a personal thing and not something that we as a society can distribute. So perhaps it doesn't make much sense to talk about distributing meaningful work. We can, however, distribute the means to meaningful work by making sure that everyone gets an education that allows them to find their own meaningful niche in the world of work. Since meaningful work is integral to happiness, it makes sense to distribute this education equally. We might say, then, that we have a social obligation to provide everyone with the kind of education that will allow them to find meaningful work, as well as meaning in other parts of their lives. What they do with this opportunity is then up to them.

There is much more that we can do if we have some control over the workplace. We can design projects and workspaces to maximize the possibility that the people working with and for us will be able to find meaning in their activities. We can create opportunities for the future growth and experience that will help someone to discover how best to make a contribution.

▶ Exercise 8.3

How can you make your own working life more meaningful? If you are a manager, what concrete steps could you take to make work more meaningful for your staff?

Worker Obligations

Since meaningful work is integral to happiness, it makes sense to say that we each have a personal obligation to seek meaning in our working lives. Since part of the definition of meaningful work is that it is socially useful, it is an obligation we owe to others as well. There are other obligations we have as workers, and we will mention some of them here. We have obligations to colleagues. These obligations can be based on a number of things—our shared humanity, our shared history as colleagues, the need for trust in shared endeavors, past promises, and professional obligations. We also have obligations to our employers, to customers, to competitors, to society, and to the environment. These obligations have similar foundations, and we can spell them out in more detail by referring back to our moral perspectives.

Kant reminds us to respect all persons. Moral rights protect certain boundaries. Utilitarianism reminds us to maximize good consequences. Virtue invites us to consider the effect of our actions on character and community. Care reminds us of the importance of personal relationships and trust. Social Contract Theory tells us that we are operating within a society and that our interactions must be based on a shared set of principles acceptable to all. Ancient texts, such as the *Bhagavad Gita*, remind us that our relationships to others, including our coworkers, not only define who we are, but also tell us what we ought to do (and also lead others to expect us to do certain things as a person occupying that specific role). All these perspectives remind us that our obligations and entitlements are reciprocal. We have them whether we are managers or managed, competitors or colleagues. The world of work has the same moral dimensions as the rest of our lives. If we leave our integrity at the office door, we will be poor leaders and we will undermine our integrity in every other aspect of our lives.

Worker Entitlements, Part Two

We've already talked about two things that may be due to us as workers—the right to a job, and the right to meaningful work. Here we want to focus on the possible entitlements of the currently employed. There are lots of things we want as workers, but what kinds of things are we entitled to as workers? The list we will consider includes the following: continued employment, safe and relatively pleasant working conditions, fairness, privacy, autonomy, the ability to choose to join or not to join a union, benefits, and the ability to live a full personal life outside of work.

We can distinguish between two different kinds of entitlements. The first is a moral right. If a worker has a moral right to something, then we have an obligation to see to it that each and every worker has access to it. This doesn't necessarily require that employers pay the entire cost of providing it, since there are other ways of spreading the cost. The second kind of entitlement is less strong than a right. If a worker has an entitlement in this sense, then the morally sensitive society and employer will try to make it possible for all workers to have access to this entitlement. Entitlements in the strong sense can be defended using the moral rights perspective, while entitlements in the weaker sense can be defended using any perspective.

Continued Employment

Many people assume that if they do a good job, they are legally and morally entitled to keep their job as long as serious economic factors do not intervene. They are surprised to find out that they live in an employment-at-will state. This means that unless you are protected by contract, your employer can fire you for good reasons, for bad reasons, or for no reason at all, as long as your employer's action does not constitute discrimination under the law. Well, this may be legal, but is it right? Here are some reasons for thinking that employees are entitled to keep their current jobs as long as they do these jobs adequately and as long as their employers can keep them without incurring substantial economic cost. First, employers make an implicit promise that employees can keep their jobs if they perform them adequately. Second, employees' lives would be made quite miserable for at least a short period of time if they were forced from their current jobs. Third, employees have made a contribution to their employers through their past labor and are thus entitled to future employment.

Let's begin by looking at implicit promises. An explicit promise is one that is made openly and more or less formally. We make such promises when we sign a contract. Implicit promises are not done in the same open or formal way, but are based more on custom. Suppose that one of your coworkers buys the newspaper every day and then leaves it on your desk when she finishes with it. If this practice continues for a number of years, you might say that she has made an implicit promise to give you her paper every day. If you miss reading about an important event because one day she chooses to give her paper to someone else, you may well have a right to be angry with her. In this case, her past actions have created an expectation in you, in much the same way that an official contract creates an expectation that its terms will be fulfilled. But is the world of work governed by implicit promises of continued employment? If we look at the past two decades of labor history, we would have to say no. People are fired and laid off for many reasons, and their termination often comes as quite a surprise. This suggests that implicit promises do not provide a very good reason for thinking that you are morally entitled to keep your current job.

The next argument for the idea that we are generally entitled to keep our jobs was that, since most of us are not independently wealthy, we would be miserable, at least in the short term, if we lost our jobs. But does this reason stand up to close scrutiny? Recall that earlier we said that everyone is entitled to have their basic needs met, but that this needn't be accomplished by giving everyone a job. The same argument can be made here. You may be miserable, but as long as your basic needs are being met some other way (for example, via unemployment provisions), you have no moral grounds for complaining.

The third argument for worker entitlement to continued employment was that workers have made a contribution through past labor, and in virtue of past contributions they are entitled to share in the prosperity of the employer. This is a version of an argument made by Karl Marx. He argued that the difference in price between raw material and manufactured products was created largely by the labor involved. Employers provide the setting for this transformation, and workers provide the labor. Because it is only through the labor of the workers that profit can be created, workers have a right to share in the profit. He thought that the ideal situation would be one in which the workers simply owned the means of production and thus shared the profit only with the other workers. Even if you do not agree about this, there is a more modest claim that you might find persuasive. If someone profits from someone else's labor, the laborer is entitled to profit also. If workers are terminated from their jobs through no fault of their own, they do not profit from their past labor.

There are other arguments for worker entitlement to continued employment one could make. One view says that if employers are cavalier about terminating employees, their current and prospective employees will feel no sense of obligation toward them. Instead, they will be quite ready to do less than a full day's work for a full day's wage and will be ready to jump ship whenever it suits them to do so. In addition, current employees will be resentful of the extra work they will likely be called on to do and fearful for their own jobs. This does not create the sense of trust and camaraderie that is needed in a successful organization.

The next argument turns on the idea of trust and community. Employees are members of a community. Their work takes up a substantial part of their time, and they forgo many other options to do their jobs. They come to understand who they are in part through the labor they perform. Their employers in the corporate culture consciously socialize them to see themselves as members of the corporate community. They may wear clothes with the corporate logo even when they are not at work. Their workday is extended with pagers and cell phones. Terminating someone with no good reason ignores their role as a member of the community.

A final argument against worker entitlement to continued employment notes that workers are free to quit a job for good reasons, for bad reasons, or for no reason at all. Reciprocity would seem to require that employers have the same freedom.

None of these arguments will cover every case. There are situations where layoffs and terminations are justified—when an employer is forced by a changing market to lay off workers, or when an employee fails to do an adequate job. And of course, one also has to consider other stakeholders involved, such as shareholders or customers. What these arguments do show, however, is that when such decisions are made, workers deserve to be seen as important stakeholders.

Safe Working Conditions

There are clear moral arguments against deliberately harming others. It violates the right to life and the right to bodily integrity. It will usually create more bad than good consequences. If it means exposing others to dangers you would not expose yourself to, it involves using others merely as means. Exposing someone to dangerous conditions in the workplace is objectionable for the same reasons. There is an additional argument we can offer here. We can often avoid dangerous environments if we are aware of them. Unsafe working conditions are especially problematic because it is often not easy to avoid them. People who work in dangerous environments do not do so because they like danger; they do so because they feel that they have no better options.

Though we may all agree that it is immoral to expose someone to unsafe working conditions, there is substantial disagreement about what counts as a safe working environment and about how much cost must be sustained to make environments safe. If we defined safety as the complete absence of any potential for harm, then nothing would be safe. Even the most innocuous object can be misused in a dangerous way if someone is stupid or determined enough to do so. To avoid this conundrum, safety can be defined in terms of the likelihood that ordinary use by a reasonably prudent person will result in harm.

How much should we be willing to pay for safety? Ordinary use of my car will result in some likelihood of harm. We can reduce this likelihood by making cars much safer than they are now, but this will come with a price tag. We could make all our SUVs as impervious to rollover as a Humvee, but this would greatly increase their cost and their contribution to global warming and other environmental harms. In addition, it would make other vehicles more vulnerable in a collision with an SUV unless we made all our cars like tanks. We have the technology to do this, but if we did, cars would be so expensive that few of us would be able to afford one. This example illustrates why we need to talk about reasonable safety—safety purchased at a cost that most rational people would be willing to bear. We can then apply this concept of safety to the workplace. A workplace is reasonably safe if the ordinary and relatively efficient operation of the workplace does not impose serious risks to the life and health of the employees. Once we've defined it this way, it seems clear that we are entitled to a safe working environment.

Suppose a workplace was safe but ugly. Are workers entitled to aesthetic improvement? At first this question seems silly, but one might argue that ugly workplaces have an effect on the emotional well-being of employees. If a workplace is sufficiently ugly, or loud, it may be stressful for the employees. At a certain level this looks like just another example of an unsafe workplace. If the ugliness or loudness of the workplace creates a certain level of stress, and it can be remediated at a reasonable cost, it seems reasonable to describe this as an unsafe workplace. Beyond this, it is not clear how one can make a moral argument that workers are entitled to a pleasant environment, though one could certainly argue that pleasant surroundings lead to improved productivity.

Fairness

Are workers entitled to be treated fairly? I think we already answered this question when we talked about fairness earlier. The workplace is a society, and just societies must treat their members fairly, though we can have many disagreements about just what policies and practices are fair.

Privacy

We think there is good reason to be concerned about privacy in the workplace. We define privacy as the ability to protect certain activities from public scrutiny and the ability to keep certain information about oneself private. Privacy is routinely challenged in the workplace. Workers are monitored by cameras, microphones, and software. They are asked to provide urine and hair samples for drug testing. They travel through their workplaces with ID badges around their necks. They are psychologically tested and profiled. Their employer has access to school, employment, and medical records. They are often unable to control any aspect of their lives if their employer decides to intrude.

The arguments given in defense of this intrusion are largely Utilitarian. In some occupations in which public safety is a concern, invasions of privacy are defended in terms of safety. In others, invasions of privacy are defended in terms of profitability. If employees are under surveillance, they will be less likely to steal, to be rude to customers, or to slack off when they are being paid to do a job. While a case can be made for public safety, it is hard to see how a case can be made for some other invasions of privacy. Though this looks like a Utilitarian argument, it ignores the effects on the employees. When we look at other moral perspectives, we have more reason for being skeptical about the moral permissibility of invasions of privacy in the workplace.

Autonomy

Autonomy is the ability to make and carry out one's own decisions about important aspects of one's life. Some decisions seem acutely personal, while others seem to have enormous consequences for us. Some other decisions seem to grow out of who we are as persons. The sphere of autonomy has often been seen to protect such decisions, and it includes decisions about sexuality, religion, politics, and morality.

There is no reason to think that autonomy is any less worthy of protection in the workplace than it is in our homes or in community life. Indeed, since coercive intrusions on autonomy are frequent in the workplace, we have additional reason to object to such intrusions. One's sexual orientation, political affiliation, religious views, family values, and moral orientation are intensely personal. If we are to respect others as persons, we should avoid coercive intervention in these spheres. This is not to say that these topics should be off-limits. Morally committed persons often have an obligation to discuss some of these issues. But many would argue that unless you work for the local church, your employer has no right to impose an official view about deeply personal issues on you.

Unions

Many states have right-to-work laws that are supposed to protect employees from mandatory union membership. They are defended in terms of an employee right to association. One might argue that a genuine right-to-work law ought to include an additional provision to protect employees who want to create a union or join an existing union. After all, if we are trying to protect an employee's right to choose whether to associate with colleagues in a union, we must protect the employee's decision whatever it is.

There are additional arguments that can be given for unions. A Utilitarian argument might point out the consequences of having unions. Virtually all of the protections that US workers take for granted were won at enormous cost by unions, and unions continue to fight for workers. All workers, whether unionized or not, benefit from this activity. Of course, anti-union forces argue that there are negative consequences of unions—the bureaucracy, the difficulty in dealing with problem employees, the acrimonious labor climate. These are real issues, but we are not convinced that unions are the only source of the problem. Many of us work for enormous organizations with unwieldy bureaucracies of their own, and nonunion employees also experience acrimonious labor climates. At any rate, a Utilitarian argument would look for evidence to support these various claims.

A fairness argument can be given in favor of unions. Employers have substantial clout and internal cohesiveness. When an employee goes up against a manager, it is not one on one, but one against many. Being a member of a union makes the odds more equal.

One argument given against unions is that unions care only about the wages, benefits, and working conditions of their members. But there is no reason to think that unions are any more likely to be narrowly self-interested than management. If we can assume that management cares about customers as well as profit, we ought to assume that unions can care about customers as well as wages, benefits, and working conditions. Indeed, improvements in working conditions often are directly beneficial to customers. Consider health care and education, for example. Better working conditions for nurses means fewer patients per nurse. This is clearly a direct benefit for patients. Similarly, teachers lobby for fewer students per teacher, and students are the direct beneficiary of improvements in this ratio.

Benefits

In the United States, many social benefits have historically been connected to work. Health care and security in one's old age have been employment benefits. This is not the only, nor perhaps the best, way to provide social benefits. For example, most European countries provide for these benefits through taxes, and independently of employment. Though we can make an argument for providing equally for basic needs, it is not clear why we should think that one's employer ought to be the one to meet these needs. One problem with doing it this way is that people who are unemployed do not have these benefits. Those who are underemployed or employed by organizations too small to provide these benefits are also deprived of them.

There are some benefits that seem obligatory. Some benefits are spelled out in employment contracts. Some benefits are the result of compensating employees for losses they sustained through their employment. Other benefits, while defensible in broad outline, seem to be distributed unfairly. Compensation, for example, has become increasingly skewed in the United States. While ordinary employees find their paychecks growing modestly and sometimes actually shrinking in real terms, top executives have been the beneficiaries of ballooning compensation packages. Contribution has been the usual justification for this inequality, but it is not clear that chief executives have been working any harder than their employees. Indeed, in some famous examples, executive compensation ballooned as profits plummeted.

The bottom line on benefits is that some are designed to meet basic needs and perhaps ought to be provided for in a way that would ensure equity. Other benefits seem the reasonable result of hard work and probably ought to continue. Still others need serious moral scrutiny, as they often seem to reward unequally.

Self, Family, and the Workplace

Personal Life

Before the Industrial Revolution in the West, work was most often done in the home and provided the worker with a sense of identity as well as a livelihood. Most non-farm workers these days find a vast separation between their work lives and their non-work lives. Current moves to create a corporate culture often bridge the gap, but at the expense of one's personal and civic life. Workers are increasingly urged to see the workplace as home. Colleagues provide family; chores that used to be done at home have moved to the office. Now you can call out for pizza, drop off your dry cleaning, and leave your child at day care all without leaving your office.

Though there are real advantages of having a "homey" workplace, there are definite downsides. Sometimes the workplace is made "like home" just to make it possible to pressure workers into spending virtually every waking moment at work (and some sleeping moments as well). The distinction between home and work blurs as workers are encouraged to telecommute after dinner after spending all day at work. They are expected to be reachable by pager and cell phone even when they are on vacation. The move to allowing workers to work at home might be seen as a good remedy to these problems, but if the ability to work in your bathrobe means that you have to be on call constantly, this would seem to undercut the advantages.

When work takes up so much of one's life, everything else suffers. In Japan, *karoshi*—suicide attributed to overwork—has become an increasing problem. In the United States, "working yourself to death" is no longer a humorous exaggeration but a frightening reality for many. Family takes a back seat when parents are forced to work long hours and endure long commutes. Civic life is undermined when no one has time to understand the issues, much less contribute to their resolution.

What are we to do? The personal solution is to refuse to work such long hours. But this solution is not without its cost. If all your colleagues in the field are working long hours, your refusal to do so will likely result in adverse consequences for your career. If one partner works fewer hours in order to spend time with the family, how will the other wage earner in the family make up the difference? In expensive housing markets, where many people find interesting and challenging jobs, how can anyone opt out?

When we stand back and look at the big picture, it is obvious that this is madness. No employee can continue to work this way without burning out. In an increasingly tight labor market, no one can afford to "throw away" workers in this fashion. Civic life is affected when no one is available to participate in it. The fragile and vulnerable—the young and the old—are neglected when there is not enough time to care for them.

This situation is in many ways similar to the early days of the Industrial Revolution. Union activity was responsible for changing many of the worst abuses. Forty-hour workweeks became the norm, and wages rose to such an extent that many families were able to live on one paycheck. Progress on this front was scaled back in the United States when the National Labor Relations Act excluded managers and professionals from overtime pay. Now many employees are described as managerial or professional. Companies pressure these workers to work long hours in order to keep up with the competition. One obvious solution would be to reclassify most of these employees. This would create a level playing field in the United States. But since the economy is global, a more permanent solution must be global.

Care of Children, Sick Spouse, or Parents

In many parts of the United States, most adults work. This has caused a crisis in our society because there are not enough family members available to care for children and ill family members. Those with sufficient incomes can often buy the care they need, but they might not be assured of good quality, and even if they can secure quality care, they may want to do some of the caring themselves. Others are simply unable to pay for care and are left exhausted and frustrated. Some have argued that this is purely a personal problem with a personal solution. Individuals and families should forgo some income and arrange to have some adults available to care for children, the sick, and the aged. There are two problems with this response. First, not every family can afford to do this. Second, even for the families who can afford this, why should any adult be deprived of the fulfillment and economic security of paid employment? This concern is underscored when we note that in many societies women would be the ones who would be expected to make this sacrifice.

Others have argued that we should see this as a social problem instead of a purely personal one. How then do we solve it? One solution that has been adopted in many countries, including the United States, is to require employers to give workers time off to deal with family illness. The 1993 federal Family and Medical Leave Act requires employers with fifty or more employees to grant up to twelve unpaid weeks off to care for a new baby or a seriously ill family member. New mothers and women with an ill family member have been taking advantage of this option. The situation is a bit different for fathers. In 1994, Kevin Knussman, a helicopter paramedic with the Maryland State Police, was denied a leave to take care of his newborn daughter. Knussman sued, and four years later he finally won his lawsuit, the first sex discrimination case under the Family and Medical Leave Act.[4] While this victory will go a long way toward protecting the legal right of fathers to such leave, we suspect that attitudes will be much harder to change. This suggests that even if we grant that something is an entitlement for workers, we need to work to create an environment where workers feel comfortable availing themselves of it.

Aging

As we write this, coauthor Rita Manning lives and works in the Silicon Valley, where youth is valued highly. Older workers are often described as dinosaurs who are not up on the latest technology. But aging is a universal human phenomenon and people still need an income even after their hair begins to gray. Should we describe protection against age discrimination as an entitlement? We think this is a fairly easy question because the mere fact of age says nothing about a worker's ability to get the job done. Discriminating on the basis of age is then a violation of equal opportunity.

But there are other more subtle issues connected with aging. Though we all age differently, and some of us can expect to reach a ripe old age without any impairment in our ability to function, the reality is that many of us will slow down in some ways as we age. Perhaps we are a tad slower or a tad more forgetful. Should our employers have to make allowances for this? One might point out here that older workers also have many virtues associated with their age. Their experiences have often made them wiser and more patient than younger workers. But insofar as aging often brings with it a general slowing down, should workers be entitled to special treatment? Here the issue no longer seems to be about age, but about disability. Though it may be true that aging workers are at greater risk of impairment, anyone can become either temporarily or permanently disabled.

Disability

Before we discuss what entitlements workers have with respect to the issue of disability, it is important to ask just what disability is. Some people have suggested that we not even use the expression "disabled" because it suggests that we have a special group of persons who are different from the "normal" persons.

Anita Silvers, a contemporary philosopher, talks about the "tyranny of the normal."[5] We privilege certain states of ability by calling them "normal" and all the rest "disability." We then debate about how much help the normal should be expected to give the disabled. She argued that we ought, instead, to think in terms of equality. We are all equally entitled to certain benefits, but we often erect barriers that exclude some. Architecture, for example, is not part of the natural world; it is a human artifact. When we design our homes and buildings using staircases rather than ramps and elevators, we have chosen to privilege those who can easily walk over those who rely on devices like wheelchairs. Thus we are creating barriers to equal participation in society. So instead of talking about "the disabled," we should be talking about persons with ability sets and the various barriers to equal access we construct.

Another way to think about disability is that it is not an essential feature of certain people. Rather, it is a state that we all go through at different times. As we age, most of us will notice that our physical and sometimes even our mental abilities are not as sharp as they were when we were younger. Pregnant women don't navigate stairs in their ninth month with the same breezy ease that they might have in their first month. People who participate in sports often find that injuries impair their ability to get around. Even if you never have the experience of pregnancy, aging, or injury, all of us experience some time in our lives when we can't navigate freely through the world. None of us was born with the ability to walk and fill our own needs. We don't think of caring for infants as charity, however. We "childproof" our homes and equip our schools to allow for full access. Removing barriers to adults with impairments is in principle no different.

So it appears that the underlying rationale for how to deal with disabled workers (or differently abled workers) is equality. Look back and see what you decided about equality. Our guess is that most of you chose to include at least equality of opportunity in your just world. Look back even further and see what moral perspectives you found most compelling. If you felt most comfortable with Kant, for example, then you are perhaps committed to a more robust sense of equality.

The United States committed itself to equal opportunity for workers (and for persons using public facilities) with the Americans with Disabilities Act (ADA). This act requires equality in all aspects of the workplace for persons who are qualified to do the job but suffer from some impairment, record of impairment, or perception that they are impaired.

Conforming to Corporate Culture

Workers are expected to conform to corporate culture in a myriad of ways. They are expected to work on days of special significance to their religions. Even with the advent of "dress down" Fridays, there are still standards for working attire. Some employees wear clothing with corporate logos even on their days off. Some workers are told to speak standard English regardless of their native tongue or particular idiom. Some workers are sometimes even told what kinds of emotions are acceptable. Have we gone too far?

One way to think about this issue is to look at the underlying reasons why we want to be able to express our individuality. Mill argued that unless we are free to express our own individuality, even when such expression is offensive, we will become a nation of sheep. Advances that will ultimately benefit all society are only possible if we encourage eccentricity. Another argument might be that unless we are free to express our individuality we will not be able to form our distinct dreams and goals. If we cannot do this, then we will never be able to fully develop as ends in ourselves. Finally, demands that we conform to corporate culture in every respect seem to indicate that our worth is a function of the role we play in the larger corporate goals. In other words, it treats us as a means to an end.

But surely there are some limits that our employers are justified in enforcing. The difficult issue is in sorting out how to draw this line. Public safety seems an obvious justification for limiting individuality. You may like your long hair hanging over your face, but your employer has the right to ask you to corral it if it keeps falling into the soup. At the other extreme, one might argue that employers are justified in enforcing any policy that would benefit the employer. This seems too broad because it implies that it is the organization and not the individual that is the locus of value. Further, insisting that employees sacrifice their individuality merely to benefit the employer seems to treat the employee as a mere means. There seems to be a compromise to be struck here. Perhaps one could argue that employers are justified in insisting on conformity to corporate culture if failure to do so would result in direct and immediate harm to serious and legitimate corporate interests.

Are Workers Really Entitled to Benefits?

So far, we've used the various moral perspectives that we've introduced in this book to make a case for various worker entitlements. But one could also make a case against certain benefits. Utilitarian considerations are often given in favor of limiting workers' benefits. Let's look at one of these arguments here. In today's increasingly global economy, the corporation that is not streamlined and efficient simply will not survive. Generous worker benefits interfere with a company's ability to price its products competitively. Thus if we insist on generous benefits, the company will fail and the workers will lose all their benefits, including their jobs.

We can make an analogous argument for public-sector and nonprofit jobs. Public-sector jobs must be funded through fees or taxes on the public. If these fees and taxes seem excessive or arbitrary, the public will be less willing to shoulder the burden; thus the activities of the public sector will be curtailed and ultimately many public-sector employees will lose their jobs. Some nonprofits are nonprofit in name only and thus have the same challenges that the private sector faces. Other nonprofits depend on philanthropy, and philanthropists will not be willing to contribute to nonprofits if they do not operate in the same lean and mean way that the private sector does.

Another set of arguments depends on a certain conception of rights. Libertarians, for example, privilege rights to liberty and property. Simply put, the owners of private-sector organizations have the right to do what they want with their own property, and this includes the right to set benefits in a way that is most advantageous to the owners. The laws of supply and demand reward the companies that can produce the most desired goods at the lowest price; thus owners have a motivation to use worker benefits solely to attract workers who are highly valued in the job market.

We invite you to think about these various views and come up with your own responses.

Exercise 8.4

Do you think that workers have a right to privacy? What does the sphere of privacy include? Compare your answers with the policies at your workplace.

Do you think that workers have a right to autonomy? What does the sphere of autonomy include? Compare your answers with the policies at your workplace.

Do you think that your work impinges on your personal life? In what ways? What personal changes could you make to shift the balance? What institutional changes would help you (institutional changes include things like changes in the corporate culture, in the law, and in social customs)?

Exercise 8.5

Do you find the Utilitarian argument in favor of limited worker benefits compelling? If so, why? If not, how would you respond to the argument? Does it follow that workers in the past had different moral entitlements than workers today have?

▶ **Exercise 8.6**

Do you find the Libertarian position on worker benefits persuasive? If so, why? If not, how would you respond?

Discrimination

Before we leave the topic of work, we want to spend some time looking at perhaps one of the most egregious and controversial examples of the way in which workers' rights to fair treatment are violated. We begin by asking you to think about a fairly lengthy and complex case. Take a day or so to think about this case and do the exercise before you read our discussion of it.

▶ **Exercise 8.7**

For this exercise, you are to imagine that you are the vice president of new acquisitions at the Morally Upright Corporation (MU). Your company has just bought Morally Bankrupt (MB), and you have heard disturbing rumors about discrimination there. You want to make sure that you can integrate this new company into the morally sensitive culture of MU. Your first task is to read the following consultant report. Then you will identify every possible example of discrimination and design a plan to end it once and for all. Write a memo to your CEO outlining your plans.

Report from Consultant Regarding Discrimination at MB

The Morally Bankrupt Company manufactures equipment for use in the hospital industry. Its equipment is not terribly high tech and workers can be trained for the factory in a matter of weeks. The company has four divisions: manufacturing and technical support, marketing and sales, engineering, and human resources and finance.

Manufacturing

Manufacturing is located in Watsonville, a city with a predominantly Latino population. There are approximately sixty people in manufacturing and they are divided into three groups: unskilled, skilled, and tech support. The people in tech support have been with the company the longest and are most familiar with the product and its problems. They make about twice what the unskilled workers make and about 50 percent more than the skilled workers. There are thirty-five unskilled workers and they are predominantly Latina. There are no special skills needed for this grade. There are fifteen skilled workers who have about three weeks of training beyond what the unskilled workers get. They are paid 50 percent more than unskilled workers. These workers are overwhelmingly male and about half are Anglo; one-quarter are Asian, and the remainder are Latino and African American. The remaining ten workers in manufacturing are tech support. These workers are drawn mostly from the ranks of the skilled workers and are all white males. Most of the workers were leery about talking to me. It seems that some workers were fired for union activity and the others are afraid that there would be reprisals for talking to me.

I asked Rod Weary, the vice president of manufacturing, about the makeup of his division. He made the following comments:

> I only hire gals for the unskilled ranks, because they do the work without giving you a lot of crap about working conditions. These Mexican ladies are great workers, too. They've got some mouths to feed and that keeps their noses to the grindstone. But you gotta make sure they're not going to be missing work because they're having babies. This is tough because I like the young ones. They're cuter than the grandmas and I just like those big brown eyes. I make them have a pregnancy test before I hire them. I don't believe in women in the skilled ranks. They might get hurt, and besides, the other workers don't like it. Now in tech support, we have to be sensitive to what our customers want. We ship all over the world and you can't just put anyone on a plane. I wish I had some Asians for our Asian markets, but Asians are just not available at these ranks. They all want to be engineers. So I do the next best thing and I hire only white males. I would love to be able to hire other folks, but our customers would throw a fit.

Engineering
This is a small division with only four engineers. There are three men and one woman. Two of the men are Asian and the rest are white. Here's

what the woman said to me: "I feel really alienated here. The men only want to talk about football, and they pay no attention to me. If I voice a good idea, no one listens. But if one of my male colleagues repeats what I just said, he gets credit for having a great idea. I also just found out that they are all making more than me."

Sales and Marketing

There are ten sales and marketing people and four admins. The people in sales are all on commission, but they do not have the same commission structure. The top salesperson is the son of the CEO and he makes 2 percent. The newest member of the team makes only 0.5 percent and covers a much bigger region. There is only one woman, and she is inside sales. There are four Asians and six Anglos. They all seem to work pretty hard, but morale is very low. I talked to one salesperson, who wished to remain nameless:

> Everything here is done on the basis of who you are. Are you the son of the boss, or his old girlfriend? I bust my butt and spend half my life on a plane, but I make only about a tenth of what some of the others make. I get the lousy territory and a crummy commission structure as well. And the whole culture is so macho. You gotta have the wife and the kids. I don't flaunt my boyfriend, but I'm pretty sure that I've paid a price for not being in the closet about it.

Another problem concerns a worker who was fired, ostensibly because he could not make his quota. I suspect that this worker might have an ADA claim because his output declined after back surgery.

Finance and Human Resources

This is the smallest division and all the decision-makers are family members. All the important decisions are made in this division and they are pretty top-down. I talked to Ben, the CEO and founder: "This is my baby. I built this company from scratch. I started out with a pretty good idea and I did some networking and brought my talented buddies on board to get the thing up and running. I always saw the company as a way to keep my family happy and employed, and it was very good to us."

Defining Discrimination

Start by reviewing what you identified as discrimination in the preceding case study. We are going to use our intuitions about what should count as discrimination to come up with a definition of discrimination. Let's begin with manufacturing.

We could start just by looking at the numbers. In a city with a predominantly Latino population, there are about sixty people in manufacturing. The thirty-five unskilled workers are Latina. The fifteen skilled workers are almost all male, half of whom are Anglo, one-quarter of whom are Asian, and the remainder Latino and African American. The ten tech-support workers are all white males and are drawn mostly from the ranks of unskilled workers.

Just by looking at the numbers, we have reasons to think that there might be discrimination at MB. It is highly unlikely that Latinas would be clustered in the unskilled ranks by chance. Similarly, since the unskilled workers make so much less than the skilled workers, it is unlikely that they are there by choice. It is not impossible, though. Perhaps they enjoy each other's company, or the work is less stressful. Since moving to the skilled ranks only requires about three weeks of training, and no special skills beyond what can be learned in those three weeks, it is unlikely that it is by mere chance that these ranks are overwhelmingly male. It seems reasonable to suppose that female workers would want the opportunity to get a 50 percent raise. Similarly, it seems unlikely that chance would result in so many non-Latinas having these jobs.

Finally, we can look at tech support. We don't see any Latinos, Asians, or African Americans in these ranks, and none of them are female. Again, it seems reasonable to suppose that everyone in manufacturing would want to move up to these jobs, which pay so much more than the other jobs in manufacturing, if given the option. There is some possibility that some workers would not want the travel associated with this job. Perhaps they have families to look after. Since women in our society are expected to be the ones with primary responsibility for children, this might explain the dearth of women in these ranks. But it is reasonable to suspect discrimination at MB at this point. We can look at the statement of Rod Weary, the manufacturing vice president, for confirmation of our suspicions.

Obviously we have to take what he says with a grain of salt. We don't know if what he tells us is true, and as soon as we look at his statement, we can see that he has some unfortunate prejudices about certain groups. He begins by admitting that he deliberately limits women to the un-skilled ranks. He hints that working conditions are not very good at MB. He goes on to make unsupported generalizations about "Mexican" women, and women in general. Finally, he says that he likes their "big brown eyes." This makes us worry that he might be sexually harassing these women.

Weary also tells us that he deliberately refuses to hire pregnant women. In fact, he makes every woman of childbearing age take a pregnancy test before he hires her. He also makes a point of not hiring older women.

Weary gives another reason for hiring only white males to be tech support. He says that his customers will only accept males, and only Asian and white males. He seems to be relying on stereotypes about Asians when he says that all Asian males want to be engineers, so we have to take this remark with a grain of salt. But suppose he is right about his customers? Would this be a justification for refusing to hire members of other groups? This is a difficult question, but answering it requires that we first come up with a definition of discrimination. Once we come up with such a definition, we can ask whether discrimination is justified when customers desire it.

There is another problem in manufacturing. Workers have been fired for union activity. Whether or not we decide to call this discrimination, it is certainly illegal.

Let's begin our search for a definition by looking at one that is fairly common: Discrimination occurs whenever people are treated unfairly. While many agree that unfairness is morally wrong, this is not a very helpful way to define discrimination because it lumps together too many different kinds of unfairness. Discrimination seems to involve a particu-lar kind of unfairness.

The employment policies at MB harm some of the workers, or deny them important benefits, and the harm and denial of benefits seem to fall on members of particular groups. In addition, the employment decisions do not seem to have anything to do with whether the employees could do the job. This suggests the following definition. We are calling it a provisional definition because, as we shall see, it will need further clarification.

Provisional Definition of Discrimination 1: (a) Actions or policies of an individual or organization which cause harm to people or result in the denial of important benefits and, (b) are based on characteristics not relevant to the task at hand, where (c) these characteristics seem to be related to membership in particular groups.

Let's now look at engineering at MB. Though there is only one woman engineer out of four, this might not be the result of discrimination since the field of engineering is still dominated by men. Similarly, the racial and ethnic makeup might not be due to discrimination, since there are not very many Latino or African-American engineers in the field as a whole. This gives us reason to take a closer look at MB, however. The principle problem here seems to be the perception by the female engineer that she is not being treated fairly. She says that she feels alienated and that others take credit for her ideas. In addition, she says that all the male engineers are being paid more than she is. She thinks that all these things are happening to her because she is a woman. This might be a case of discrimination. One suspects that not everyone will have the same reaction to this example.

There are two questions we need to raise here. The first is whether the female engineer's perceptions are accurate. The second is whether MB ought to be held responsible for the all the actions of its employees if those actions result in a member of a particular group being harmed. The first question is an important one, and any resolution of the problems at MB will require a closer look at engineering. It also suggests a revision of our definition of discrimination. We shouldn't merely take people at their word when they say have been harmed. It seems reasonable to insist on some evidence of harm. We can incorporate this into our definition by inserting the word "demonstrable" in front of "harm" in clause (a).

The second problem is how much we should blame organizations for the actions of their members. Obviously we want to blame individuals for their own morally deficient behavior, but sometimes we can hold organizations at fault as well. It seems reasonable to blame organizations for the actions of their members when these actions are in conformity with established policy or organizational culture. The first thing to notice here is that established policy and organizational culture are not the same thing. An organization might have a written set of guidelines, but a culture that is very different. In this case, it seems reasonable to hold the organization responsible when its members are following culture, whether or not it is written down and whether or not it is the same as the more formal guidelines.

It's a bit tricky when actions are not clearly in conformity with established guidelines. There are two kinds of cases where it seems reasonable to hold organizations morally liable when their members are at fault. The first is where the organization should have known what was going on. In some cases, we expect supervision of employee behavior. The second case is where managers are discriminating. The behavior of managers is closely associated with the organization itself, and managers have varying degrees of power to act in the organization's behalf. We can add another clause to our definition to capture this insight: "Discrimination can be deemed to be committed by an organization if it was done by someone in a managerial role or if someone in such a role knew or should have known it was occurring." We can now amend our definition.

Provisional Definition of Discrimination 2: (a) Actions or policies of an individual or organization which cause demonstrable harm to people or result in the denial of important benefits and, (b) are based on characteristics not relevant to the task at hand, where (c) these characteristics seem to be related to membership in particular groups; moreover, (d) the discrimination can be deemed to be committed by an organization if it was done by someone in a managerial role or if someone in such a role knew or should have known it was occurring.

Let's move on to sales and marketing. One thing to note is that different treatment is not necessarily discrimination. Perhaps the CEO's son makes a bigger commission because he is a better salesperson. There are moral arguments that can be made for different commission structures. A Utilitarian, for example, might point out that the entire organization benefits if sales are robust, and that commission is a powerful motivator for increasing sales. One might make different arguments for more equal commissions, too. Here, we might bring in principles of justice.

In any case, regardless of the moral status of differences in pay, mere difference is not enough to show discrimination. What about basing differences in treatment on sexual orientation, as the complaining salesman alleges? It certainly appears to fit our provisional definition. The salesperson is harmed because of his sexual orientation, which doesn't seem to have anything to do with the performance of his job. Unfortunately for him, there are no federal laws banning discrimination based on sexual orientation, though there are several states, including California, that do ban it.

What should we say about the salesperson who was let go after his back surgery? One might argue, on the one hand, that he was let go because he could no longer do his job as well as he could before. On the other hand, one might argue that with some help or a transfer to a different position he might have been able to continue to be productive. Thus it looks like the ADA could apply in this case.

There is another issue here and this comes up in finance and human resources as well. This is the question of nepotism. Is nepotism discrimination? We can look at the argument made by the CEO. He says that he built the company in order to benefit his family. We think that arguments can be made on both sides about the moral status of nepotism. We don't believe that a case can be made that nepotism is discrimination, though. One crucial feature is missing. When we looked at the case of Latina workers, we noted two things. One is that they are treated unfairly because they are Latinas. Another is that Latinas are relatively disadvantaged in our society. This second feature is missing in cases of nepotism. Though non-family members are relatively disadvantaged within the organization, not being a member of this particular family is not the same as being a member of a group that is relatively disadvantaged in our society. This leads to the final qualification in our definition of discrimination: Discrimination is experienced by members of relatively disadvantaged groups.

We can now state our final definition of discrimination:

Definition of Discrimination: (a) Actions or policies of an individual or organization which cause demonstrable harm to people or result in the denial of important benefits and, (b) are based on characteristics not relevant to the task at hand, where (c) these characteristics seem to be related to membership in particular relatively disadvantaged groups; moreover, (d) the discrimination can be deemed to be committed by an organization if it was done by someone in a managerial role or if someone in such a role knew or should have known it was occurring.

Before we leave our analysis of the problem at MB and move on to how to respond to the problem, we want to raise one final concern. The salesperson is quoted as suggesting that the boss's old girlfriend is favored in the department. This might well be an example of sexual harassment, as we shall see when we turn to that subject later in this chapter.

Responding to Discrimination

We have now identified the most egregious forms of discrimination practiced at MB. Now we need to be creative about ending it. First, we need to think about our overall goals. Here are the main options: to compensate victims of past discrimination, to punish those who have discriminated against others, to prevent future discrimination, and to create relative equality between disadvantaged and advantaged groups. Look at your plan and see what goals your plan was designed to further.

Let us begin with the first goal. Should MU compensate the Latinas at MB for the discrimination they suffered while employed at MB? To decide, first let's review the harm they suffered. The most obvious problem was that they were deprived of the opportunity to earn substantially more money. Let's assume that unskilled workers earn just a little over minimum wage, that is, $6 an hour, or $12,000 a year. Suppose that the average Latina worked for MB for three years. Assuming that the average unskilled worker would have moved up to become a skilled worker after one year, each worker lost an average of $12,000 in wages as a direct result of discrimination by MB. Since there were thirty-five Latina unskilled workers, this comes to $420,000 in lost wages for unskilled workers alone. Think what these women could have done with these lost wages. They could have sent a child to college. There are a number of ways we could compensate these women. First of all, we could write them each a check for the wages lost. Second, we could give them first priority for advancement to the skilled and tech-support ranks. If you did not include compensation for lost wages in your plan, ask yourself why not.

Another goal might be to prevent future discrimination. Did you include this goal in your plan? Setting up goals and timetables is the most cost-effective way to do this, and this might explain why this particular strategy is so popular. Let's look briefly at some other alternatives. We might bring in consultants to educate the managers about the evils of discrimination. While we think this is a worthy goal (and we would be happy to offer our services), we are not convinced that it would be effective by itself. This strategy assumes that discrimination occurs because of ignorance. We think this is sometimes the case, but it is more likely that individuals discriminate because they just feel more comfortable interacting with people "like them," or because they have strong negative feelings about other people. In addition, practices grow up which make discrimination part of the culture of institutions.

There are also pressures outside the organization that lend support to discrimination. Perhaps women are discouraged from studying math and science as girls and are less likely to study engineering as a result. Perhaps customers really do have racist and sexist preferences. Maybe local schools shortchange the local population. If we are serious about ending discrimination, we need to address these larger issues. Education as a stand-alone strategy assumes that people can be taught to give up their prejudices. We are not convinced that Rod Weary will benefit from this instruction, and unfortunately, the world has to deal with its Rod Wearys.

Goals and timetables begin to look like a very cheap and quick response to discrimination when we see what a complex issue it is.

The most ambitious goal is to create relative equality among groups. When we look at MB, we see that several groups are often victims of discrimination: African Americans, Latinas, Asians, women, persons with disabilities, gays, and lesbians.

Federal Laws against Discrimination

In the United States, concern about discrimination is addressed in both federal and local laws. The primary federal law about discrimination is Title VII of the Civil Rights Act of 1964. It bans discrimination based on race, color, gender, and national origin. It has more recently been interpreted to ban sexual harassment as a form of gender discrimination. Federal law also bans other types of discrimination: discrimination based on age, pregnancy, citizenship, disability, and union membership. If an organization is found guilty of discrimination, there are a number of remedies that a court can order: rehiring or promoting workers, compensating workers, paying damages for emotional suffering and mental anguish, changing policies so that discrimination won't recur, and paying workers' legal fees. One of the things courts cannot do is require organizations to institute quotas, since quotas were outlawed by the Supreme Court in the *University of California Regents v. Bakke* decision.[6]

In the Americans with Disabilities Act (ADA), federal law treats disability much like race or gender. The ADA requires that reasonable accommodation be provided for workers with disabilities. What counts as a reasonable accommodation is a gray area that will be the subject of litigation for some time. In our Morally Bankrupt case, we might argue that the salesperson who had back surgery could have performed his job with some accommodation that would neither be excessively costly nor unreasonable in other ways. We don't have all the details, but we can guess that the stress on his back might have caused him to cut back on travel, and this might account for the falloff in productivity. Instead of letting him go, Morally Bankrupt could have offered him a reasonable accommodation. For example, he could have been given video-conferencing equipment to substitute for some of his travel. Allowing him to fly business class instead of coach might have relieved his difficulty traveling.

Sexual Harassment

The understanding of discrimination in the US legal system has been expanded to include sexual harassment because this practice makes the workplace (and the schoolyard) unfair to women by limiting their participation. Though there have been cases of same-sex sexual harassment and harassment of men by women, the most common case is harassment by men against women. In what follows, we will discuss this common case, but a similar analysis could be used against the other cases as well.

The moral arguments against sexual harassment are essentially the same as the arguments against discrimination, since sexual harassment is a form of discrimination. Sexual harassment is any unwelcome sexual advance or conduct on the job that is either a condition of continued employment or promotion or creates an intimidating, hostile, or offensive working environment. Some examples of practices that have been ruled sexual harassment under the law include obscene comments, obscene behavior, a dress code that puts special burdens on women, coerced sex, refusal of management to discipline for sexual harassment, and preference given to an employee who consents to advances (this last type of sexual harassment comes to mind as we recall the statement of the salesperson at MB).

The causes of sexual harassment are varied and include sexual stereotypes and the desire for control in the workplace. Sexual stereotypes come into play when men make assumptions about what women desire. Some men, for example, might assume that women like to be complemented and touched and made to feel sexy. They may also assume that real men have to be the pursuers. Some women accept certain stereotypes and thus do nothing to discourage the harassment—they may accept the stereotype that says that a good woman does not complain, for example. A more pernicious cause of sexual harassment is hostility about women's entry into workplaces that were formerly all male. Finally, some people try to control their environments by demeaning others, and since many women find sexual harassment humiliating and hurtful, this is an effective strategy for limiting the agency of women.

The effects of sexual harassment accrue to the individual worker in the form of loss of job, wages and/or position, retaliation, and stress. The effects on women as a group include limiting the job options for women, reinforcement of patterns of discrimination, and the constant vigilance that it imposes on women.

The Civil Rights Act of 1964 prohibited discrimination in employment based on race, color, religion, national origin, and sex. In 1980, the Equal Employment Opportunity Commission (EEOC) provided regulations prohibiting sexual harassment. Sexual harassment was acknowledged by the Supreme Court as employment discrimination in 1986,[7] and monetary damages were allowed by the Civil Rights Act of 1991. One interesting issue that remains to be settled is what standard we should use to decide when conduct is unreasonable. Reasonable men and reasonable women may have very different views about what constitutes sexual harassment. Most recently, the reasonable woman standard has prevailed.

Employers are legally liable for sexual harassment by supervisors, whether or not management knew about it, and by coworkers, if management knew or should have known about the harassment. Policies that have been effective against sexual harassment include a statement with the following provisos: a notice that sexual harassment will not be tolerated, a definition of prohibited behavior, and a spelling out of penalties. Other elements of an effective policy include clear reporting guidelines, prompt and confidential investigation with results made known to both parties, a strong policy against retaliation, and proper training and monitoring.

If you or someone you know is a victim of sexual harassment, here are some helpful strategies. First, confront the harasser. It may turn out that he is unaware that his behavior is troubling. If the harassment continues, you will need to collect evidence. Keep a journal in which you document your recollections of each incident, talk about the incidents with your friends and coworkers, contact or organize a support group, and get a copy of your work records to forestall retaliation. If all else fails, use formal complaint procedures, either the ones available in your organization or through your state EEOC office.

▶ **Exercise 8.8**

Get a copy of the sexual harassment policy of an organization you belong to. How does it define sexual harassment? What do you think of this definition? What procedures are followed in cases of alleged sexual harassment? What do you think of these procedures?

Conclusion

In this chapter, we've presented some of the moral issues connected to the world of work. We've tried to present multiple perspectives and an example of how to use the moral perspectives from earlier chapters to decide what is right and to justify that decision. There are two other dimensions of human life that we think are both important and fraught with moral quandaries—the world of family and friends, and the global world. We will address these two dimensions in our next two chapters.

▶ **Study Questions for Chapter Eight**

1. What is meaningful work?
2. How did Robert Bellah distinguish between a career and a vocation?
3. How would a Utilitarian answer the question of whether everyone is entitled to a job?
4. How would various principles of justice weigh in on the question of whether everyone is entitled to a job?
5. Here is the list of possible worker entitlements: continued employment, safe and relatively pleasant working conditions, fairness, privacy, autonomy, the ability to choose to join or not join a union, benefits, and the ability to live a full personal life outside of work. Describe and briefly discuss each using some key concepts from this text.

6. What is discrimination?

7. Use the definition of discrimination to identify examples of discrimination at Morally Bankrupt.

8. Briefly describe the history of federal discrimination law.

9. What is sexual harassment? Briefly describe the history of federal law on sexual harassment.

NOTES

1. Karl Marx, *The German Ideology* (originally written 1845–1846) (Amherst, N.Y.: Prometheus Books, 1998).

2. Aristotle, *Nichomachean Ethics* (originally written circa 335–322 BCE), translated by Terence Irwin (Indianapolis: Hackett Press, 1985).

3. Robert Bellah, *Habits of the Heart* (Berkeley: University of California Press, 1996).

4. *Knussman v. State of Maryland,* 272 F.3d 625, 634.

5. See Leslie Pickering Francis and Anita Silvers, eds., *Americans with Disabilities: Exploring Implications of the Law for Individuals and Institutions* (New York: Routledge, 2000); Anita Silvers, David Wasserman, and Mary Mahowald, *Disability, Difference, Discrimination: Perspectives on Justice in Bioethics and Public Policy* (Lanham, Md.: Rowman and Littlefield, 1998).

6. *University of California Regents v. Bakke,* 438 U.S. 265 (1978).

7. *Meritor Savings Bank v. Vinson,* 477 U.S. 57 (1986).

CHAPTER 9

Family and Friends

In *The Euthyphro*, Euthyphro is on his way to take his father to court for murder when Socrates comes upon him. There are reasons to question whether the charge against his father is fair. But one of the questions this dialogue raises is whether it is ever morally defensible or even morally obligatory to put our family members in harm's way.

Some would argue that it is never morally defensible because loyalty is a primary virtue when it comes to one's family and close friends. Confucius is said to have reacted negatively to the thought of turning in one's father for stealing sheep—instead, he replied that in his village, fathers covered for their sons and sons covered for their fathers.[1] Others would argue for a more nuanced position, perhaps focusing on why you were putting your family member or friend in harm's way. In the case of a family member who has committed a crime, we think it depends on two factors: the seriousness of the crime, and the consequences to the family member of your action. In cultures where family honor is primary, the family member might be sacrificed if needed to protect family honor.

Special Obligations

One of the fundamental questions in this debate is whether we have special obligations to family and close friends that we do not have to strangers.

There is a flourishing debate in moral philosophy today about special obligations. This is by no means a new conflict, or a merely Western one. Indeed, the ancient Chinese philosopher Mo Tzu quarreled with the

Confucians over just this point. He argued for a universal concern for all, whereas the Confucians thought familial love obligated you to your immediate family in a unique way distinct from the emotions and obligations you have in regard to others in society. Here we will just try to sort out the types of answers that would be given by the various moral perspectives we introduced earlier.

Utilitarianism

One might expect a Utilitarian to say that we have no special obligations; in every case we have an obligation to maximize utility. A Rule Utilitarian might allow for special obligations if rules allowing or requiring special obligations would maximize overall utility. In either case, Utilitarians would need to look at the actual consequences of social practices that privileged family and friendship in this way. It's unlikely that Utilitarians would think of this as an all-or-nothing issue. It's far more likely that they would find that under certain conditions privileging special obligations would maximize utility.

Suppose, for example, that your son, who is graduating from high school, wants a BMW convertible badly. Even if you could afford the car, and even if getting it wouldn't be a hindrance to healthy character development for your son, do you really have an obligation to get him the BMW? We leave this question for you to answer, but note that if you decide to use Utilitarianism to answer the question, you will have to look at all your other options and see which one would maximize utility, not just for you and your son, but for all concerned. One thing to add here is that a prominent Utilitarian, Peter Singer, has argued that we do not have the obligation to spend this kind of money on our children, but we do have an obligation to needy people all over the world. He said that discharging that obligation requires that a minimum of 10 percent of the income of people in the developed world be donated to those in dire need.[2]

Kant

At first glance, the question of special obligation looks less murky if we take a Kantian perspective. Kant argued that all human beings are moral equals and that we must treat all persons as ends in themselves. This appears to foreclose the possibility that we have greater obligations to some than to others. This strikes many as counterintuitive. Charles Fried tried to solve the problem with his famous example of the drowning wife. Suppose that there are two people drowning, one of whom is your wife, and you can only save one. Are you justified, on Kantian grounds, in saving your wife?

Fried argued that you are justified in such a choice because you happen to be the spouse on the scene, rather than the spouse of the other victim. Thus a kind of randomizing event has occurred that preserves the moral equality of the two people drowning.[3] Bernard Williams argues that this is asking one question too many. He criticized this Kantian solution because it failed to capture our intuitions that in this case, we think that the good husband, the *morally* good husband, would dive in to rescue his wife without thinking that doing so would require any moral justification at all.[4] The husband who needed to stop and think about whether he was justified in prioritizing his wife is thus asking one question too many.

Virtue

There are multiple virtue traditions, and thus multiple virtue perspectives, on the issue of special obligation. We begin with Aristotle. Recall that he suggested that being virtuous is a matter of acting "at the right time, toward the right objects, toward the right people, for the right reason, and in the right manner."[5] Later in the same work he explicitly stated that loyalty to one's friends and family members is limited: "We must, as a general rule, repay good deeds rather than do favors for our bosom companions."[6]

Confucius treated family with special reverence, but noted that the family was the foundation of the state. Though he clearly argued that we have special obligations to our families, they are not unlimited. Unlimited obligation would conflict with the idea of the family as the foundation of the just state. Confucius would also add that people have certain obligations to their parents that they do not have in regard to the parents of others. This highlights an important part of Confucian social philosophy—

not only is the self ("who" we are) defined by relationships, but our duties to specific people are affected by the relationships we hold in regard to them. The virtuous individual is one who can deftly and artfully uphold the relationships in which they find themselves.

The Christian virtue tradition, with its emphasis on equality in God's eyes, seems to be incompatible with a strong concept of special obligation. The story of the Good Samaritan illustrates that the good person is the one who recognizes obligations to strangers. On the other hand, the fourth commandment says, "Honor thy father and mother."

For all these virtue traditions, the best interpretation seems to be that it is morally permissible, perhaps even morally obligatory, to recognize a special obligation to one's family and close friends, as long as this special obligation does not conflict with one's other obligations.

Care

Coauthor Rita Manning has a detailed discussion of this question in her book on an ethic of care.[7] Here, we'll just summarize. On one hand, care is fostered and developed in intimate settings—through the giving and receiving of care. So we do have special obligations to intimate others. On the other hand, the foundation of care is the importance and moral equality of persons. Thus, responding to the needs of others is a central part of being a caring person. The bottom line is that we do have a special obligation to family and friends, but this obligation can sometimes be superseded by the pressing needs of strangers.

Social Contract

In the Original Position behind the Veil of Ignorance, we don't know anything about ourselves, but we do know basic facts about humans. Presumably, then, we know that we live and thrive in intimate personal relationships. So it looks like we would allow for some special obligations. At the same time, our concern about the least well off suggests that we would limit these obligations in support of our quest for relative equality. Rawls's second principle of justice, for example, requires that we allow everyone an equal opportunity to succeed in their life plans, regardless of family income and wealth. Making this a reality would probably require that we share family resources, perhaps by taxing wealthy families to provide for the support necessary for children of poorer families to achieve their goals.

All of these perspectives seem to allow for special obligations, with the possible exception of Kant, though it's not clear how we draw these limits. We leave it to you to settle this difficult question for yourself.

▶ **Exercise 9.1**

Suppose that you found out that your sister had stolen $40 from her place of employment. Should you turn her in? Suppose she stole it from your mother? Now suppose that she stole it to buy a prescription drug for her child that she couldn't otherwise afford? Do these additional features make a difference? Why or why not?

Obligations to Family: Neglect and Abuse

Even if you don't think that you have special obligations to family and friends, we think that most readers will agree that we can have obligations to persons on other grounds—for example, past promises, role responsibilities, past harms and/or benefits, and need. Failing to meet these obligations is often described as neglect, and direct harm to family members is described as abuse. In this section, we will discuss the issue of abuse.

Child Abuse

Child abuse can best be understood through three lenses. First, we can view it as a failure to discharge obligations owed to the child. Next, we can understand it in terms of harms done to the child. Finally, we acknowledge the special wrongness of harm done to children by noting their vulnerability.

Understandings of what is owed to children by their parents have varied throughout history, and they vary widely both between and among different social traditions. Rather than attempt to adjudicate these differences here, we shall try to understand parental obligation through the perspective of contemporary North American legal and social-science discussions of what constitutes child abuse.[8]

The obligations toward children generally assumed in discussions about child abuse include the obligation to provide food, clothing, shelter, education, health care, and an emotionally healthy environment. Positive duties to provide the minimum conditions necessary for self-esteem and autonomy are often asserted in discussions of what constitutes an emotionally healthy environment. Another way to describe such an environment is in terms of one's freedom from the harms that we will discuss in the next section.

Neglect is failure to fulfill the obligations a parent owes to the child, so an understanding of this concept begins with an understanding of parental obligation. Since there are different views about parental obligation, there are different views about what constitutes neglect. There is virtually unanimous agreement that failure to provide the material conditions for continued relatively healthy existence is neglect. There is, however, great disagreement about how far to extend this concept. Liberals argue that failure to provide a child with the education that will allow a fully autonomous life is neglect, while traditionalists argue that we neglect children when we fail to provide them with a positive aversion to certain life choices. Alice Miller came down on the side of the liberals for a different reason. She argued that a child can either be autonomous or dependent on parents (and later parent substitutes) for validation and self-esteem. Failure to provide conditions of autonomy are not mere neglect, but count as positive harm.[9]

Early discussions of child abuse focused on physical abuse. Later discussions extended the notion of harm to include sexual exploitation, excessive criticism, lack of appropriate affection, treating the child as a parent or spouse, exposing the child to the abuse of another (usually the abuse of the mother by the father or other male), exposing the child to an alcoholic parent (though this can be analyzed in terms of the harms that alcoholic parents are likely to inflict), and exposing the child to other harms through a lack of parental supervision.

The issue of child abuse is divorced from the issue of parental intention in many respects, largely because the harm is reckoned so severe as to make parental *mens rea* (intention) irrelevant. If the child is harmed through an action or omission of the parent, the parent is usually deemed to be at fault, even in cases where the harm is caused by factors beyond the parent's control. One example is harm caused by lack of parental supervision. Here, the parent's financial and emotional ability to provide such supervision is often overlooked.

The last feature of child abuse we will discuss is the vulnerability of children. Children are vulnerable in two ways. First, they are relatively powerless. They are physically, legally, and financially dependent upon their parents or parent surrogates. Second, they are emotionally vulnerable. Children depend on the love of their parents and parent surrogates. When a child is hurt by a parent, the hurt is magnified in several ways. First, the child suffers a harm. But the child experiences the harm in a particularly damaging way. The child begins to see him/herself as the cause of the harm. It is inflicted by a figure that is essentially all-powerful and the source of justice in the child's world. The child then begins to view him/herself as deserving of the harm.

Further compounding the injury for the child is the need to protect him/herself from future harm. If the child views him/herself as the cause of the harm, then the child may attempt to change his or her nature or behavior in order to assert control over the infliction of future harm. When this strategy is ineffective, as it is bound to be, since the child is not really the cause of the abuse, there is an increase in both the child's self-blame and in the child's vigilance about trying to control the situation in order to avoid future abuse. This complex perception is reinforced by the abusing parent, who is likely to displace his or her own anger and shame onto the child and explicitly tell the child that he or she is deserving of the abuse, or at least the cause of the abuse.

▶ Exercise 9.2

Spanking is illegal in many European countries, while it is still legal in the United States. Do you think spanking is child abuse? Why or why not? If you think it is child abuse, do you think it ought to be illegal?

Medical sources indicate that millions of children in the United States are overweight, due in large part to decreased physical activity and poor diets. Some cases have come to light in which state agencies have threatened to take a child away from his or her parents because they continue to "fail" in providing their child a healthy diet. Given that the harms of extreme obesity among children include increased risk of diabetes, asthma, and conditions that risk early mortality, what should the state do to protect children from "abuse" that centers on extremely bad diet and exercise? If there are limits or boundaries for such protection, what are they? What sort of obligations does a parent have to his or her child in the realm of health?

Elder Abuse

Elder abuse can be analyzed on an analogy with child abuse. The frail elderly are vulnerable to abuse in similar ways. They are physically weaker than their adult children and caretakers. Many experience varying degrees of dementia and thus lose control over fundamental decisions—about their finances, health care, and physical environment. Even where they are of sound mind, when they are dependent—financially, emotionally, or because they can no longer carry out the details of daily life without help—they are at the mercy of their adult children and caretakers. The elderly parent is often treated not as an adult and a parent, but as a child.

One might argue that child abuse is especially egregious because the child is in his or her formative years and thus the damage will be, if not permanent, at least quite difficult to alleviate. Further, the harm cuts to the very core of the child, affecting, as it does, the child's sense of self. Elderly parents, in contrast, are not dependent on their adult children for their sense of self. We want to challenge this difference. While we certainly do not want to minimize the child's special vulnerability to harm, we wonder if we can ever distinguish between formative and nonformative years. Child abuse inflicted by parents is especially damaging because of its effects on self-perception. Similarly, one might argue that elder abuse inflicted by adult children is more damaging than abuse by non–family members for much the same reason. Being a parent is a large part of one's life; it is a role that parents fill until they die. One may retire from one's job, but one never stops being a parent. Consequently, being a parent is a central part of a parent's identity, and a large part of the parent's self-esteem is based on how good a parent they have been.

There is another disanalogy between child and elder abuse. In the case of child abuse, there is no question that the child is an innocent victim. Although the child's behavior may be the occasion for the abuse, there is no reason to think that the child is deserving of the abuse. In the case of elder abuse, one might make a case for saying that the elderly parent deserves some punishment, either in virtue of present behavior or past child abuse or neglect. Here abuse is distinguished from punishment by the seriousness of the harm.

▶ **Exercise 9.4**

In the United States, the vast number of Alzheimer's patients are cared for at home by their families. These families are given little state support in the United States, so this task is enormously draining and difficult. Elder abuse occurs among all segments of society, but sometimes it is at least partly a result of the incredible stress that families with few resources are under. Do you think that we, as a society, have an obligation to do something about this? If so, what? If not, why not?

Parent Abuse

We turn now to the discussion of parent abuse. By "parent abuse" we refer to the abuse of non-frail parents, who may or may not properly be described as elderly, by their adult offspring. This definition distinguishes parent abuse from elder abuse. It also points to an important disanalogy with child abuse and elder abuse: Parent abuse does not involve acts or omissions directed at people who are vulnerable to their potential abusers either physically or financially.

This is not to say that parents are not vulnerable to emotional harm. Still, given their relative immunity to some forms of harm from their children, one might wonder why we are calling it abuse. Some reasons for calling it abuse are the following. If you look at the evolution of discussions about child and elder abuse, they both involve making visible practices that were previously unseen and unremarked upon. Describing these practices as abuse also involves a criticism of these practices. Describing harm to adult parents as abuse is a way of getting people to see this as deeply morally problematic and largely invisible.

In an earlier era and in many parts of the less-developed world, parents became frail and elderly soon after their children became adults. In relatively prosperous societies, the experience is usually quite different. People are living longer and spending many of these years as relatively healthy and independent parents of adult children. It is perhaps in part because of this new reality that philosophers haven't really thought much about whether we owe obligations to our parents after we have reached adulthood and what those obligations might be. Still, in our analysis we can draw on the few general discussions that do exist in the philosophical literature as well as the more detailed debates in jurisprudence (for example, about filial responsibility statutes and grandparent visitation).

On the one side we see arguments that adult children have obligations to their parents. These discussions appeal to reciprocity, role responsibility, and social utility. Aristotle made an appeal to reciprocity. Confucius appealed to role responsibility in his discussion of filial piety. Contemporary defenders of filial responsibility statutes often appeal to the cost savings that can be realized if families recognize an obligation to their impoverished parents. Since we are concerned with parents who are not necessarily impoverished, we might rework this argument in terms of the social utility of families with strong intergenerational ties.

The reciprocity argument can be stated in the following way. Parents invest a tremendous amount of time, money, attention, and love in raising a child. The child benefits from this parental investment and thus should reciprocate by caring for the parents when they are in need. Critics like John Locke have argued that the reciprocity argument fails because the implied contract was entered into voluntarily by just one of the parties.

The child did not ask to be born. There are two main objections that one could make here. First, it assumes that reciprocity must always be understood on the model of legal contracts. Second, it implies that there are no duties of gratitude.

There are two responses that critics of reciprocity could make on the issue of gratitude. One might argue that the expression "duties of gratitude" is a misnomer. If something is a gift freely given, the only obligation thus incurred is the obligation to express thanks. Second, one might acknowledge that there are duties of gratitude but that they apply only to goods transferred to someone who seeks or values such gifts. One can then argue that a child simply does not exist when the gift is first offered and thus cannot be said to seek or value it. It is only after living for a considerable amount of time that one can decide whether the gift was worth getting.

Jane English offered a different objection to reciprocity arguments. She argued that ties of affection rather than obligation ought to motivate relations between parents and child. Though we agree about the value of ties of affection in this case, we do not think the two are mutually exclusive. Rather, we think we can argue that both are important in relations between parents and children. One might even add that we can have obligations to develop affection, though such an obligation would have to depend on the possibility of generating affection where none currently exists. Another advantage of asserting obligation is that even in cases where affection does exist, one can marshal social support for discharging obligations. One cannot similarly marshal support by appealing solely to desires or feelings of affection. The Family and Medical Leave Act was ultimately acceptable to Congress because there was a general recognition that caring for ill family members and new babies is an obligation and not just a desire based on ties of affection.

To sum up, we think one can plausibly defend the reciprocity argument, though we would reject a picture of reciprocity based on a contract model. Still, it might appear that this argument does not quite fit our case, since we are interested in whether children owe anything to their relatively healthy, financially secure parents. One solution involves a version of the reciprocity argument that we call the caring friendship reciprocity argument. This argument involves adding an element from an ethic of care to the standard reciprocity arguments. In a caring, reciprocal family, parents, like good friends, respond generously to their children when they are in need. Like the parents, the child can expect a period when the parents are likely to need a great deal of assistance. There will be other moments when they are content with the child's affection. The child's needs are most pressing when the child is a minor but may continue to arise throughout the lifetime of the parents. The child is at first incapable of the reciprocity that is called for in a friendship, but later becomes more and more capable of returning the parents' generosity and care through acts of generosity and care on the child's own part.

We can now add arguments from role responsibility and social utility. There are varying ways we organize social interaction, but an important and useful way of doing so is through the assignment of social roles and corresponding responsibility. Role responsibility is not the final appeal, however. Arrangements of roles that systematically disadvantage a class of persons, such as the gendered division of labor that disadvantages girls and women, are clearly morally problematic. In order to show that a role responsibility is morally defensible, one would need to show that such an assignment is compatible with a Kantian concern for persons. One could plausibly argue that a construction of parent–child roles that includes friendship and reciprocity between parent and adult child meets this challenge.

One final argument for the claim that adult children have obligations to their parents is that the recognition of such obligations maximizes social utility. Caring, reciprocal relations between family members allows them to take care of needs that might otherwise be borne by the public sector.

▶ **Exercise 9.5**

Do you think that you have obligations to your parents? If so, what are your obligations? What reasons do you have for thinking that you have these obligations? Do you think they still have obligations to you, even if you're an adult? If so, what are their obligations? Why do you think they have these obligations?

Friendship

We've already introduced the topic of friendship in our discussion of family. If family obligation can be based on reciprocity using the model of caring reciprocity, then it seems reasonable to use the same model to describe the obligations of friendship.

Obligations in Friendship

Friends delight in each other's company and seek it out. They do not count the kindnesses they offer each other with an eye to a strict balancing of accounts, but rather give what they can and in doing so try their best to summon up the spirit of true affection and respect. They recognize obligations based on their friendship, and they recognize the obligation to sustain the friendship. They note that friendship cannot be sustained through the mere expression of feeling, but requires careful nurturing and acts of random kindness. This model of friendship is informed by an ethic of care. In a caring friendship, friends attend to each other with a commitment to being mutually responsive. They try to understand each other in a sympathetic fashion. They are aware of the complexity of human relationships and honor their own relationship as well as the complex web of relationships that sustain them. Finally, they try to adjudicate disputes with an eye to preserving harmonious and supportive relationships.

Note that this understanding of friendship assumes several things about true friendship. First, it assumes that the relationship between friends is reciprocal. This doesn't mean that each friend is counting up what he's done for his friend, but that they each care for the other and do their best to return favors in a spirit of concern and respect for each other. Think about some of the "friends" you've had in the past. The person who always wanted something but never seemed to be there when you needed something wasn't a true friend on this view of friendship because he or she didn't understand the need for reciprocity. The person who demanded that you give them exactly what they gave you didn't understand that reciprocity has to exist in the context of real care and respect.

Second, our understanding of friendship assumes that real friends have moral integrity. They aren't in it just for themselves, and they aren't trying to use another person to get what they want. We can express this in Kantian terms: They recognize their friends as ends in themselves and never merely as means. Aristotle made a similar point about friends when he said that true friends are moral equals.[10] Lastly, our concept assumes that friendship is something that must be cultivated.

Challenges of Friendship

Like family, friendship also brings with it difficult moral dilemmas. Loyalty is one of these dilemmas. Though we think that we have an obligation to be loyal to our friends, we often find ourselves torn between loyalty and our belief about what is right. Another kind of problem is the problem of conflicting loyalties. We have all found ourselves in the crossfire of a nasty divorce or a nasty breakup between two people that we consider friends. How do we remain loyal to both? Should we remain loyal to both? If not, which friend do we remain loyal to? Another problem arises when the demands of friendship exceed our ability or willingness to shoulder them. Suppose a friend becomes seriously ill and we find it difficult emotionally to be around her. Is it okay for us to drop her as a friend? Finally, what are our obligations when we simply grow apart from our friends, when our values and goals no longer seem compatible?

We are not going to answer these questions for you, but we would like to suggest that the moral perspectives we've looked at through this book will help you answer them. But no perspective will yield the perfect answer in every case. If a perspective promised to give you the right answer all the time without any real searching on your part, it would seriously underestimate the complexity of moral life.

Use the perspectives, both individually and collectively, to inform your decisions. As you live with your decisions, reflect back on how you arrived at them. This will help you to assess the moral perspectives as well as your decisions. If you find yourself thinking that your decision turned out to be the right one, that's a reason for trusting the way you're using the moral perspectives. If you're unhappy with your decision, think again about how to balance the moral perspectives as you make future decisions.

Conclusion

We've now looked at the most intimate part of your moral life. There are still many questions that we haven't addressed about family and friendship, but we have tried to model how to use the moral perspectives introduced earlier as a way to answer these further questions for yourself. In the final chapter, we will look at the biggest picture: your obligations as a global citizen.

▶ **Study Questions for Chapter Nine**

1. What is a special obligation? Why might someone think we have special obligations?
2. What would a Utilitarian think about special obligations? A Kantian? A virtue theorist? A care ethicist? A Social Contract theorist?
3. What feature makes child abuse especially morally reprehensible?
4. How does elder abuse compare with child abuse? How does it differ?
5. How does parent abuse differ from child and elder abuse?
6. Why might someone think we have obligations to our parents? Consider the reciprocity, friendship, role responsibility, and social utility arguments here.
7. Why might someone think we have no obligations to our parents? Respond to the arguments you listed above.
8. What is true friendship?
9. How might loyalty create moral problems?

NOTES

1. Confucius, *The Analects*, 13:18.
2. Peter Singer, *Practical Ethics*, 2nd ed (Cambridge: Cambridge University Press, 1993).
3. Charles Fried, *An Anatomy of Values: Problems of Personal and Social Choice* (Cambridge: Harvard University Press, 1970), 227.

4. Bernard Williams, *Moral Luck* (Cambridge: Cambridge University Press, 1981), Chap. 1.

5. Aristotle, *Nichomachean Ethics* (Indianapolis: Library of Liberal Arts, 1962), Bk. 2, Chap. 6, 1106b, 20.

6. Ibid., Bk. 9, Chap. 2, 1164b, 30.

7. Rita Manning, *Speaking from the Heart: A Feminist Perspective on Ethics* (Lanham, Md.: Rowman and Littlefield, 1992).

8. Before looking at these discussions, we want to note an important way in which the discussion of child abuse is coded by race. The increasing prevalence of trying children as adults is evidence that there are important and frightening cultural trends at work. First is the assumption that children, or at least some children, are not significantly different from adults. Second is the way the discussion is coded in racial terms. A recent California proposition allows for "gang members" to be tried as adults. We think a persuasive case can be made for saying "gang member" is a code used to denote African American and Latino youth. One might argue that the mutual existence in US culture of concern about child abuse and demands that we try and incarcerate children as adults is either evidence of schizophrenia or racism. Though we think this is an important issue and one which anyone concerned about children needs to address, we will not return to it here.

9. Alice Miller, *The Drama of the Gifted Child* (New York: Basic Books, 1996).

10. Aristotle, *Nichomachean Ethics,* Chap. 9.

CHAPTER 10

Global Citizenship

We live in an increasingly global world, and we participate as citizens in increasingly diverse cities, states, and countries. Many of us live and work in diverse environments with people from all over the world, many of whom actively live according to some of the concerns voiced by the traditions described in Chapter 5. We live in a global economy where the citizens of relatively wealthy countries consume products produced in distant factories. At the same time, they worry about their high-paying jobs following factory jobs offshore. We live in a world where war and terrorism threaten our lives and our sanity. We live on the same planet where environmental damage knows no national boundaries. Humans have a need to understand their environments and feel safe and comfortable. Change and complexity is often frightening to us. For this reason, we often think of our global environment as a challenge while we often fail to notice the obligations we have as global citizens. But globalization can also be a source of great opportunity. Global citizenship and global markets provide a wealth of new ideas, new alliances, and new friends.

In this chapter we will begin by discussing the general question of whether we have obligations to distant strangers who live under different governments. We will then turn to some substantive problems: global poverty, immigration, war and terrorism, and the global environment. As in previous chapters, we will not be telling you the right answer to these challenges, but noting some things that perhaps you may not have thought about and reminding you how you can use the concepts and strategies we've laid out in earlier chapters to decide for yourself. We begin with the concept of global citizenship.

Global Citizenship, Global Obligations

When we think of the role of citizen, we usually think of membership in political communities as defined by voting: We might think of ourselves as citizens of a city, state or province, and country. Citizenship in this sense is concentric—we belong to a small group that is itself a part of a larger group, which is part of a yet larger group, and so on. Our membership in these groups carries with it both obligations and privileges. In a democratic society we have a say in our political communities and we're given some benefits, such as protection from harm. Recall when we talked about Social Contract Theory that this was the very justification for political communities—we give up our right to settle everything for ourselves in exchange for being protected by the larger community that results from such individual decisions. Recall that this doesn't license just any state—things like the extent of democracy, limitations on power, and fairness must be part of the just state. Given this picture of citizenship, the idea of global citizenship makes sense—we give up the right to unilateral action in the international arena in exchange for a set of benefits that cannot be gained any other way. We have not yet addressed the question of whether such a move would be prudent or whether we have an obligation to organize ourselves in this way.

The question of prudence is an interesting one when we look at nations. Recall that in Chapter 2, we rejected narrow self-interest as a foundation for morality, but we acknowledged that prudence is defensible. Prudence is usually thought of as a virtue, and it means taking reasonable care of oneself. When we think of prudence in the case of an individual person, we think of that one person taking care of him or herself. In the case of national prudence, we think of people acting on our behalf, and often at our behest, to take care of all the people who are members of the nation. So prudence here sounds more like a kind of altruism. The question is whether it is morally defensible to take care of one particular group of people and ignore or perhaps even harm other people in the process. This is the question of whether we have special obligations.

You will recall the discussion about special obligations in Chapter 9 and our suggestion there that one could defend this idea under some moral perspectives. A Utilitarian would find special obligations defensible if admitting these obligations resulted in greater overall utility. We examined this claim in the context of family and friendship, and we can make analogous observations here. As long as there is inequality between nations, it's hard to see how privileging special obligations in every case can maximize utility. If no nation acknowledged any obligations beyond obligations to its own citizens, then rich nations would take care of their citizens and ignore, or even exploit, the citizens of poor nations. Poor nations would be unable to provide for their own citizens and would be hard pressed to protect themselves from the demands of rich nations. One might argue that this is the situation we have now, with poor nations saddled with crippling debt to the developed world and being forced to slash social programs and investments in the future in order to pay back this debt. This is especially troubling when we note that the debt to be repaid is at interest rates that are far higher than current market interest rates.

A defender of an ethic of care might privilege special obligations because intimate caring relationships are the foundation of morality. But here, too, note that there are limits to one's actions. Though one is obligated to respond in a caring fashion to one's close relational partners, this does not license harming others. This is so because we are all entitled to care. Kant and the moral rights perspective speak even more clearly about our global obligations. We have obligations to persons, and such obligations are not limited by geography. Rawls's social contract view invites us to put ourselves in the shoes of the least well off. When we take this perspective globally, we probably would find ourselves in the shoes of people who are suffering extreme poverty and war, perhaps even genocide. Though Rawls himself drew a different conclusion, we think that his position suggests that citizens of the developed world have strong obligations to persons in the developing world.

Some people have argued that the stability of nations requires that governments and their citizens put compatriots first. Patriotism becomes the primary virtue here. But notice that when we talked about virtue we noticed that it is possible to do the wrong thing if our virtues are not properly balanced. Loyalty, for example, can get us into trouble if it leads us to harm someone, even if we are doing so out of concern for a friend or family member. Patriotism, in our opinion, is a lot like loyalty. It is possible to do the wrong thing out of a concern for one's compatriots. Thus patriotism, like loyalty, must be balanced with other virtues, among them non-maleficence, which is the disposition to do no harm.

Poverty and the Global Economy

Before we turn to the issue of our global economic obligations, it is important to make some basic points about obligations. There are a number of factors that play a role in our ordinary understanding of when and why we have moral obligations. First, we recognize an obligation to compensate those we've harmed unnecessarily. Second, we usually recognize an obligation of reciprocity when we benefit from someone else's actions. Finally, we recognize obligations to keep our promises. These don't exhaust our obligations, but they are important for talking about the issue of global economic obligations.

We begin with the issue of harm. Thomas Pogge has argued persuasively that both global economic and global political arrangements are organized to benefit the members of rich nations, and that this creates undue harm for the members of developing nations. He pointed to several factors, but the most important is that the international economic and political order legitimizes in two crucial ways autocratic rulers who loot their own countries. First, it recognizes these rulers as legitimate sellers of the natural resources of their nations. Second, it recognizes these rulers as able to incur debt on behalf of their nations. The consequence of this dual recognition is that people who are only interested in looting the country for their own benefit are both tempted to gain control and supported in their rule after they have gained control, regardless of how they came to power. To make matters worse, they buy weapons from the developed world to maintain their power.

Pogge used the examples of Saudi Arabia and Nigeria. In both cases, the rulers are able to sell their nations' oil and put the proceeds in their own bank accounts. Nigeria is no longer under the control of the military dictator General Sani Abacha, but it is still forced by the international finance markets to service the debt he incurred, in spite of the fact that he used the money to enrich himself. Servicing the debt means that the country is hard pressed to invest in basic nutrition, health care, education, and infrastructure. In this way, rich nations are directly harming the people from developing nations.

Perhaps you are still skeptical. Pogge invited his readers to imagine what might happen if Microsoft's headquarters were taken over by gangsters who attempted to sell Microsoft products and keep the proceeds. They might be able to sell a few truckloads, but quite quickly law enforcement would arrive to return control to Microsoft's legitimate managers. Anyone who bought from the gangsters would be guilty of receiving stolen property and the property would be returned to Microsoft. But a dictator can seize power in a country, declare himself the legitimate ruler, and, in far too many cases, be recognized by the international order and thus begin selling the country's resources and incurring debt on its behalf. And to make matters worse, the people of these dictatorial regimes are criticized for having bad governments.

Of course, not all countries in the developing world are badly ruled. There are many countries that are democratic and whose citizens are hard working and frugal. But there, too, we see signs of the harm inflicted by the international order. For example, developing countries do not have the same bargaining power in international trade negotiations as developed countries and thus are forced to live with the results of deals that increase their poverty. A good example is agricultural products. The United States, the European Union, and Japan heavily subsidize their own farmers, who can then undercut the prices that farmers from other countries can get on the world market for their agricultural products. Since most developing countries are heavily dependent on agriculture, this is a devastating loss. The United States has recently offered to lower its subsidies if the EU countries and Japan would do likewise, but so far no real reform is in sight. And agriculture is but one example among many.

In addition to the harm inflicted on poor countries by rich countries, people from developed countries benefit from the uneven playing field.

Consumers can buy more for less, and companies can increase their profit margins by cutting labor and environmental costs.

Finally, there is the issue of promising. In the United Nations, all the nations of the world agreed to make substantial progress toward the eight Millennium Development Goals by the target date of 2015. These goals are: (1) to eradicate poverty and extreme hunger, (2) to achieve universal primary education, (3) to promote gender equality and empower women, (4) to reduce child mortality, (5) to improve maternal health, (6) to combat HIV/AIDS, malaria, and other diseases, (7) to ensure environmental sustainability, and (8) to develop a global partnership for development. In order to meet these goals, rich nations pledged to contribute 0.7 percent of their gross national product (GNP) to development assistance. To put this figure in perspective, Jeffrey Sachs noted that the promised US contribution is what the United States spends each year in the war in Iraq. The United States made the same promise in the Rio Summit on Sustainable Development in 1992 and in the Monterrey Consensus in 2002. Still, US development assistance to other nations averages just 0.15 percent of the annual US GNP.

Individuals, Corporations, and Global Obligation

We've argued that a number of moral perspectives and general views about obligation commit us to saying that rich countries have obligations to the people in developing countries.

Utilitarians would point out that if every person is to count as one, and no one as more than one, then when we look to our obligations national borders are not terribly relevant. Thus, if our actions contribute to overall suffering, we are at fault, and if our actions contribute to an amelioration of such suffering, we are doing the right thing. Kant and moral rights theories tell us that each person is, qua person, equally valuable, and thus that we must treat all people as moral equals. This means that if it is wrong to kill an innocent compatriot, it is wrong to kill an innocent foreigner. Care reminds us that we are all, as living, aware creatures, entitled to care. Thus we cannot sacrifice someone in a distant land to benefit our near and dear relational partners. Virtue reminds us that the good person has the right mix of virtues and thus that we go astray when we fail to balance loyalty or its national equivalent, patriotism, with the commitment to do no harm. Finally, Rawls reminds us that morality requires taking the perspective of the least well off, and in this case, persons in rich nations must enlarge their perspective to include the perspective of persons in poor countries.

We've tried to make the case that rich countries have obligations to developing countries. What does that tell us about the obligations we have as individuals? One might argue that citizens of democratic countries have the same commitments their nations assume, because in a democracy government speaks for the people and can make commitments on their behalf. Individuals in rich countries have a number of ways of discharging their obligations. They can lobby their governments to live up to their promises; they can change their consumption patterns; and they can volunteer or contribute to organizations that are working to ameliorate the effects of the global economy on people in developing countries.

Corporations, which are legal persons in the United States, can be thought of as having similar moral obligations, but they also are capable of both inflicting more harm and of creating more good than individuals acting alone. Thus it would seem that they have the same sorts of obligations as those we sketched above: to maximize good consequences, to treat all persons in a similar caring and respectful fashion regardless of where they live, to behave in a virtuous manner, to consider the perspective of the least well off, to avoid harm, to respond in a reciprocal fashion to those who benefit them, and to keep their promises.

▶ Exercise 10.1

Get together in a group of your fellow students. Brainstorm over some of the ways that corporations can help reduce poverty in other countries. Are there moral limits or guidelines to how you think they might go about doing this? Should they be able to make a profit from such endeavors, or reap the positive publicity from their actions? Discuss the complex interaction of motives, corporate values, and consequences involved in this issue.

Immigration

The issue of immigration is closely aligned to the issue of global poverty because global poverty is perhaps the major reason why immigration is such a potent issue. Rich nations fear and resent immigrants, while at the same time they rely on them to work for low wages. The justification for immigration policy is similar to the justification for global economic justice. Those who favor equal respect for persons might be expected to favor an open borders policy, whereas Utilitarians would favor whatever restrictions would maximize utility. Defenders of care might point to the needs that motivate immigration and to the past harms and promises that might justify it. Defenders of the virtue tradition might be expected to argue for the importance of protecting traditional societies and virtues. Principles of justice come into play as we note that membership in society is itself a good that can be distributed and that immigration policy lays out the rules that govern its distribution.

Michael Walzer offered a rich discussion of immigration, so we will spend some time on his account. He began by noting that the most important good to be distributed is membership in the community: "It is only as members somewhere that men and women can hope to share in all the other social goods—security, wealth, honor, office, and power—that communal life makes possible." He then presented a number of principles that one could use to justify immigration policies. We will focus on just four because we think these are either the most defensible or the most common:

1. Global socialism: All human beings are already members of a global state. Thus there should be no limits on the movement of people across national borders. There should be no bar to entry; individuals and families ought to be able to join (within the constraints of market) whatever state they choose.
2. Club: Only original members choose themselves; all others are to be chosen by members by appeal to standards adopted by members.
3. Family: We are obligated to offer membership to "particular groups of outsiders, recognized as national, ethnic" or political "relatives."

4. Mutual aid: Membership should be granted "if (1) it is needed or urgently needed . . . [and] (2) if the risks and costs of giving it are relatively low."

Global socialism relies on the idea of moral equality of persons. One argument against it is that it might make the lives of current residents of rich countries much more difficult than under a more closed-door policy. The club rationale is not clearly morally defensible, though it is common practice to make immigration policy by merely appealing to the wishes or interests of current residents. There may well be good arguments for doing so, but the fact that they already belong doesn't seem to be a very good reason. It would appear that we can apply the same kind of argument to the family rationale as we used in our discussions of families in the previous chapter. There we saw that there are some justifiable reasons for prioritizing one's family, though this doesn't justify priority in all things; nor does it justify harming others. The mutual aid rationale seems compatible with all our moral perspectives, though the requirement of only minimal risk would need further justification. Let us now look at what Walzer concluded.

He argued against global socialism for a number of reasons. This policy would be incompatible with patriotism; it might actually undermine our efforts to deal with poverty in other countries; it would undermine stable cultures and the efficient working of political institutions; and it is insensitive to the desire of most people to remain in their home communities. He offered two further arguments for borders. The first is that it is important to protect national territory because "the link between people and land is a crucial feature of national identity . . . [and] because so many critical issues . . . can best be resolved within geographical units, the focus of political life can never be established elsewhere." The second argument is that it is important to protect ways of life; without such protection, "there could not be communities of character, historically stable, ongoing associations of men and women with some special commitment to one another and some special sense of their common life."

So it seems that there are some good reasons for having borders. But how do we justify policies about emigration and immigration across borders? We can now turn to Walzer's next three rationales. The argument against the club rationale is fairly obvious. As it stands, it is indifferent to the policies that the current members might choose, and it is also indifferent to the past practices that resulted in the current constitution of the club. Both the family and the mutual-aid rationales seem defensible on a number of grounds, especially if we understand the family rationale as including past harm and promising.

It would seem, then, that rich countries can justify opening borders to people to whom they have an established relationship and to those with pressing needs. The hard question is whether they are justified to closing borders to people in either category. Walzer appealed here to the arguments for territory and way of life: We are justified in closing the borders if doing so is required to protect the territory and way of life of the rich countries. Territory is important to societies because we depend on them for the resources we need. Our long association with our territory might also make us the best stewards of it. One might point out that we aren't always the best stewards of our own territory, nor is it simply a matter of hard work that a people enjoy the resources associated with their political territory. We also have to be careful here to limit the idea of "way of life." If we include material wealth as part of the way of life, it seems that we are turning our backs on the basic idea of moral equality.

Some other features of way of life might be more defensible. If it is true that humans flourish best in societies with some shared core values, and if it is also true that societies are most stable when they have such shared values, then it seems reasonable to require immigrants to agree to commit to these shared core values. Similarly, it seems reasonable to restrict emigration when such emigration undermines such shared core values. The suggestion that rich nations focus considerable resources on local responses to poverty might then be both an obligation of mutual aid and a reasonable response to pressures of immigration.

One might argue here that this general discussion of immigration is insufficiently detailed to tell us much about how to respond to our current crisis of immigration. But if we take the long view, and look back at the history of immigration policy in the United States, we may find that using such a general principle can help the United States to put its past policy into sharper focus. By evaluating past policies in a new light, we may be able to design better policies for the future.

For example, we would reject the Chinese Exclusion Act of 1882 because it violated moral equality and cannot be justified in terms of the protection of way of life. We would note a similar problem with the 1921 US quotas on immigration from Russia, the Middle East, Africa, Australia, New Zealand, and the Pacific and Atlantic Islands. The policy of immigration quotas based on past immigration history unfairly privileged immigrants from Europe, because past policies explicitly restricted immigration from non-European countries. This policy was not changed until 1965. The 1975 Indochina Migration and Refugee Assistance Act facilitated the immigration of Southeast Asian immigrants and was largely defended in terms of US involvement with this region during the Vietnam War. Note that these are the types of reasons Walzer described in the family rationale. Similarly, family reunification policies target actual families and thus also can be defended in terms of the family rationale.

There is one further question we need to ask here. Even if we have a general principle that helps us to decide what is a defensible policy about the movement of people across borders, what should their status be after they have crossed the border? Many people have argued that immigrants should only be granted the status of "guest worker"—staying a limited amount of time and with no chance to become a citizen. We can start answering this question by examining the idea of being a guest. Guests are supposed to wait for an invitation for a visit of limited duration, but once invited, they are free to accept; during the visit they are free to come and go, within limits; and they are treated with special courtesy and not expected to do the work that is ordinarily expected of regular members of the household. It's pretty clear that guest workers are not "guests" in most of these senses. If we are to treat these immigrants as ends in themselves, then we are not free to see them as mere machines who exist solely for our financial advantage.

What then are our obligations? Walzer argued that if we allow immigrants, we ought to allow them to become citizens. His argument is that anyone who is subject to the coercive power of the state has a right to be represented by the state. Immigrants are even more subject to state power than citizens; thus, under this argument, they have a right to representation. If we couple this claim with his earlier claim that citizens have a right to protect their way of life and territorial integrity, then rich countries are justified in limiting citizenship to those who are committed to respecting the territorial integrity and core values of the country to which they wish to immigrate.

Obviously, there are a lot of questions that we haven't raised, and there are many defensible views that we haven't even addressed. In this discussion of immigration, we have given you an example of how you might use moral perspectives to think about the issue, and we've given you one argument to consider. We hope that you can now construct and justify your own substantial view on this difficult issue.

Violence: War and Terrorism

One of the most difficult and enduring global questions concerns the nature of violence. As we think about relations between nations, we look to discussions about war. Increasingly, our concern about global violence concerns the actions not of nations but of individual groups. When these actions target innocent civilians, we describe this as "terrorism." Before we look at questions about war and terrorism, we want to back up and ask the larger question about the moral permissibility of violence.

Pacifism

Pacifism is the view that violence against persons is never justified. The genesis of this view in the West is often traced to Christ. The secular figure in this debate in the West is Kant. If we are all moral equals, then we should see others as ends in themselves. Thus we are not justified in treating others as existing merely for our use. Treating someone violently is a way of coercing them to do something for us that they would not otherwise choose to do. Thus it is a violation of respect for persons. There is another defense of pacifism that is more in the spirit of Utilitarianism. Violence always begets more violence; thus it is better to renounce violence, even if it appears that we can maximize short-term social utility by resorting to violence.

The primary objection to pacifism is that even if one renounces violence, there will still be others who want to achieve their ends through violence. If the pacifist refuses to respond violently, then the pacifist (and those under his or her protection) will be especially vulnerable. One response to this argument is that there are other ways to resist. Mahatma Gandhi stressed noncooperation. One might point then to the nonviolent rebellion of India against British rule as clear evidence that this can be a powerful strategy. Still, most critics of pacifism are unconvinced that this strategy can be relied upon in all situations. But even if one rejects pacifism, it does not follow that anything goes. Indeed the tradition of Just War Theory argues that there are moral standards in war.

Just War Theory

Just War Theory had its genesis in Grotius's *De Jure Belli ac Pacis* (1625) and has been incorporated in the Geneva Convention. Its current and perhaps most influential spokesperson is Michael Walzer. Just War Theory includes the following points:

1. A war is just war only if it is a last resort and is waged after all other options have been exhausted.
2. It must be waged by a legitimate authority.
3. It must be fought to redress a wrong.
4. It must have a reasonable chance of success.
5. It must have as its ultimate goal the establishment of a peace preferable to the peace that existed before the war.
6. The violence used must be proportional to the injury being redressed.
7. Weapons must discriminate between combatants and noncombatants. Civilians must never be targeted, and all care must be taken to avoid killing civilians.

Each of these conditions must be met before a war is declared to be just. A full discussion would take an entire book, and there are many such books on the topic. Here we offer just a brief sketch. Condition number one is fairly obvious, but its consequences are quite practical given the current US policy of defending preemptive war. Condition two is more complex. Usually a war is considered unjust unless it is declared by a legitimate authority. Again, the United States provides a good example of how complex this condition can be in practice. The Constitution requires that Congress declare war. But Congress has not officially declared war since World War II. The situation can be even more complex than this. For example, is a country at war if it is run by a dictator who is opposed by the vast majority of the population? Condition three rules out wars of aggression, but it leaves vague the issue of what constitutes a wrong and how serious the wrong must be. Conditions four, five, and six seem to be consistent with the Utilitarian view that one must maximize overall social utility. The final condition is the only option compatible with treating persons as ends in themselves. In modern war this condition is difficult to fulfill, and for that reason some have argued that it is no longer possible to wage a just war.

We have seen then that Just War Theory derives its strength from some of the same moral perspectives we've looked at earlier. Like all moral principles, it is not obvious how to put them into practice. In our opinion, this is not an indictment of the principles but a reason for recognizing both that their application will require careful thought and that not everyone will agree about the application.

Terrorism can be defined in contrast to just wars. It is violence undertaken with a political aim, but it violates condition seven. Any politically motivated violence that deliberately targets civilians is clearly terrorism and is a violation of the fundamental principle against harming innocent persons. There has been much debate about whether the other conditions must also hold in order for a war to be just. Condition two is notably controversial; the idea of "state terrorism" turns on precisely this concept. Some would argue that even legitimate authorities can commit terrorist acts.

Obviously, we've just scratched the surface about these difficult issues, but here again, we've tried to sketch out the basic arguments and show how you can use different moral perspectives to think about them constructively.

Exercise 10.2

One perennial issue in times of national danger, including our current era as we face dangers posed by terrorism, has been the tension between personal liberty and national security. Thinking about the issues connected to terrorism and the United States' efforts to combat it, discuss the moral issues in terms of the major moral theories presented in this book. What values are in conflict? Are there ways to compromise and uphold both values, or must one be subordinated? Explain your reasoning from the basis provided by one of the moral theories elucidated in earlier chapters.

Exercise 10.3

Think about a moral theory we've discussed that would come to the opposite conclusion from the one you argued for in Exercise 10.2. How does this other moral theory lead to this conclusion on terrorism and how one ought to respond to it?

The Environment

While there are many lively debates about the global environment, there is almost universal agreement that this is a problem that can only be effectively addressed by global action. There are two very different kinds of issues that must be addressed: factual and value. We leave the factual issues to you, but keep in mind that it is impossible to do the right thing in the absence of sound evidence. This is especially true when you are dealing with an issue as complex as the global environment. Here we want to focus on some basic disagreements about values.

In this section, we'll be looking at worldviews about the relation between humans and the natural environment. We divide them into three general categories: domination views, stewardship views, and holistic views. Let's begin by looking at some versions of each.

Domination Views

All domination views share the assumption that the earth exists for the purpose of humans. Here we distinguish between two very different views that make quite different assumptions and have different implications for action and policy.

> **D1:** We have the right to do whatever we want with the earth and its nonhuman creatures because we can.
> **D2:** We ought to use the earth and its nonhuman creatures as a resource for the well-being of humans, including future generations.

Stewardship Views

> **S1:** We have a responsibility to take care of the earth including its nonhuman creatures.

Holistic Views

> **H1:** We ought to take care of the earth and recognize that we are part of it.

Underlying Values

Before we sort out these views, we need to address some preliminaries. We can make two distinctions about the values underlying these different views. The first is the difference between intrinsic value and instrumental value. Something is intrinsically valuable if it is valuable for its own sake. Something is instrumentally valuable if it has value only because it promotes something else that is itself intrinsically valuable. We are now in a position to see what values underlie each of the views above.

The second distinction we can make is between objective and subjective value. When we say something is objectively valuable we are saying that there is something about the world that makes the thing valuable. When we say something is subjectively valuable we are saying that its value consists solely in the fact that we value it. With this in mind, let's look at the values that lay beneath the surface of the views listed above.

D1 does not seem to presume that anything is valuable. In fact, like all "might makes right" views, it is cynical with respect to the question of value. It is because there are no real objective values that we can do whatever we can get away with.

D2 assumes that humans are intrinsically valuable and that this is an objective fact. The rest of the natural world is instrumentally valuable—it is valuable only insofar as it supports human life.

S1 seems to assume that the natural world is intrinsically valuable. Since we are seen as stewards of this intrinsically valuable thing, this view is compatible with the view that we are merely instrumentally valuable. But it is also compatible with the view that we are, like the natural world, intrinsically valuable. If we are all intrinsically valuable, then it looks like we have both an obligation to the natural world and a right to it. In other words, we are not mere stewards; we are justified in using the natural world to support human life as well.

H1 is puzzling. Holistic views are compatible with many different views about what is valuable. For example, we could assume holism as a fact about the world—we are simply intimately affected by what happens in the rest of the natural world. On this view, we could assume that only humans are intrinsically valuable. This view looks very like D2. Another alternative is that the natural world, as a holistic entity, is the only intrinsically valuable thing. What then do we say about its parts?

We can now further distinguish stewardship and holistic views.

Stewardship Views.

S1: We have a responsibility to take care of the earth, including its nonhuman creatures. The earth is intrinsically valuable, whereas humans are only instrumentally valuable.

S2: We have a responsibility to take care of all the creatures of the earth because every creature is intrinsically valuable. Because humans are also intrinsically valuable, we also have a right to use the rest of the natural world to sustain human life and culture.

Holistic Views.

H1: We ought to take care of the earth and recognize that we are part of it. This is a mere fact about the earth. Humans are the only intrinsically valuable creatures but we ought to be careful in how we use rest of the natural world, because our use of its resources might have unintended consequences.

H2: The earth itself is the only intrinsically valuable thing. We have a responsibility to promote its well-being.

Though there are many different value disagreements at play in controversies about the global environment, we think that one must first become clear about these basic values. At this point, we invite you to ask yourself which of the views above you hold. Notice that your previous commitments are relevant here. If you are a Kantian, for example, it is likely that you will reject a holistic view because a Kantian thinks that only humans have intrinsic worth. A Utilitarian could adopt a holistic view but would need something like a concept of well-being to stand in for utility. Vandana Shiva is an Indian environmentalist who argues for a holistic view using a number of perspectives, including respect for persons, Utilitarianism (with the welfare of all natural creatures being the measure of utility), and Hinduism.

Let's now explore some issues and see how our different commitments play out. Population increase is an obvious one here. If you are committed to a holistic view, you will be in favor of any policies that reduce the negative effects of humans on the well-being of the environment. If you hold a domination view, you will focus your attention on the carrying capacity of the earth. Note that people with these two views might still be able to compromise, but before they could even have a meaningful dialogue they would have to see where their disagreements were.

Another difficult issue is global warming. This might be one where compromise is most easily achieved because it doesn't matter what your views are about the relative status of humans. Whether you hold a domination, stewardship, or holistic view, global warming is a bad thing. Now the controversy begins to seem more familiar: How do we bring about compromise when self-interests collide and trust is lacking? We leave the issue of the global environment with more questions than answers. What we hope is that you can now see how to find and discuss the fundamental value issues. This is the beginning of compromise, and in these issues compromise is surely in everyone's best interest.

▶ **Exercise 10.4**

Many consider environmental issues to be of vital importance but not relevant to our daily lives. Others have argued that environmental issues do radically affect the style of life that we've become accustomed to. Consider two examples—owning domestic animals and the consumption of meat products. Are these unethical uses of animals? Some say that both infringe on animal autonomy and place them in a subordinate role to human interests of culinary pleasure and companionship. What do you think? Think through and justify your natural reactions with one of the moral theories we have discussed.

Conclusion

One thing that is a special challenge for all the issues we've discussed in this chapter is that solving them requires global dialogue and compromise. We've already discussed the key elements to getting along. Effective and ethical communication is a cornerstone. We build on it by developing our ability to assess consequences. In a global setting, this requires coming to see how people from diverse perspectives will be affected and how they will assess the different options.

Regardless of our differences, respect for each other is both a requirement and a way of smoothing out our interactions. When people come from diverse perspectives and backgrounds, we need to do some detective work to see the many ways respect and disrespect can be exhibited. We learn to be fair in our interactions with others, keeping in mind what it might be like to be in the shoes of someone quite different from ourselves. We develop the virtues needed in our shared community. We consciously work to build a caring and harmonious community. Finally, we work in global communities to develop and continually reinvent a shared code of ethics that we can commit to in spite of our many differences.

▶ Study Questions for Chapter Ten

1. What are some moral theories that support special obligations to developing nations? Can you think of theories that would not support such obligations?
2. How might existing practices in international relations lead to harming citizens of unstable and developing countries?
3. Why is the issue of immigration a moral issue?
4. What are four principles discussed by Walzer that could be evoked to argue for a particular side in the immigration issue?
5. What is pacifism?
6. What are the key points to Just War Theory?
7. What are the main "views" taken toward the environment in environmental ethics?
8. What is the difference between intrinsic and instrumental value?

Index